lonely planet

ULTIMATE UNITED KINGDOM TRAVELIST

THE TOP 500 EXPERIENCES IN THE UK... RANKED

Introduction

Tiny pubs, giant cathedrals, inky lochs, eccentric rituals, world-class museums and rollicking festivals that proceed whatever the weather... While the United Kingdom may not always seem so united, its four constituent countries and countless little islands comprise a powerhouse of history, culture and intrigue. But where to start? That's where this book can help. Here you'll find our pick of 500 of the most memorable, beautiful, surprising and downright compelling experiences to be had in England, Northern Ireland, Scotland and Wales (and a sprinkling of Channel Islands for good measure). And what's more, we've ranked them in order of their brilliance.

How did we come up with our selection? We started by compiling every highlight in the Lonely Planet guidebooks to Great Britain and Northern Ireland. Every sight, attraction and experience that had caught our writers' attention over the years was included. We then asked everyone in our UK office, plus 20 leading figures in the country's travel sector, to reveal their favourite spots and experiences. The contents of family holidays, school trips and weekends away were diligently documented. Then the voting began. We asked everybody in Lonely Planet's UK community to vote for their 20 top experiences. And, with hundreds of votes cast and a bit of mathematical alchemy, we ended up with a score for each of the 500 experiences in this book, and one very clear winner.

Each entry listed gives a taste of what to expect from the sight or experience, plus some practical advice to start planning your own trip. Turn to our guidebooks and lonelyplanet.com for more detailed directions.

This is Lonely Planet's Ultimate United Kingdom Travelist. We think this country is pretty special, and hope this book will inspire and invigorate your travels within it. Just don't forget to pack a brolly.

01–99 Contents

100–199

200–299

300–399

400–500

01—99

© David Monteith - Hodge / Photographise
© Edinburgh Festival Fringe Society

Edinburgh Festival performances from the Lemon Bucket Orkestra (left) and Wiz Productions (below). Right: the city's High Street during the Fringe

© David Monteith - Hodge / Photographise / Edinburgh Festival Fringe Society

ESSENTIAL ARTS FESTIVALS

↓

Held in mid-Wales every spring, the Hay Literary Festival is an international exposition of all things books

☛ page 97

↓

WOMAD (World of Music and Dance) first hit its global groove in England before expanding into other lands

☛ page 134

↓

For a more genteel cultural gathering, but with plenty of top-drawer art, head down to Cornwall's Port Eliot Festival

☛ page 224

© James Ratchford / Edinburgh Festival Fringe Society

See the greatest shows on earth at the Edinburgh Festival Fringe

01

EDINBURGH // Walking down the cobbled Royal Mile, set against the brooding backdrop of Edinburgh Castle and a congregation of medieval rooftops, it isn't the knife-throwing unicyclist that first stops you in your tracks. Neither is it the a cappella choir rehearsing in the shadows of St Giles' Cathedral, nor the gussied-up collective of artists including bare-chested Korean drummers, a karaoke version of *Macbeth*, a soap-bubble circus and a group of preening Thai ladyboys. Even the camera-ready crowds lining up to take photos aren't surprised by them. Instead, it is the zombified drag queen, pulling balloons from between her buttocks, that brings the street to a standstill.

At such times, there's no shame in being baffled by the world's largest arts festival. Now well into its 70s, the annual, three-week-long Fringe comes with a packed programme of some 3500 shows, 1900-odd premieres and around 55,000 performances stretched across 300 citywide venues. In previous years, the Royal Botanic Gardens has hosted a 'pianodrome' built from 55 recycled pianos. A repurposed 1960s' caravan has become a comedy club. The top deck of a bus has welcomed poetry recitals, and a chicken coop – with a capacity for only three – has hosted the world's smallest-ever comedy show. In some cases, public convenience has been forsaken in the name of art – believe it or not, even toilets have been used as an unlikely venue. Quite simply, the Fringe floods the city with art and nowhere beats it for spectacle or scale. Strangeness, too. Come August in Edinburgh, everything seems brighter, barmier and more colourful.

To negotiate such a minefield of creative freedom, it's best to tackle the Fringe over several days, dipping in and out of shows aided by word-of-mouth reviews and tips picked up in the pub. There is theatre, comedy, dance, circus, cabaret, opera, music and spoken word, and whatever the time of day, an acrobat, trapeze artist, contortionist or tried-and-tested bagpiping busker will be pleased to entertain you. Plan ahead too much and you'll miss the freedom of spontaneity, but come ill-prepared and you may find the hot tickets already sold out. In previous years, you could have seen the likes of Dudley Moore and Peter Cook, Robin Williams, Rowan Atkinson, Mike Myers, members of Monty Python or Sir Billy Connolly for less than a fiver.

Still bewildered? Simply step through the looking glass and prepare to be dazzled by the greatest show of arts and culture on Earth. You won't have seen anything like it and – unless you return year on year, like a local – you never will again.

☛ SEE IT ! ***The Edinburgh Festival Fringe runs for three weeks throughout August. At the big four venues (Assembly, Gilded Balloon, Pleasance and Underbelly) 2-for-1 previews are the norm in the first few days, while the Fringe Half Price Hut on The Mound is a safe bet for last-minute bargains.***

02

Take a world tour of treasures at the British Museum

LONDON // Some museums are travel destinations in themselves. The British Museum – the first ever public national museum – is the envy of the world, with good reason in some cases, considering the many treasures obtained under questionable circumstances in colonial times.

Yet this miraculous museum started life as a humble cabinet of curiosities, assembled by 18th-century physician and hot-chocolate inventor, Sir Hans Sloane. As a condition of bequeathing his treasures to the nation, he ordered that they be open for free to 'all studious and curious persons', a tradition that persists to this day.

Early on, the collection was dominated by natural history, books and drawings, but the kleptomaniac zeal of the colonial period saw it stuffed with gifted, borrowed and purloined treasures from across the globe, from mummified Pharaohs to the Parthenon Marbles, alongside the greatest treasures unearthed in the British Isles.

Putting disputes over ownership to one side, visitors today are transported on a whirlwind world tour of human creativity. If human beings have made it, somewhere in the world, there's a chance you'll find an example among the display cases. One side effect of this globetrotting collection is that the museum speaks to the culture of almost everyone who walks in the door.

The museum also has its finger on the pulse of modern archaeology, hosting temporary exhibitions in the Reading Room, beneath a geodesic canopy designed by Norman Foster.

There's far too much to take in on one trip; if you only have a day, make a beeline for the Egyptian treasures, the Parthenon Marbles and quirky British antiquities such as the Sutton Hoo helmet and the Lewis chessmen.

SEE IT ! ***The British Museum is a short stroll from Tube stations at Russell Square, Holborn and Tottenham Court Rd; avoid the crowds on weekends and public holidays.***

Opposite & above: designed by Foster + Partners, the British Museum's Great Court is an exhibit in itself. Below: statues in the Ancient Greece collection

© Stuart Stevenson / Getty Images

The sun sets over the Giant's Causeway, County Antrim, a landscape that's become part of Irish lore

03

Step ogre-sized strides over hexagonal stones at the Giant's Causeway

NORTHERN IRELAND // The descent down from the cliffs to the strange rocks of the Giant's Causeway feels at once timeless – the scene has remained the same for countless centuries – and unrepeatable: the moody skies, the light and the temperament of the sea are constantly changing. Equally exhilarating when cloaked in fairy-tale mist as when bathed in bright sunshine or whipped by howling winds, uneven stacks of hexagonal basalt columns stand in neat clusters along the water's edge, emerging from the shore like tightly packed tower blocks in a city skyline. The low rumble of the ocean builds into a roar as white-tipped water creeps up and crashes over the rocks, lapping the stones as it retreats. Northern Ireland's only Unesco World Heritage site is shrouded in a sense of magic, myth and natural wonder.

Legend has it that Irish giant Finn McCool built a causeway across the sea as a way to reach his rivals in Scotland. One day, the Scottish giant Benandonner followed Finn back to Ireland, but he was tricked by Finn and retreated home to Scotland, ripping up the causeway behind him. Giants aside, scientists put the formation of the rocks down to volcanic activity some 60 million years ago. As the lava flow cooled and hardened it contracted, creating a honeycomb pattern.

After clambering over the pillars on the shore, check out the Organ, a rock formation resembling organ pipes, and the Chimney Stacks headland, which looks like industrial chimneys on the edge of the ocean. A clifftop path leads to the Amphitheatre viewpoint and down the Shepherd's Steps to the shore; there's also a minibus that runs to the rocks from the visitor centre, where you can learn more about the causeway's history, geology and legends.

SEE IT ! ***The Causeway is immensely popular: to see it with fewer crowds come early in the morning or after 4pm and avoid the peak months of June to August. A pleasant way to reach the Giant's Causeway (and avoid paying the combined parking and visitor centre entrance fee) is to walk or cycle the 3 miles from Bushmills. Alternatively, take public transport.***

The Roman baths that gave the English city of Bath its name are among the best-preserved examples in the world

04

Experience how the Romans bathed in Bath

SOUTHWEST ENGLAND // If there's one thing the Romans liked better than anything – except perhaps straight roads, good sanitation and gladiatorial gore – it was a nice hot bath. And 2000 years ago, when Britain was under Roman rule, they built a sumptuous bath complex at a site known as Aquae Sulis (present-day Bath), taking advantage of the area's geothermal hot springs, which warm the underground water to 46°C (115°F).

Though now swallowed up by the modern city of Bath, most of the structure is still standing – including bathing pools, changing rooms, the original hypocaust heating system and the central Great Bath, lined with lead and filled with 5.2ft of steaming, geothermally heated water. In fact, it's one of the best-preserved Roman bathhouses in the world, and gives a fascinating glimpse into their everyday lives (and fastidious ablution habits). The only disappointment is that it's no longer permitted for people to take a dip here – but you can get pretty close to a bona fide Roman bathing experience at the Thermae Bath Spa nearby, complete with its postcard-worthy panoramic rooftop pool.

SEE IT ! *To dodge the worst crowds, avoid weekends and all of July and August. Buy tickets online to bypass the queues.*

© Joe Daniel Price / Getty Images

05

Below: giant strides along the Wall's Milecastle 39. Bottom: Hadrian's Wall runs through Northumberland National Park

Retrace the Romans' footsteps along Hadrian's Wall

NORTHEAST ENGLAND // Hot on the heels of Bath's namesake thermal baths is another mighty Roman legacy – an enormous defensive wall stretching 73 miles across Britain. This phenomenal feat of engineering was built under Roman emperor Hadrian between AD 122 and 128 to keep out Scottish Picts. Rising to a height of up to 15ft, with a width of almost 10ft, it took 15,000 men six years to construct it from local whinstone (dolerite). Only 10% survives today, but what does makes an unforgettable impression.

Along the wall were 80 mile-castle forts, with observation turrets between them. Larger forts were built in the south, with 16 more lying astride the wall, which you can visit today. Staggering remains that serve as reminders of the Romans' advancements include the hospital at Housesteads Fort, ventilated granaries and barracks, as well as flushable communal latrines.

Exploring sections of the wall is easy thanks to good rail and road access (including buses), but if you're up for an adventure, you can complete the national Hadrian's Wall Path walking trail along its length in about a week.

SEE IT ! *Carlisle and Newcastle-upon-Tyne are ideal launch cities. Visit in summer (but bring waterproofs all the same).*

© Justin Foulkes / Lonely Planet

© Alice-photo / Shutterstock

© Dave Head / Shutterstock

Opposite from top: the Tate Modern is housed in a former power station; a typical British pub

06

Make a British weekend of it with a Sunday pub roast

Fewer and fewer people in Britain start Sunday with a trip to church, but the roast lunch is still a lock. For visitors, it's a must-do experience. It doesn't matter whether you're in a centuries-old, windowless pub in London or at a large country inn with tables sprawling over a lawn, you'll be among friends and families laughing, drinking beer and tucking into plates of hot sliced roast beef or pork, Yorkshire pudding, roasted potatoes and assorted veggies, all slathered in gravy. Warming, filling and indulgent, it's comfort food par excellence. But more than that, it's a reassuring experience, a weekly ritual where the nation stops time, staves off the start of the working week and lives in the moment. Grab a plate and take your fill.

EAT IT ! ***After you've tried the local pub(s), go haute cuisine at the Michelin-starred Star Inn, Main St, Harome, near Helmsley.***

07

Discover a powerhouse of modern art at Tate Modern

LONDON // London's art galleries were once stuffy, nostalgic, Portland-stone institutions, heavy with history. But when Tate Modern opened in 2000, in the hollowed-out shell of the decommissioned Bankside Power Station, modern art finally got an address to be proud of.

Now housing the Tate's art collection from 1900 to the present day, the gallery has exploded beyond its original footprint, with new galleries inside the power station and the Blavatnik Building rising behind like a twisted ziggurat. Inside, you might see anything from permanently displayed Rothkos, Dalís and Picassos to visiting masterpieces by Monet, Matisse and Warhol, and eccentric installations from the likes of Ai Weiwei, Rachel Whiteread and Anish Kapoor. Before you leave, head to the top-floor viewing deck for stunning city views.

SEE IT ! ***Tate Modern is close to Blackfriars Tube and mainline stations. Alternatively, visit as part of a walk along the South Bank.***

07

FULLER SMITH & TURNER
CHISWICK ALES & STOUT
FULLER'S
THE CHURCHILL ARMS
THE CHURCHILL ARM
CHURCHILL ARM

06

08

Marvel at the mighty megaliths of Stonehenge

SOUTHWEST ENGLAND // Just what were ancient Britons playing at when they hauled these giant stones into place all those millennia ago? Stonehenge, on Salisbury Plain near Amesbury, is a monumental, undeniably mind-boggling achievement. Built in stages between around 4500 BC and 1500 BC, Stonehenge's massive stones (some weighing 25 tonnes) were probably erected using a system of sledges, rollers, pivots and pulleys; some were transported here from the Preseli Hills in Wales, 140 miles away.

But despite decades of academic study, no one really has the foggiest why Stonehenge is there. Oriented around the solstices, it forms part of a larger sacred site, including barrows, burial mounds, earthworks and a ceremonial pathway, the Avenue. But what did this site mean to its builders? Is it a temple? A sacrificial centre? A place of healing? A memorial to the ancestors? An astronomical timepiece? The truth is, nobody knows. And standing in the shadow of the stones, feeling their power and presence, it's impossible not to let your imagination run wild.

☛ SEE IT ! ***Salisbury has good rail and bus links, and pre-arranged Stonehenge tours. Admission is via timed tickets; to step inside the circle, pre-book a Stone Circle Access Visit, or come at solstice or equinox time.***

MYSTERIOUS MONOLITHS

↓

The stone houses at Skara Brae in Scotland are older than the Great Pyramid

☛ page 35

↓

Stonehenge's more accessible relative, Avebury is the biggest stone circle in the UK

☛ page 146

↓

Aligning with the stars on the Isle of Lewis, Callanish's standing stones are another puzzle

☛ page 235

09

Find poetry on the shores of Lake Windermere

CUMBRIA // England's largest natural lake – 10.5 miles from Ambleside to Newby Bridge – is at the heart of the Lake District and its most popular destination. People come in search of the scenic splendour and bucolic experiences that inspired Wordsworth, Coleridge and the English Romantics.

You can visit Wordsworth's house at Rydal Mount, or ride across the lake on a 19th-century steamer (sketchbook and pencil optional) just as the Victorians did. For more modern pursuits, the adventure centre at Brockhole, on the eastern side, has a zip wire running between 250-year-old oak trees.

Most activity is focused on the twin towns of Windermere (on a hill overlooking the lake) and busy Bowness-on-Windermere, which is home to the boat docks, a cluster of shops and the World of Beatrix Potter, which brings to life the most famous creations of the writer who dedicated her life to the preservation of the Lake District.

Far more evocative is Wray Castle, the mock-Gothic structure used by Potter's family as a holiday home. It's now empty but the lake views from the battlements are impressive; get there by boat from Bowness.

☛ SEE IT ! ***Windermere is in the South Lakes. Arrive by train at Windermere or by car via the A591 from Junction 36 on the M6.***

Top: the purpose of the enormous stones at Stonehenge remains a riddle. Bottom: a wintry view of Windermere in the Lake District

08

09

© Michael Roberts / Getty Images

10

Explore Pembrokeshire Coast National Park

SOUTH WALES // There's more to Wales than sheep, drizzly valleys and place names that are impossible to pronounce for outsiders. If you haven't been to the Pembrokeshire Coast National Park in the country's 'wild west', you are missing a trick. Wholly deserving of its number 10 Travelist slot, this ravishing stretch of cliff-flanked coves, thrashing seas, wildflower-freckled moors and hedgerowed tracks leading to one-pub villages still feels like a great escape. Life around here moves in the slow lane.

You've come for the beaches? Wise choice, you're in for a treat. Tenby in the south offers a classic dose of ice-cream-licking, bucket-and-spade fun. But the further west you head, the wilder it gets, with the likes of crescent-shaped Barafundle Bay, reached on foot through the dunes, surf-hammered Freshwater, and tucked-away Marloes with its high sea cliffs, shipwreck and boats heading over to puffin island, Skomer. A terrific base for beach-hopping and coastal-hiking is St Davids. Britain's smallest city is charm personified, with a whopping medieval cathedral, lanes staggering down to the sea, and a couple of highly stylish, architect-designed hotels, including art-slung former windmill Twr Y Felin and one-time Victorian convent Penrhiw.

Break up drives by striking out on the 186-mile Pembrokeshire Coast Path, which dips and rises over kissing gates and windy clifftops to smuggler's coves, wooded hollows where brooks burble, and Neolithic burial chambers. To up the adventure, go coasteering with the pros at eco-lodge Preseli Venture. Or turn your focus inland to the lonely Preseli Hills, a windswept range of rocky outcrops, low-lying peaks capped with prehistoric standing stones, and moorland flecked with gorse and heather.

SEE IT ! ***Driving gives you freedom to explore. Or take the train to Pembroke or Haverfordwest, then buses along the coast.***

Above: steps to Traeth Llyfn beach. Below: flowers bloom on the Pembrokeshire cliffs. Opposite: the surf breaks at Marloes Sands

© Michael Roberts / Getty Images

© Pete Seaward / Lonely Planet

Opposite, from top: festivalgoers flock to Glastonbury's main Pyramid Stage; punting past King's College on the River Cam

11

Go punting to see Cambridge at its blissful best

EAST ANGLIA // What gondolas are to Venice, punts are to Cambridge. These broad, flat-bottomed boats are propelled by a pole from a platform at the back. When done skilfully, progress is a thing of beauty. When done badly, everyone ends up in the water. Hence the appeal of punt tours, where your chauffeur, often in waistcoat and boater, pushes you on an idyllic route, drifting along the Backs (the rear of the colleges), past improbably grand buildings framed by bridges and lawns. Slide under the Bridge of Sighs, glide past gothic King's, marvel at the splendour of St John's. Or, if you're itching to try it yourself, heed the local advice: adopt a wide stance, bend the knees, steer with the pole and don't fall in. Oh, and hold on to that pole, especially around Clare Bridge – students sometimes snatch them for a laugh.

TRY IT ! *Fleets of punts sit waiting to be hired around the Silver St and Magdalene St bridges but you can also book ahead.*

12

Turn on to the music, mayhem and mud of Glastonbury

SOUTHWEST ENGLAND // Founded by dairy farmer turned entertainment impresario Michael Eavis, the majestic, marvellous, mud-drenched musical extravaganza that is the Glastonbury Festival of Contemporary Performing Arts has been held on and off every summer since 1970 on Eavis' own farm near Pilton in Somerset, within sight of the legendary Glastonbury Tor. From humble beginnings, the event has ballooned into the UK's biggest music festival, hosting more than 150,000 revellers and dozens of stages (not to mention art workshops, experimental theatre, comedy, crafts and more). It's a wild, weird, wonderful world of its own, and a rite of passage for every self-respecting British music fan. And no, watching it on the telly absolutely does not count.

SEE IT ! *Tickets sell out in minutes once on sale (usually the previous October). Join the website frenzy and hope for the best.*

12

11

Opposite, from top: the Millennium Bridge stretches across the Thames to St Paul's Cathedral; the white sands of Pentle Bay, Tresco

13

Be wowed by Christopher Wren's still monumental St Paul's Cathedral

LONDON // Even the Blitz failed to diminish London's great cathedral. Volunteer firefighters damped the flames, preserving St Paul's through a firestorm almost as destructive as the one that led to its construction. Hemmed in today by skyscrapers, the cathedral looks as imposing as it did in 1697, when Sir Christopher Wren opened it following the Great Fire of 1666. Wren himself resides in the crypt, alongside such luminaries as Wellington, Turner and Reynolds. The standout feature is the dome, reached via passageways and stairs, opening to an outdoor gallery offering dizzying views. In the chapels below, you can wander past ornate marble altars and iridescent stained glass, in the footsteps of royals and dignitaries married or buried here through the centuries.

☛ SEE IT ! ***St Paul's has its own Tube station, but it's more atmospheric to approach from Ludgate Hill, with the grand facade rising above the surrounding offices.***

14

Find paradise close to home in the western outpost of the Scilly Isles

SOUTHWEST ENGLAND // Land's End is where the British mainland finally runs out: a craggy finger of black cliffs and booming surf jutting out into the blue Atlantic. But the very end of the British Isles is to be found 28 miles further west on the Isles of Scilly, an archipelago of more than a hundred islands. Five (St Mary's, Tresco, St Martin's, St Agnes and Bryher) are inhabited; the rest are deserted and can only be visited aboard sightseeing boats. Better still, charter your own yacht, and live out those Robinson Crusoe fantasies as you discover the island's remotest coves and quietest beaches. Whether you decide to sail or sightsee, there are few destinations to match the scenery of the Scillies: paradise is not too strong a word.

☛ SEE IT ! ***The St Mary's Boatmen Association runs cruises to the outer islands from St Mary's. Summer is busy: come (by ferry, plane or helicopter) in spring or autumn for a more tranquil experience.***

13

14

Opposite, from top: fresh produce on the stalls of Borough Market; a performance of *King Lear* at Stratford-upon-Avon's Royal Shakespeare Theatre

15

See Shakespearean sights in Stratford-upon-Avon

MIDLANDS & THE MARCHES // The proud and pleasant home of the greatest-ever writer in the English language, this Warwickshire market town cashes in on the drama: opening to the public not only William Shakespeare's half-timbered birthplace, but also his granddaughter's husband's house, his son-in-law's house, his wife's old digs, his school and the church where he is buried.

Stratford-upon-Avon is at the vanguard of drama in the UK to this day. The Royal Shakespeare Company operates three theatres – the Royal Shakespeare, the Swan and the Other Place – where acclaimed plays from the prince of playwrights and his contemporaries are performed. Shakespeare'd out? The town touts plenty more 16th-century architectural charms than just the addresses with Bardic ties.

SEE IT ! ***Stratford-upon-Avon is 9 miles southwest of Warwick. Theatre tickets are best booked well in advance.***

16

Take a foodie foray through London's Borough Market

LONDON // Once a humble wholesale fruit and veg mart, Borough Market has become London's foodie epicentre, blowing holes in Britain's reputation for stodgy, stolid cuisine. The atmospheric location under the railway arches was created in the 1850s, but it wasn't until the 1980s that the market made the leap to artisan epicureanism. Today, there's nowhere better to browse for homegrown produce, exotic imports and rare breeds. Most visitors make a lunch of it, grazing on everything from Asian stir-fries and wild boar sausages to oysters and pungent cheeses, and sipping single-origin coffee or a cheeky Belgian Trappist ale. With the maze of stalls and phenomenal crowds, it pays to come early to get a head start on the lunching office workers from Wednesday to Friday, or the legions of tourists on Saturdays.

SEE IT ! ***London Bridge (not Borough) is the nearest Tube station. The market is open Weds–Sat and the stalls are mobbed at lunchtime.***

BOROUGH MARKET
BOROUGH MARKET
CANNON & CANNON
British Charcuterie
WILD BEEF
ANY 3 for £10
DORSET SAUCISSON SEC
CANNON & CANNON BRITISH CHARCUTERIE
CANNON & CANNON BRITISH CHARCUTERIE
3 × £10
RUSTIC WILD GAME
BRITISH CHARCUTERIE
WILD VENISON CHORIZO
VEAL (lemon & thyme) SALAMI
AIR-DRIED GOAT LEG
ANY 3 for £10
KENTISH CHORIZO
SUFFOLK CHORIZO
& MANY MORE (just ask)
FENNEL & GARLIC SAUCISSON
100% BRITISH CHARCUTERIE
TASTING TODAY!
• WILD SCOTTISH VENISON CHORIZO
• KENTISH COBNUT SALAMI
• WELSH VEAL, LEMON & THYME SALAMI
SUPPORT BRITISH PRODUCERS
16

15

© Helen Hotson / Shutterstock

Left: a riverside cottage in the cinematic foothills of Buachaille Etive Mor mountain in Glencoe, Scotland

17

Step into your own movie in Glencoe

HIGHLANDS & ISLANDS // Glencoe at dawn on a softly lit winter's day presents a portrait of a country dressed in its fullest finery – an image Scots love the rest of the world to see. Its snow-dusted hills, frozen waterfalls and lost valleys are suggestive of a mythical place created by an ambitious god. A rutting deer bellows across the moorland. A snow goose soars above a drifting canoe on a sea loch. A climber ropes up for a day above the clouds on the famed Aonach Eagach. It is a bold, adventurous context, and from every angle Glencoe offers a feast of Scottish storytelling.

The unforgettable entry point – the pyramid-shaped guardian Buachaille Etive Mor – is a fitting introduction. It is your archetypal Scottish mountain: its paths and precipices present dangerous obstacles for climbers and hikers; there's a life-affirming view from its top; and the location – overlooking Loch Etive and Glencoe Mountain Resort (ground zero for skiers and mountain bikers) – is classic movie fodder. You may recognise it from the James Bond film *Skyfall*, or from the Harry Potter series, extensively shot around the glen.

For all the silver-screen credentials, there is also an echo of grief and a hint of a macabre past. In the hush of the Glencoe Folk Museum, you'll find a shocking reminder of the infamous Glencoe Massacre, which saw 38 members of Clan MacDonald butchered in their beds following the Jacobite uprising. Yet far more than history, it is the natural drama that Glencoe remains proud of today. Glimpsed through the car windscreen – or on a mountain path, preparing for an old-fashioned adventure – the blissed-out faces say it all.

SEE IT ! ***Glencoe is a 93.5-mile drive north of Glasgow on the A82. For midge-free weather and smaller crowds, visit in April, May or September.***

Dry-stone walls are a prominent feature as they wind across the bucolic landscape of Wensleydale, North Yorkshire

18

Have an outdoor adventure in the Yorkshire Dales National Park

YORKSHIRE // Find a perfectly preserved slice of 1950s England in the Yorkshire Dales: picture-postcard villages of honey-coloured stone, with sheep grazing on the green, set against a distinctive landscape of flat-topped hills, stepped skylines and broad valleys patchworked with lush pastures and little stone barns. This countryside has served as a backdrop to British TV period dramas like *All Creatures Great and Small* and movies such as *Calendar Girls* and *Harry Potter and the Deathly Hallows*.

Protected as a national park since the 1950s, the Dales are a magnet for outdoor adventurers, offering some of Britain's best walking, mountain biking, caving and wild swimming. The limestone country in the southern part of the national park displays fine examples of karst scenery, including the natural amphitheatre of Malham Cove (#77 on this list) and the beetling crags of Gordale Scar. You can descend, if you dare, into the depths of Gaping Gill, a 328ft-deep cave shaft (open for a week in May and a week in August), or climb to the top of Whernside (2415ft), the highest summit in the Dales.

SEE IT ! ***The main Dales gateways are Skipton and Richmond. Good bases in the park include Settle, Grassington and Hawes.***

© Martin McCarthy

© Helen Cathcart / Lonely Planet

19

Catch your breath on Arthur's Seat

EDINBURGH // Imagine a stupefyingly wild landscape of rolling hills, basalt cliffs and glassy lochs, behind which lies a once-upon-a-time castle and a row of fairy-tale turrets crowding the skyline. This is the seemingly impossible view from Arthur's Seat, the 335-million-year-old extinct volcano rooted at Edinburgh's centre. It is the rampant Scotland you've been dreaming of, complete with snaggle-tooth ruins, mussed-up gorse ridges and a ridiculous measure of excitement as you finally reach the 823ft summit.

☛ SEE IT ! ***Situated southeast of Edinburgh's Old Town, Arthur's Seat is a 3-mile round trip from Holyrood Palace.***

20

Promenade with the people on London's South Bank

LONDON // The capital owes its existence to the toffee-coloured waters of the Thames, and the section of the Thames Path that traces the South Bank offers a view of London's most prominent landmarks: the Tower of London, St Paul's, Shakespeare's Globe, Tate Modern, Parliament, the Shard... Start from Shad Thames, whose hulking wharfs recall the days when tall ships moored in the heart of London, then follow the South Bank past royal relics and brutalist cultural venues to Parliament, for a transect through London, past, present and future.

☛ SEE IT ! ***Start at Tower Hill Tube, on the north bank, for a chance to see the Tower before the crowds swell.***

Durham Cathedral stands on the banks of the River Wear from where it looms over its host city

© stocker1970 / Shutterstock

21

Contemplate 1000 years of ecclesiastical history at Durham Cathedral

NORTHEAST ENGLAND // Soaring heavenward, Durham's colossal cathedral is a marvel of earthly achievement. An architectural game changer, it pioneered pointed stone arches, and today it's a Unesco World Heritage site along with nearby Durham Castle, home to the city's prestigious university.

Over a millennia of history is chronicled here: the community of St Cuthbert arrived in 995 from Lindisfarne (Holy Island) with Cuthbert's miraculously preserved body, and built an Anglo-Saxon cathedral. After the Norman Conquest, Benedictine monks arrived in 1083; construction on the cathedral as it appears today began a decade later. The exquisite 1175-built Galilee Chapel shelters the tomb of the 8th-century Northumbrian monk, Venerable Bede, who introduced the AD system for numbering years. The 218ft-high central tower dates from 1262 (though it was rebuilt in 1470) – climb the western towers for views across the city. Back on ground level, look out for the original Sanctuary Knocker, on the northern door, which medieval felons used to gain 37 days' refuge in the cathedral before standing trial.

SEE IT ! ***Direct trains to Durham run from cities including Newcastle (in less than 20 minutes), Edinburgh, London and York.***

Chemmy Alcott's Top Five Places

Four-time winter Olympian Chemmy Alcott is the only British female skier to ever win a run in a World Cup. She is now a presenter and commentator for the BBC and Eurosport, while still competing in physical challenges.

01

PAINSHILL PARK, COBHAM – I live just outside London and spend a lot of time in the city, so like to escape to the quiet. Painshill Park is divine, I do an amazing yoga class then walk; in autumn the leaves are so colourful.

02

ISABELLA PLANTATION, RICHMOND PARK – Before my mum passed away in 2006 she used to volunteer at the Isabella Plantation. Visiting in spring, finding the secret ponds surrounded by magical colours, always helps me remember her energy.

03

PETERSHAM NURSERIES, RICHMOND – My godmothers and I always have our catch up here. It's a lovely Balinese greenhouse with the best coffee and cake, and I can while away hours there writing and reflecting.

04

THE LANES, BRIGHTON – I spent a lot of time in Brighton when I was younger and love revisiting the quirky lanes, sitting in the cafes people watching and finding some amazing handmade treasures in the tiny boutiques.

05

LOCH LOMOND, SCOTLAND – My in-laws live near here and I just love going for a day out on the boat. This summer we went to the Loch and had the most wonderful siesta on a secluded beach looking out over the water.

22

Solve the mysteries of Skara Brae

HIGHLANDS & ISLANDS // The Orkney Islands' Skara Brae is Britain's Pompeii. Forming the best-preserved Neolithic site in Western Europe, its cluster of eight Unesco-listed stone houses was occupied from about 3180 BC to 2500 BC. Remarkably, it's older than both the Great Pyramid of Giza and Stonehenge, yet is still a work in progress – excavations are ongoing and its next chapter is yet to be written.

SEE IT ! ***Skara Brae's Visitor Centre is open year-round and can be reached by car, or by taking a bus to Sandwick on the Bay of Skaill.***

© Padmayogini / Shutterstock

23

Be one with the bard at Shakespeare's Globe

LONDON // No matter that it's not on the site of Shakespeare's original theatre, or that it was cooked up by a Hollywood movie actor, the Globe Theatre is a fitting tribute to Britain's most-loved playwright. The building is a faithful recreation of the theatre where Shakespeare trod the boards as a young actor, based on 16th- and 17th-century plans. Seeing a show here offers a glimpse of Elizabethan theatre in all its turnip-throwing glory. True to historical form, the Globe has launched a string of modern talent, include Mark Rylance, the first artistic director here in the 1990s.

SEE IT ! ***The Globe is an essential stop on the South Bank walk between London Bridge and the Southbank Centre.***

© Saffron Blaze / Getty Images

24

Discover Harry Potter on Edinburgh's Royal Mile

EDINBURGH // The Royal Mile is a big, booming boulevard, with bagpipes warbling as you stroll past a procession of tight-quartered towers and crooked tenements that would make the wizards and witches from Harry Potter feel at home. Both its curtain-raiser, Edinburgh Castle, and its grand finale, the Palace of Holyroodhouse, bookend the street with drama, but there's extra magic in the spaces in-between. Discover the Hogwarts-like majesty of St Giles' Cathedral, spot ghosts in Greyfriars Kirkyard, or browse Victoria St, a Diagon Alley-style wynd that inspired JK Rowling.

SEE IT ! ***Running downhill from Castle Esplanade, the Royal Mile is easiest to explore from west to east.***

The hexagonal *The Hive* by sculptor Wolfgang Buttress at London's Kew Gardens is based on the structure of a real beehive

25

Breathe deep in the green bower of Kew Gardens

LONDON // In the heyday of the British Empire, London's botanical gardens were a hotbed of intrigue, as colonial botanists smuggled in seeds and cuttings from across the globe in the hope of breaking the horticultural monopolies of rival powers. It was through these gorgeous gardens that rubber made its way from Brazil to Ceylon (Sri Lanka), breaking Portuguese control of the world's bottle stoppers, rainproofs and tyres.

Kew's towering 19th-century glasshouses rank among Britain's best-loved buildings, especially the Palm House, which allows a mature tropical rainforest to flourish. These Victorian wonders have been joined by contemporary glasshouses hosting everything from alpine blooms to agave cacti. Kew sprawls over 121 hectares, offering miles of walks through ornamental gardens and woodland glades dotted with ginkgos, monkey puzzles and coastal redwoods. In between picnicking and ambling through the forest canopy, you can drop into a number of historic follies, from mock-up Greco-Roman temples to a 10-storey Chinese pagoda built by Sinophile architect William Chambers.

SEE IT ! ***Take the Tube to Kew Gardens station, or a boat from Westminster Pier (April to October).***

© Travellinglight / Alamy

Left: a tidal pool on the beach of Yorkshire's Robin Hood's Bay, a village rich in historical and natural intrigue

26

Enjoy a rock-pool ramble at Robin Hood's Bay

YORKSHIRE // So picturesque it hurts, this ancient fishing village seems to tumble down the North Yorkshire sea cliffs in a cascade of whitewashed cottages and red pantile roofs. A maze of narrow lanes leads off the forbiddingly steep main street (do not try to drive down here; use the car park in the upper village), tempting you to explore. In the process of getting pleasantly lost, you'll stumble across quaint craft shops, artists' studios, cosy tearooms and even a tiny cinema, before popping out on a terrace with an unexpected view of the sea.

The origins of the village's name are shrouded in mystery, but they have nothing to do with the hero of Sherwood Forest; locals call the place 'Bay Town', or simply 'Bay'. It was a notorious haunt of 18th-century smugglers who brought contraband tobacco and spirits ashore under cover of darkness; learn more about its history in the volunteer-run Bay Museum.

The old coastguard station at the foot of the main street marks the eastern end of the Coast to Coast Walk and houses a National Trust visitor centre with displays on the region's natural history. It's also the starting point for rock-pool rambles on the foreshore, and for longer hikes along the rugged and scenic 'Jurassic coast' – the rocks here are noted for the fossilised remains of ammonites, ichthyosaurs and plesiosaurs. Footpaths lead north to Whitby (6 miles) and south to the spooky sea cave known as Boggle Hole (1 mile); at low tide you can stroll along the sand at the foot of the cliffs. Here you'll find one of England's most delightful youth hostels (YHA Boggle Hole), complete with welcoming cafe, set in a heritage water mill at the back of a smuggler's cove.

☛ SEE IT ! ***The village is 6 miles southeast of Whitby. It's a 2.5-hour walk, or travel by bike or a 10-minute bus ride.***

© Artem Vorobiev / Getty Images

27

Lose your head amid the horrible histories of the Tower of London

LONDON // Assembled over nearly 1000 years ago, the Tower of London has been the stage for more murders and mysteries than a *Game of Thrones* box set. William the Conqueror laid the foundations. Henry VI and Edward V were murdered here. Anne Boleyn and Catherine Howard, wives of Henry VIII, lost their heads on Tower Green. Everyone from Thomas Cromwell, Walter Raleigh and Guy Fawkes to Rudolf Hess and the Kray Twins spent time imprisoned in the Tower's cells.

As one of the world's premier tourist attractions, the tower is always busy, but a cheerful contingent of Beefeater guards (and their pet ravens) keep everything moving smoothly, ensuring you won't face too long a wait to gaze on the diamond-encrusted Crown Jewels, or the priapic suit of armour of Henry VIII.

SEE IT ! ***Tower Hill station is on the doorstep. Combine a visit with a stroll over Tower Bridge to the cafes around City Hall.***

© Susan Lansdell / Alamy

28

Let Holkham Beach soothe your soul as you sink your toes in its fine sands

EAST ANGLIA // Low tide reveals a seemingly endless sweep of white-gold sand stretching towards a distant sea. The highest tides create a dazzling lagoon, thanks to a crescent-shaped basin filling up fast. And this is just part of a 14-sq-mile nature reserve of dunes, marsh, pinewoods and scrub. Long, straight Lady Anne's Drive leads to ribboning pathways that snake through forests, past bird hides and on to a cinematic shore – Gwyneth Paltrow wandered here in *Shakespeare in Love* and it's an unrivalled spot for a windblown, sand-dusted stroll under the blue dome of a north Norfolk sky. Afterwards, join the locals at the Victoria, at the gates of Palladian Holkham Hall. In this atmospheric inn, the food comes from the surrounding Holkham Estate, the pints are perfect and you can warm yourself beside a fire.

SEE IT ! ***Holkham sits on the A149, a rolling road running along Norfolk's shore and linking beaches, bird marshes and villages.***

Top: the rock arch of Durdle Door on Dorset's Jurassic Coast. Below: Man O' War Beach lies just to the east of the arch

© artherng / Getty Images

29

Wild swim under Durdle Door

SOUTHWEST ENGLAND // Is there a more famous arch in Britain? All right, maybe Marble Arch. But apart from that one? Named after an Old English word 'thirl', meaning to bore, drill or pierce, Durdle Door is one of the most famed – and photographed – sights on the Dorset coastline. Some 200ft high and 10,000 years old, this graceful rock arch has been carved out from the nearby limestone cliffs by the relentless pounding action of the sea. It takes on different forms depending on your view – from one angle, it looks like a horse stooping its head to drink; from another, it resembles the outline of a monstrous sea dragon rearing up from the waves. Or if you're more prosaically minded, it just looks like a cool thing to kayak or swim through – although currents around the arch can be strong, so take extra care, don't swim alone, and watch the tide times carefully. Lulworth Cove itself is equally dramatic: a near-perfect horseshoe, scattered with white pebbles and numerous rock pools, ideal for exploring at low tide.

SEE IT ! *Durdle Door is part of the privately owned Lulworth Estate, about 40 minutes' drive from Poole. There is a small car park nearby, and a steep path leading down to the beach from the clifftops.*

© Manfred Gottschalk / Alamy

Opposite from top: York Minster's imposing Gothic facade; playing with fire at Bonfire Night in Lewes

30

Bask in the medieval magic of York Minster

YORKSHIRE // Choose a bright morning to visit York Minster, northern Europe's largest medieval cathedral and one of the world's most beautiful Gothic buildings. Stand before the high altar and bask in the sunlight streaming through the Great East Window. At 77.8ft by 30.8ft, it is the world's largest medieval stained-glass window, completed in 1408. Its size matches the epic theme depicted therein: the beginning and end of the world as described in Genesis and the Book of Revelations. Some 92,400 hours of restoration work were completed in 2018, returning this masterpiece to its original beauty. Don't miss the minster's Undercroft, a basement maze littered with Roman and Norman remains that chart 2000 years of history on this site, including a Roman culvert that still carries water to the nearby River Ouse.

SEE IT ! ***Climb the 275 steps to the top of the Minster's tower for breathtaking views over the city of York.***

31

Remember Bonfire Night in Lewes

SOUTHEAST ENGLAND // Nowhere else in the UK celebrates Bonfire Night quite like this small East Sussex town, which becomes something of a full-blown riot each year. Events here commemorate the Lewes Martyrs, seven Protestants burned at the stake in 1556, as well as the infamous 5th November Gunpowder Plot. All seems normal (save the 'No Popery' banner strung up in the cobbled town centre) until nightfall, when bonfire societies from across the region parade through the streets carrying torches, burning crosses and effigies of Guy Fawkes, the Pope and modern-day politicians and rabble-rousers. Exploding firecrackers land at your feet as locals loudly chant: 'Burn him!' After a few loops of the main street, the societies head out to the South Downs where the effigies meet their fiery fate.

SEE IT ! ***Book accommodation well ahead. Lewes is small so you'll likely have to stay in a neighbouring village or in Brighton.***

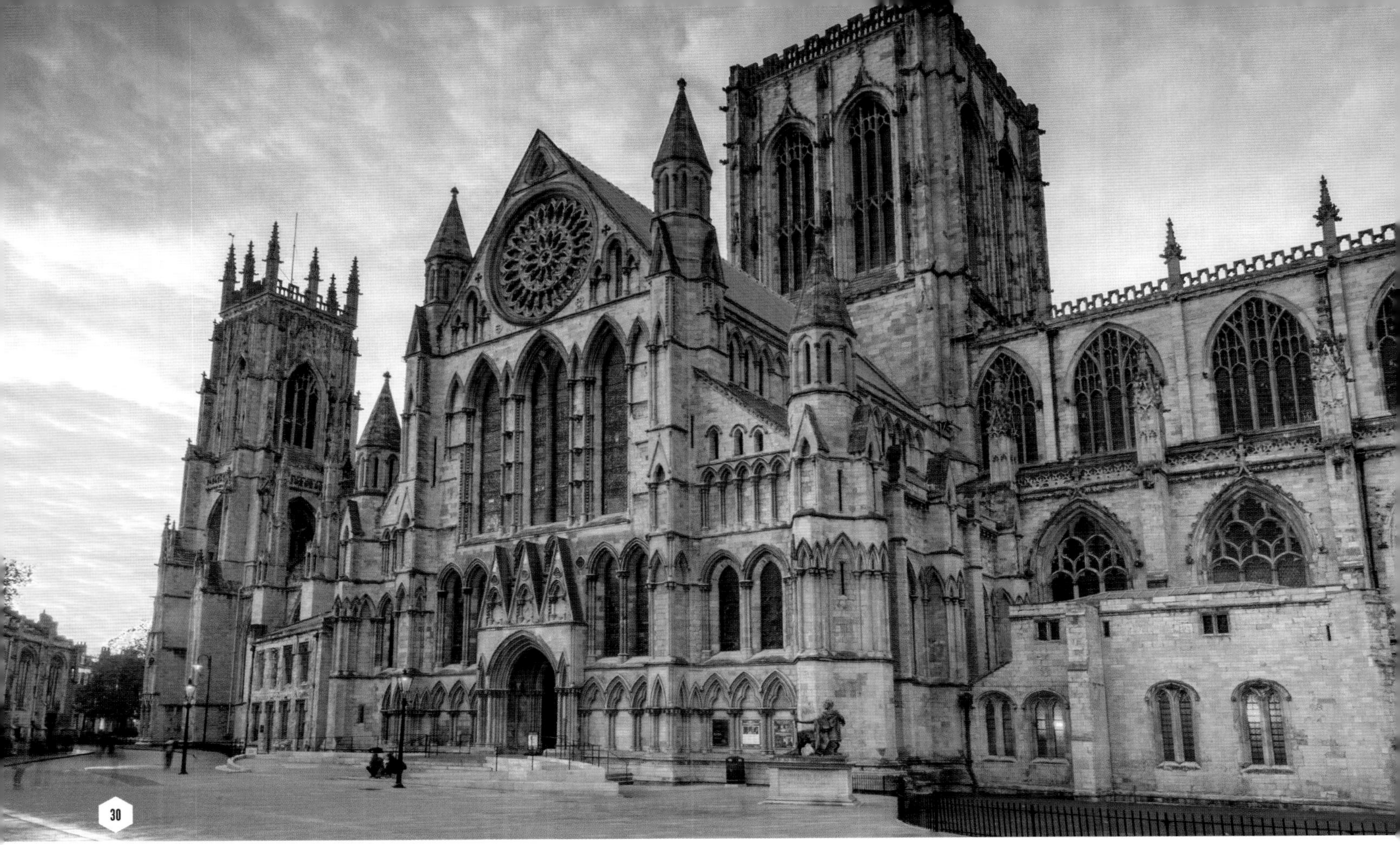

30

31

© Jason Batterham / Shutterstock

Different perspectives of the stately exterior and sweeping grounds of Derbyshire's 16th-century Chatsworth House

© Jo Jones / Shutterstock

GLORIOUS MANSIONS

↓

The birthplace of Winston Churchill, Blenheim Palace is the only non-Royal, non-episcopal country home in England to hold the title of palace

☛ page 90

↓

A work of theatrical grandeur, Castle Howard played a starring role in 1980s TV series *Brideshead Revisited*

☛ page 105

↓

The coronation place of Scottish monarchs, Scone Palace (pronounced 'skoon') featured in *Macbeth*

☛ page 252

© Georgethefourth / Shutterstock

32

Allow the grandeur of Chatsworth House to take your breath away

MIDLANDS & THE MARCHES // Incurable romantics have been drawn to this stately Derbyshire delight for centuries, not least us here at Lonely Planet, who voted Chatsworth House number one mansion on our UK best-of list. The setting helps. Just outside the dale-ensconced town of Bakewell, vistas around the property unfold on to the Peak District National Park's foothills, framed by a swathe of the Derwent Valley, of which 105 wondrous acres are the estate's very own.

Then, there is the pedigree. Chatsworth House has belonged to the Cavendishes, among Britain's most politically influential aristocratic households, from 1549 to this day, making it one of the longest continually occupied residences by the same family: 16 successive generations, including today's incumbents the Duke and Duchess of Devonshire, have stamped their character upon it. The Cavendish clan ensured a lavish legacy for their estate. William, first of the family to bear the title of Duke, embarked on the jaw-dropping Painted Hall in 1689: in a shrewd move, he flattered then-king William III by decorating the hall in scenes from Julius Caesar's life, and got promoted to Duke the year the room was complete. The sixth Duke, an avid collector, added an entire North Wing centred around a purpose-built sculpture gallery to accommodate his burgeoning collection of busts. Sculpted works, including those by Anthony Gormley and Elisabeth Frink, add a modern touch to the superb artefacts collection.

Then, of course, there is its indelible association with one of the most famous love stories ever penned in English: Pemberley, address of a certain Fitzwilliam Darcy in Jane Austen's *Pride and Prejudice*, is thought to be based on Chatsworth.

☛ SEE IT ! ***Chatsworth House is 3.5 miles northeast of Bakewell and 11 miles west of Chesterfield, which has the closest railway station.***

33

Hike the 630 miles of the South West Coast Path

SOUTHWEST ENGLAND // Britain might be a tiddler compared to many of its European neighbours in terms of square acreage, but it's a different matter when it comes to coastline. At some 7723 miles, it has one of the longest coastlines of any European nation. Roughly a tenth of that encircles the southwest peninsula, home to the South West Coast Path. Running for 630 miles from Minehead in Somerset to Poole in Dorset, the trail tracks the full diversity of coastal landscape: rock towers, white beaches, hidden coves, pebble banks, coastal lagoons, sheer cliffs, wildflower-speckled headlands. It can be done in sections, or as one epic multi-week adventure, breaking the journey at campsites, pubs or B&Bs. By the end, you'll be footsore and knackered, but you'll see corners of the UK most ordinary folk may never reach.

SEE IT ! ***The South West Coast Path Association publishes an annual guide and has an excellent website, packed with useful information and route-planning tools.***

© Meibion / Alamy

34

Go Victorian with dinner and a show in Theatreland

LONDON // Shakespeare and Burbage may have laid the groundwork at the Curtain and the Globe, but it was the opening of the Theatre Royal on Drury Lane in 1663 that triggered the meteoric rise of London's Theatreland. The Victorian love of melodrama sealed the deal, ushering in a golden age of gala openings and gushing reviews. Today, Theatreland tussles with Broadway for the biggest names, and people fly in from all over the planet just to take in a show. Runs here can be epic – *Les Misérables* played to packed audiences for 21 revolution-filled years. Every season brings new openings; some of them soar, some fall flat, but the thrill of watching the curtain rise endures, as does the buzz of eating in one of the West End's restaurants before a performance.

SEE IT ! ***Covent Garden, Leicester Square and Piccadilly Circus Tube stations are lined up through the heart of Theatreland, offering easy access to the bright lights and pre-theatre menu deals.***

© Grant Rooney / Alamy

© Andrew Thomas / 500px

35

Take a roll across Beachy Head and Seven Sisters white cliffs

SOUTHEAST ENGLAND // A natural rollercoaster carved from Sussex chalk, the Seven Sisters cliffs gleam out from the coast like some celebrity's XXL-size teeth. Viewed from the hamlet of Cuckmere Haven, the vertical, snow-white rock creates one of the south's most memorable spectacles. Heading east, these white cliffs culminate in Beachy Head, a massive chalk headland that looms over the resort of Eastbourne. The cliffs are a superb day hike from Eastbourne and are literally and figuratively the high point of the 62-mile South Downs Way.

☛ SEE IT ! *Bus 12 runs between Brighton and Eastbourne, stopping at Cuckmere Haven and occasionally Beachy Head.*

© Chris Dorney / Shutterstock

36

Fall under a spell on the Making of Harry Potter: Warner Bros Studio Tour

SOUTHERN ENGLAND // No fantasy land has captured the world's imagination quite like the witch-and-wizard Britain of JK Rowling's Harry Potter books. A hush descends as your group is led through time-worn wood-carved doors to Hogwarts' sweeping Great Hall – the first of many spellbinding sights on the famed Warner Bros studio tour, from Dumbledore's office and Diagon Alley to Sirius Black's motorbike. The star is a shimmering 1:24 scale model of a turreted Gothic castle, used for Hogwarts exteriors (and requiring 86 artists in its creation).

☛ SEE IT ! *The studio is 20 miles northwest of London. Take the train from London Euston to Watford Junction, then a shuttle bus.*

© Daniel Alford / Lonely Planet

37

Buckle up for a storied, picturesque North Coast 500 adventure

HIGHLANDS & ISLANDS // The words 'road trip' may make you roll your eyes, but this edge-of-the-world loop from Inverness is a reminder that the concept is simply about going back to the basics. Over 516 miles, the beautiful Sutherland coasts and Caithness skies shift things up a gear, and there are Insta-ready stags in the rear-view and the forgotten-by-time beaches of Wester Ross to explore up ahead.

Mostly, the North Coast 500 offers just one route to follow, namely a choice of clockwise circuits from Inverness Castle, via the crofting villages of Wick, Durness, Lochinver, Ullapool and Torridon. However, adding to the adventure, the road map delivers storied castles, single-malt whisky distilleries, sea lochs, snorkelling sites and sandy bays. Truly, it's as if the locals have included all of these diversions to keep you here as long as possible.

TRY IT ! *The NC500 is wildly popular – drive the route in winter, not from June to August.*

© Philip Bird LRPS CPAGB / Shutterstock

38

Feel the cultural buzz in boho Soho and creative Covent Garden

LONDON // Cultured, creative and crammed into the heart of old London, Soho may trade on its libertine past, but it's still one of the capital's buzzy quarters. Though traces of Paul Raymond's 1960s striptease empire linger in parts, Soho has rebranded itself as a hub of movie post-production. Casual visitors are more likely to be drawn to the flamboyant, friendly gay scene along Old Compton St, the quirky music and bookstores around Charing Cross Rd, a scattering of restaurants on the backstreets, and the pizzazz of Theatreland.

Just west, bohemian gives way to big brands around Covent Garden, whose grand piazza was laid out by neoclassical master Inigo Jones. The covered market mixes tourist-oriented knick-knacks and energetic street performances, but there's more interesting shopping to be had in venerable institutions such as Stanfords, just off Mercer St.

SEE IT ! *Skip crazily busy Covent Garden Tube for the easier stroll from Leicester Square or Tottenham Court Rd.*

© Oscar Dominguez / Alamy

© Justin Foulkes / Lonely Planet

39

See (and smell) the thousands of seals on Blakeney Point

EAST ANGLIA // The 4-mile-long shingle spit of Blakeney Point juts out to sea off the north Norfolk coast, curving around a bewitching shore of beach, creek and marsh. Here on the crunchy shingle sit thousands of seals; the largest colony in England, with some 2700 pups born each winter. Boats departing from picturesque local harbours let you enjoy this remarkable sight – furry blobs basking in the sun as far as the eye can see. As the boats edge closer, features come into focus; flapping flippers and ultra-cute snouts and eyes.

SEE IT ! *The best times to visit are between July and August when the common seals pup. Trips are popular – book ahead.*

40

Explore England's rooftop in the Lake District

CUMBRIA // If you want to witness the world from above, Cumbria gives you the choice of England's 10 tallest peaks. There's Helvellyn, which is a 9-mile ascent from Striding Edge – one of the best ridge walks in the country – that takes you 3116ft into the sky. Down below are the dark crags and shimmering lakes of the Lake District. Helvellyn's bigger brothers are Scafell and Scafell Pike, the tallest of them all, with unparalleled 360-degree views. This is the best mountain climbing in England, with views to match.

SEE IT ! *Uncertain weather is the biggest danger for climbers, so let people know where you're going and carry all safety equipment.*

The Fairy Pools of Skye are a collection of crystal-clear pools at the foot of the Black Cuillins; they are popular with wild swimmers

Adam Seward / Alamy Stock Photo

41

Believe in the impossible on a hike to the Fairy Pools

HIGHLANDS & ISLANDS // When Samuel Johnson wrote of an archetypal Hebridean island set about with primitive wilderness, relics and stories, he was referring to the Isle of Skye. The writer spent a month on the largest of the Inner Hebrides, his research forming part of his lauded 18th-century travelogue, *A Journey to the Western Islands of Scotland*, and there's a compelling argument little has changed since. It remains wild, untamed and grander than any of its neighbours. This is an island that dwarfs its rivals, in the mind's eye and in reality.

Everything about his description of Skye can be found on a walk to the Fairy Pools. It is one of the island's most popular natural attractions, beginning by following the gin-clear River Brittle past pools and waterfalls swollen from snowmelt and heavy Atlantic rains. You'll skim past heathery knolls and peat moors, hopscotch across the river on stepping stones, and be rewarded with a fine view of the Black Cuillins and a stunning whirlpool. This is where you'll almost certainly see those brave enough stripping off for a mad dash wild swim. Maybe, you'll spot a fairy, too.

Such beauty has its upsides and its downsides. The pools' popularity on social media has led to an influx of grab-and-go visitors, many of whom show little regard for the area's fragile ecology. The car park also strains under visitor numbers – it's not uncommon for the single-track road to be gridlocked by cars obtrusively parked on roadside verges. The good news? A community takeover means new facilities are in the pipeline and such problems will – hopefully – be better managed in future. In the meantime, stick to the path and leave only footprints.

SEE IT ! ***The Fairy Pools walk is a 1.5-mile round trip, with around 1300ft of lung-emptying ascent. Paid parking is available in the Forestry Commission car park signposted 'Glumagan Na Sithichean'.***

© Loop Images Ltd / Alamy

42

Stalk with highwaymen on Hampstead Heath

LONDON // Mercifully resistant to urban sprawl, the vast, naturally wild green space of Hampstead Heath is cherished by Londoners. With a historical reputation for highwaymen, and a modern reputation for naughty liaisons after dark, this is where the capital comes to let its hair down, typically followed by a pint at one of the 16th-century coaching inns. In times past, the dome of St Paul's dominated the panorama from Parliament Hill, but today Wren's masterpiece has been engulfed by glass-clad towers – that said, the views from here are still the best in London. Also here are the Hampstead and Highgate ponds, a collection of pools that serve variously as wildlife reserves, model boating ponds and open-air swimming pools for those willing to brave temperatures that can dip as low as 1°C.

☛ SEE IT ! *Hampstead Tube is handy for Hampstead Village but quite a stroll from the heath – take the Overground to Hampstead Heath or Gospel Oak instead.*

© Neil Wakeling / 500px

43

Spend a night on ice in Cairngorms National Park

HIGHLANDS & ISLANDS // The walk is harder going than you thought, your rucksack – packed with shovel and supplies – hurts your back, and a winter's wind is harrying you across the mountain ridge. Yet the prospect of reaching the gully ahead, where you'll dig a snow hole, then shelter overnight in a sleeping bag with a stove and bottle of Speyside malt, drives you on.

A night in a snow hole may be a little much for many visitors, but micro-adventures and awe-inspiring moments are easily enjoyed in Britain's largest national park, with or without a little extra legwork. Caledonian pine trails lead to lochs for canoeing and kayaking; Ben Macdui, the UK's second tallest peak, offers touching-the-void assaults; and Cairngorm Mountain is a boon for skiers and boarders. Endless outdoor fun? There's simply no time to take it easy.

☛ SEE IT ! *Aviemore, 30 miles south of Inverness, is the best place to base yourself. A car is recommended.*

44

Embrace your inner Goth in bewitching Whitby

YORKSHIRE // When a cold east wind whips in off the North Sea, shredding the mist among the gravestones and gables of the medieval clifftop abbey, it's easy to see why Bram Stoker chose Whitby as the setting for Count Dracula's landfall. Stoker regularly visited Whitby (a blue plaque marks his digs), and despite movie versions focusing on Transylvania, much of the original story was set here. The town has since embraced its Gothic reputation, with guided ghost walks, shops selling Victorian-style jet jewellery, and a summer steampunk festival.

SEE IT ! ***For maximum gothic ambience, visit during one of two annual Goth Weekends (late April/early May and late Oct/early Nov).***

45

Take on Snowdon, the loftiest summit in Wales or England

NORTH WALES // True, this is Wales' (if not Britain's) most traipsed hike and with 500,000+ annually trekking up, Snowdon can feel more like rush hour than a remote ramble. But it is Britain's highest mountain south of Scotland, and views are sublime, with steel-blue Llyn Lydaw lake sparkling at the forefront of a mountainscape sliding magisterially away to sea. And if it rains? The summit has a cafe! And a station with trains running back to civilisation. Not many mountains can claim that.

SEE IT ! ***Llanberis is the most popular start point for hiking up Snowdon, and jump-on point for the train ride up.***

Alan Novelli / Alamy Stock Photo

46

Meet dinosaurs and Darwin at the Natural History Museum

LONDON // In a magnificent Romanesque building, the Natural History Museum elevates the subject to fine art. Beneath a soaring vaulted ceiling, a skeletal blue whale dives into the hangar-sized central hall, while around the galleries, terracotta fish and reptiles writhe across the walls, above specimens of dinosaurs, diamonds and dodos. Some of the specimens were collected personally by Charles Darwin, so pay homage to his statue on the stairway, then beat a trail to the gallery of ichthyosaurs, dug out of the Lyme Regis cliffs by Mary Anning.

☛ SEE IT ! ***South Kensington Tube offers easy access to the Natural History Museum, Science Museum and V&A.***

The sun goes down beyond the Worm's Head promontory on the Gower Peninsula in South Wales

47

Gasp at the coastlines of the Gower Peninsula

SOUTH WALES // When it comes to Welsh beaches, the Gower Peninsula has some of the fairest of them all. This is Swansea's pride, joy and not-so-little secret, where butterscotch sands shift with the tides, limestone cliffs roll on to wild, wave-lashed headlands, and fragile dunes and salt marshes, threaded through with the faintest of paths, bristle with marram grass and bright-purple orchids. Pretty special, huh? Well, poet, writer and Swansea lad Dylan Thomas certainly thought so. He wrote many a short story rhapsodising the pull of Gower locations like Worm's Head and three-mile Rhossili Bay. Pick your own spot and you, too, will likely be smitten: perhaps by the fizzing surf of Llangennith or deliciously secluded coves like Pobbles and Tor Bay. Yes, those winding lanes get chock-a-block in August and the odd stray sheep is par for the course, but it's worth it. If you're game enough to strike out on the Wales Coast Path, you'll soon grasp why the Gower became the UK's first official Area of Outstanding Natural Beauty back in 1956 – it still hasn't lost its touch.

SEE IT ! ***The Gower is southwest of the M4 and Swansea, which has the nearest train station. Buses trundle along the coast.***

© WALVAUS / Alamy

The Giant's Head, Lost Gardens of Heligan © 1998 Pete Hill & Sue Hill. peteandsuehill.co.uk. Image © khd / Shutterstock

48

Roar the dragons to victory at the Principality Stadium

SOUTH WALES // Football? Forget it. For many of the Welsh, rugby is much more than just the number-one sport, it is a virtual religion, and this stadium, by far the country's largest, is its principal cathedral. Home of the Welsh national rugby union side and host of the 1999 Rugby World Cup, it has adapted to serve as a venue for major events from the Champions League final to boxing clashes. The stadium sports some impressive stats – 34 bars and 74,500 seats – but no numbers compare to coming out above the pitch for a Six Nations match as *Cwm Rhondda* (*Bread of Heaven*) or *Hen Wlad Fy Nhadau* (*Land of My Fathers*) echoes around the arena and the thrill, hope or expectation of victory for the Dragons is palpable in the (regularly rain-drenched) air.

☛ SEE IT ! ***The Principality Stadium (formerly Millennium Stadium) is on Westgate St in central Cardiff, south of Bute Park.***

49

Uncover Cornish secrets in the Lost Gardens of Heligan

SOUTHWEST ENGLAND // This is Cornwall's very own, real-life secret garden. At the end of the 19th century, the magnificent gardens of the Tremayne family near Mevagissey were one of Cornwall's horticultural wonders, but WWI took a heavy toll: many of the estate workers never returned from the trenches and the gardens sunk into disrepair. But in 1990, record producer turned renaissance man Tim Smit (the brains behind the Eden Project) decided to reclaim the gardens from the undergrowth, helped by an army of volunteers. Three decades later, Heligan has been restored to its luxuriant landscaped glory, with winding paths, elegant lawns, lakes, kitchen gardens, acres of woodland, a working farm and even a 'Jungle Valley', filled with tropical plants that thrive in the gardens' unique microclimate.

☛ SEE IT ! ***Heligan is 7 miles from St Austell. Summer can be busy, so time your visit for spring blooms or autumn foliage.***

© Aeypix / Shutterstock

Opposite: Christ Church dining Hall at Oxford University set the template for Harry Potter's Hogwarts

50

Unravel Oxford history at Christ Church College

OXFORD & THE COTSWOLDS // If you visit just one British university college, make it majestic, ever-so-slightly haunting Christ Church – though Cantabrigians will inevitably try to lead you astray! Literary heritage, movie mania, immense arts riches and outstanding architecture collide in Oxford's largest college, which has also long been one of its wealthiest, complete with its own cathedral and gallery and the city's most inspiring quadrangle. Throw in a graduate cast starring the likes of Sir Christopher Wren, Charles Dodgson (Lewis Carroll) and an army of British prime ministers, and Christ Church's perennial popularity is indisputable.

Strolling these hallowed halls feels like winding the clock back a few centuries and entering a bygone era. Christ Church was founded in 1525 by Cardinal Wolsey, though its church (so important that it doubles as the city cathedral) has stood here since the 12th century, on the site of a shrine to St Frideswide. It's easy to imagine Lewis Carroll dreaming up *Alice's Adventures in Wonderland* (whose protagonist was inspired by Alice Liddell, the daughter of the Christ Church dean of his time) in the 1860s, or Christopher Wren skilfully perfecting the Gothic-style Tom Tower in the late 17th century (its Great Tom clock still chimes 101 times at the original 9.05pm curfew time). Beyond, the college meadow ripples into the distance flanked by the Thames and Cherwell rivers.

Last but not least, instead of touring the Harry Potter Warner Bros studios near London, you could opt to see the inspiration for the Hogwarts dining hall in all its glittering original glory at Christ Church, whose Great Hall is a Renaissance masterwork resting under a hammer beam roof (sadly no magical changing Harry Potter skies) and accessed via an exquisite fan-vaulted staircase.

SEE IT ! ***The cathedral celebrates evensong at 6pm most days; at other times, it's only free to enter for services or prayer.***

© David Levenson / Alamy

© Valdis Skudre / Shutterstock

51

Mix champers and champions at Wimbledon

LONDON // London's sports calendar is fast-paced and frenetic, but Wimbledon drops things to a more genteel pace, the occasional racquet-throwing tantrum notwithstanding. Sure, there are grunts and the odd expletive, but how many other sporting events can be enjoyed over champagne and strawberries in the (fingers crossed) English sunshine? The British leg of the Grand Slam tournament shifted from June to July a few years back, ensuring the best chance of idyllic weather to accompany the season's best summer fruit. The biggest challenge is getting tickets. Unless you are well connected, try the public ballot, held the August before the tournament. If that fails, tickets change hands for monster sums online, or you can camp through the night for a spot in 'The Queue' on the day.

☛ SEE IT ! *Southfields Tube is slightly closer than Wimbledon Park or Wimbledon; come to Church Rd the night before to join The Queue.*

52

See the Peak District framed from Stanage Edge

MIDLANDS & THE MARCHES // An amalgamation of the words 'stone' and 'edge', Stanage Edge's etymology becomes clear as you near it: a near-unbroken line of escarpment that heightens the drama of the surrounding landscape. Small surprise, then, that this ranks among England's best climbing spots, as well as being a haven for hikers and beauty-spot-lovers. A backdrop of more quintessential British wilderness could scarce be countenanced. The moody 4-mile curve of cliffs separates the fetching Hope Valley from the barren moorland above. Below Stanage Edge, the woods and farmland that became one of Charlotte Brontë's key inspirations (North Lees Hall here was the basis for Thornfield Hall in *Jane Eyre*) fall away to the handsome village of Hathersage and one of England's most ravishing rural rail routes.

☛ SEE IT ! *Hathersage, with a train station on the Manchester–Sheffield line, has round-trip hikes of about 7 miles on Stanage Edge.*

Kate Humble's Top Five Places

Kate Humble is a TV presenter and narrator, specialising in wildlife programmes for the BBC. She is currently president of wetland conservation charity WWT and runs Humble by Nature, a rural skills school on a farm in the Wye Valley. Her book, Thinking on my Feet, *is out now.*

01

MID-WALES – Encompassing the Cambrian mountains and the Elan Valley, mid-Wales often gets overlooked, but it's gorgeous. Last year I did the Wye Valley walk – it was pure off-the-beaten-track, unsung beauty.

02

STAMFORD, LINCOLNSHIRE – I'd never heard of this place before I went there to do a theatre event recently. It's a really beautiful town, small and quintessentially English with beautiful limestone buildings and pedestrianised streets. A real surprise.

03

GOWER PENINSULA – For me, this is an unbeatable part of Britain's coastline. Thanks to the National Trust and lack of people, it's a wonderfully wild mix of sand beaches and moorland filled with wild ponies and sheep.

04

ISLE OF MULL – I always think of the Isle of Mull as our mini equivalent of the Masai Mara. Otters are frequently seen here, and white-tailed eagles were introduced here too; they are jaw-droppingly amazing birds.

05

MAINSTREET TRADING COMPANY, ST BOSWELLS, SCOTTISH BORDERS – This is my favourite shop in Britain. It's an old department store that's been turned into a beautiful bookshop, cafe and deli. It's so well curated it feels like a tiny museum.

53

Cast adrift on Loch Lomond

HIGHLANDS & ISLANDS // Scotland's most famous loch is the largest stretch of freshwater in Britain. It has inspired poets and songwriters and its 'bonnie banks' are etched in the imagination of Scots worldwide as an almost mythical Shangri-La, loaded with ludicrous scenery. Part of the Loch Lomond and the Trossachs National Park, its Highlands-in-miniature setting is as good as it gets for outdoor purists. Hikers summit craggy Ben Lomond (3196ft), while the shingle beaches and rhododendron forests below pack out with mountain bikers, dog walkers and picnickers. In summer, long-distance trekkers tackle the first stages of the breathtaking West Highland Way (96 miles).

To see the 24-mile loch at its most atmospheric, catch a boat from Balmaha to the tree-covered islands across its midriff. As you approach, you'll smell blooming heather, spy thickets of Scots pine, or perhaps land on an island where William Wallace sought refuge. Small wonder Scots are smitten.

☛ SEE IT ! ***The National Park Gateway Centre is located in Balloch. Autumn is the ideal time to visit.***

© Barrie Sheerman / Alamy

© Shaun Walby / 500px

54

Take a walk with fossilised dinosaurs on the Jurassic Coast

SOUTHWEST ENGLAND // Steven Spielberg got it wrong: never mind some faraway South American island, *Jurassic Park* should have been shot on the south coast of Dorset. Once, the whole of this area sat at the bottom of a deep, temperate ocean, and the region's rust-red sandstone cliffs are brimming with the remains of ancient dinosaurs who died long ago, sank to the ocean floor and became fossilised. Giant ammonites, trilobites, plesiosaur bones and even the occasional ichthyosaur have been revealed by the fast-eroding cliffs, and after every high tide or heavy storm, you'll see scores of fossil hunters combing the beaches in search of prehistoric treasure. While we can't promise you a T-Rex tooth, we can at least guarantee an entertaining and educational day out.

SEE IT ! ***Guided fossil-hunting is on offer in the town of Lyme Regis. Winter is the best time to come, as storms often expose fossils.***

55

Be a pilgrim and take the causeway to otherworldly Lindisfarne

NORTHEAST ENGLAND // Venturing out to windswept Lindisfarne (aka Holy Island) is a mystical experience – the causeway that connects it to the mainland appears like a mirage, rising up from the dunes, salt marsh and mudflats only at low tide. St Aidan founded a monastery here in 635; after it was ransacked by the Vikings in the subsequent two centuries, the monks fled, taking the illuminated Lindisfarne Gospels (housed in London's British Library) and St Cuthbert's body (now in Durham Cathedral). Although a priory was re-established in the 11th century, it too was abandoned during the 1537 Dissolution.

Today there's a palpable sense of spirituality as you wander the priory's shadowy, skeletal ruins and Lindisfarne's 16th-century clifftop castle. Afterwards, warm up with a glass of mead at St Aidan's Winery.

SEE IT ! ***Lindisfarne is reached by road from Newcastle and the Northumberland coast, but tides prevent road access twice a day.***

56

Pitch a wild camp among granite tors on Dartmoor

SOUTHWEST ENGLAND // Smack bang in the middle of Devon sits the great, stark, largely treeless expanse of Dartmoor. Characterised by hills, bogs, lakes, little villages and distinctive granite outcrops known as tors, which have been sculpted into strange shapes by the blustery Dartmoor weather, it's a cracking place to indulge your inner call of the wild – and, conveniently, one of the few places in the UK where you're allowed to wild camp.

TRY IT ! *Wild camping is allowed on Dartmoor as long as you pitch at least 330ft from the road, avoid farmland and archaeological sites, and ensure your tent isn't visible from any nearby buildings.*

57

Experience the grandeur and tragedy of Titanic Belfast

NORTHERN IRELAND // Since long before Jack and Rose played out their ill-fated love affair in James Cameron's epic drama, the tragic story of the *Titanic* has intrigued us. More than a museum, the Titanic Experience is an unmissable, multimedia extravaganza that charts the ship's design, construction and doomed maiden voyage through high-tech exhibits that explore the ship in the context of Belfast, the city in which she was built. Take a ride through the shipyard, walk the decks and get to know the passengers. It's almost like sneaking aboard.

SEE IT ! *Titanic Belfast is in front of the huge slipways where the ship was built and launched. Tickets include entry to the SS* Nomadic.

58

Island-hop Scotland's western seaboard

HIGHLANDS & ISLANDS // In days gone by, the Inner Hebrides was a destination solely for crofters tending to blackface sheep. Nowadays, the lure of beaches, distilleries and clifftop castles can't keep those in-the-know away. From the south, an itinerary could start with whisky tastings and deer sightings on Islay or Jura, before pinballing north via Mull and Iona for dolphin spotting and a date with royal history. There is unbeatable kitesurfing on nearby Coll and Tiree, too, plus a feature few other places can match: the beautiful Atlantic to the west.

SEE IT ! *Ferry tickets and itineraries are available from Caledonian MacBrayne.*

© Nieuwland Photography / Shutterstock

Atlantic puffins nest in their thousands on the island of Skomer off the Pembrokeshire coast

59

Mingle with sociable puffins on Skomer

SOUTH WALES // Come rain (most likely) or shine (if you're lucky), a little boat bumps across to Skomer off the coast of Pembrokeshire in southwest Wales. The word is out among seabirds, grey seals, dolphins, porpoises and even the odd whale that this entrancing little island of shaggy, luxuriantly green sea cliffs and pristine waters is the go-to place for a little escapism. Most famously it's the nesting ground of 10,000 pairs (and counting) of puffins. Few places in the world offer such close encounters – we're talking right up to your feet – with these dinky, comical birds, whose wingbeat is so ludicrously fast (400 per minute) it's as though God inserted the wrong batteries.

On the circular four-mile trail of the island, you'll see puffins preparing their nests, bringing sand eels in for their newly hatched pufflings and grumbling and growling in their burrows. Stay overnight at the Old Farm for a chance to glimpse dive-bombing Manx shearwaters as they return from sea under the cloak of darkness. The island has 300,000 pairs, the world's largest colony.

SEE IT ! ***Queue for the first-come, first-served tickets with Dale Sailing in Martin's Haven. Get there at 8am to secure your seat. June and July are peak months for puffins.***

60

Tackle the world's largest fortress at regal Windsor Castle

SOUTHERN ENGLAND // Windsor's 1000-year-old, 1000-room castle is the largest and oldest occupied fortress in the world, its mighty turrets and battlements looming above the Thames. Having played host to 39 British monarchs, it's a vital part of British history – if only the walls could talk! This fantastical palace-within-a-medieval-castle was founded as a timber-and-earth fortress in 1080 by William the Conqueror, but each successive ruler left their mark. The result is an architectural fusion, from flamboyant baroque to straight-lined Perpendicular Gothic, and lavish rooms stuffed with armour, weapons, chandeliers, royal portraits and more. Windsor Castle is one of the Queen's favourite homes and it was on the steps of the 15th-century St George's Chapel here that Meghan Markle unveiled her wedding dress designed by Clare Waight Keller.

SEE IT ! ***Windsor is less than an hour by train or car from London. Time your visit to catch the theatrical changing of the guard.***

Vivek Singh's Top Five Places

***Vivek Singh is one of Britain's most respected modern Indian chefs. As well as being executive chef and CEO of five restaurants, he has published six cookbooks and regularly appears on shows such as BBC's* Saturday Kitchen.**

01

THE COTSWOLDS – I take everyone who comes to visit us to Bibury, the prettiest village in England. We always take a photo there and it goes up on our wall at home. It's surreal to look at our photo album and see how our children have grown up.

02

LUCKNAM PARK HOTEL & SPA, BATH – This is where I love going to relax. It's a secluded country house with a fantastic Michelin-starred restaurant, wonderful spa and lots of land for a country walk or exploring on horseback.

03

OXFORD – 'Going to Oxford' is an aspiration most Indian parents have for their children. That was never going to happen for me, but opening Cinnamon Kitchen at Westgate Oxford is a close second!

04

SNAPE MALTINGS, NEAR ALDEBURGH – It's home to Britain's most spectacular expanses of reeds, water and vast skies, so it's great for long walks. You can see otters, birds and the odd seal, plus there are lots of quaint shops, and great restaurants and cafes.

05

PADSTOW, CORNWALL – This is a mecca for seafood-lovers; indulge in some of Rick Stein's fish and chips or visit Paul Ainsworth at No 6. Relax and enjoy sandy beaches, go for walks or take part in water sports.

61

Go on a deer-spotting safari on Exmoor

SOUTHWEST ENGLAND // Exmoor is all too often eclipsed by its more dramatic neighbour, Dartmoor. But for those in the know, Exmoor is perfect for peace and quiet, with numerous trails, pretty coastal villages and attractive beaches. It's also a super place to watch wild red deer – especially in autumn during the rutting season, when outlandishly antlered stags bellow and clash heads in a battle to become alpha male. The best way to see them is to take a 4x4 safari with a local guide – pack binoculars and a telephoto lens.

☛ SEE IT ! ***Exmoor runs from west Somerset to north Devon. Book deer-spotting safaris at Exmoor Wildlife Safaris or Red Stag Safaris.***

62

Hit the regal road to Brighton's ostentatious Pavilion

SOUTHEAST ENGLAND // Understated elegance and a low-key lifestyle? Not for King George IV, responsible for Brighton's zany Royal Pavilion. The future king had this extravagant pad built in the late 18th century, and there's really no place like it in the rest of the realm. The design inside and out blends Regency styling with Indo-Islamic motifs and the odd huge writhing dragon, golden-scaled ceiling and faux minaret. England's finest chinoiserie led Queen Victoria to call the palace 'a strange, odd Chinese place' but most visitors are simply blown away.

☛ SEE IT ! ***Brighton is well served by train from London and by bus from most major towns in the southeast.***

63

Brave the shadowy depths of Oxford's Pitt Rivers Museum

OXFORD & THE COTSWOLDS // A feast of curious anthropological finds from across the globe, Oxford's cavernous, dimly lit Pitt Rivers Museum feels like Lara Croft territory. About 20,000 eccentric artefacts amassed by Victorian General Pitt Rivers fill period glass cases, though the collection now numbers at least 300,000. Expect musical instruments, voice disguisers, protective amulets and suspended canoes, and – more macabre and, of course, popular – shrunken heads, pierced skulls and a bottle believed to imprison an evil witch.

☛ SEE IT ! ***The Pitt Rivers Museum is in central Oxford. Keep an eye out for free tours and object-handling sessions.***

paul weston / Alamy Stock Photo

© Dave and Les Jacobs / Getty Images

© Justin Foulkes / Lonely Planet

Left: The 3010ft Tryfan peak in Snowdonia National Park is a magnet for the adventurous and outdoorsy

64

Lace your best climbing boots for reconnoitring tricky Tryfan

NORTH WALES // The hiking, scrambling and climbing mecca of Tryfan ranks among Britain's most distinctive peaks, characterised by the ribbed lines of rock shooting up its slopes to erupt into three big bumps on the summit. Only the sixth-highest mountain in Wales at 3010ft, it is nevertheless among the most popular with adventure-lovers, thanks to the variety of routes up.

Grade I, II and III scrambles and the renowned rock-climb of the Milestone Buttress get pulses quickening. The easiest (although nevertheless lung-busting) route to the top runs from the Ogwen Cottage outdoor centre on Llyn Ogwen along the north ridge: still classed as a scramble rather than a hike and thus perhaps proving the old saying true that you can't get up Tryfan without using your hands.

Outdoorsy types often reckon the best way of taking in Tryfan to be the Brochlwyd Horseshoe: a clamber extended to include the 3260ft Glyder Fach and Bristly Ridge to the southwest, and a candidate for Britain's best high-altitude leg-stretch because of the surrounding summit views. Scramblers on the north ridge route should certainly pause along the ascent at the giddying Canon Stone, a rocky protrusion jutting out at a 45-degree angle into thin air above Llyn Ogwen. And once up top, having oohed and aahed at the panoramas of the Ogwen Valley, it is a rite of passage to leap between the two monoliths of Adam and Eve, a feat said to gain the leaper the 'Freedom of Tryfan'.

From Bethseda, 5 miles north of Llyn Ogwen, the A5 threads through the valley in a rocky picture show of adrenaline rushes: zip lines through slate caverns, climbing and canoeing await.

SEE IT ! ***Access Tryfan's easiest ascent by taking the A5 7 miles south from the North Wales Expressway to Ogwen Cottage.***

© mkos83 / Shutterstock

© Brian Blades / Shutterstock

65

Straddle time itself at the Royal Observatory

LONDON // Greenwich is so much more than just a grand collection of magnificent maritime monuments; this is where time itself begins. Britannia would never have ruled the waves without the discovery of longitude, still measured to this day from the prime meridian marked on the ground at the Royal Observatory.

The ingenious chronometers invented by John Harrison, which helped ships accurately calculate their position for the first time, are displayed inside the observatory, alongside other landmark navigational timepieces. Despite being founded by Charles II, the observatory itself is arguably less of an attraction than the views over the park, Naval College and river. Almost everyone pauses to stand on the line of 0° longitude, straddling the eastern and western hemispheres.

SEE IT ! *National Rail and the DLR serve Greenwich station, but the Cutty Sark DLR stop is slightly closer to the action.*

66

Stand on top of Britain on Ben Nevis

HIGHLANDS & ISLANDS // By mid-morning, you are climbing a steep path, a staircase of natural design. It is dangerous terrain, but fuelled by a panorama that encompasses the river glens of Loch Linnhe, Loch Leven and Glencoe, you get a second wind. Here and there a red stag roars, or a snow bunting settles on heather blushing purple and pink. Then comes the grand reveal: the 4406ft top of this 'mountain of heaven'. The easiest route to the summit is the Mountain Track, an old pony route that leaves from the Glen Nevis Visitor Centre (10.5 miles). Experienced hikers, meanwhile, prefer the Carn Mor Dearg Arete scramble, which boomerangs over the top of the UK's eighth highest mountain to the summit (11 miles). Yes, London has its Big Ben, but Scotland has one, too.

SEE IT ! *Start from the Glen Nevis Visitor Centre, where you'll find parking and information, including a weather forecast.*

67

Boost your wellbeing in the Malvern Hills

MIDLANDS & THE MARCHES // Perhaps it's the perspective you gain from this spine of grassy, wooded upland that makes it such a tonic (13 counties are visible from the ridgetop, including glimpses of the Severn Estuary, Welsh mountains, Cotswolds and three city cathedrals). But the Malverns have been a wellness getaway since Victorian times, when thousands flocked to the waters of Great Malvern. The area still has 70 springs and wells at which to sample the fabled water, and the hills erupt dramatically from the surrounding plains.

SEE IT ! *Great Malvern, right below the hills, is connected by train to Worcester, 8 miles northeast.*

68

Start the day with a full English breakfast

LONDON // The local British caff, with its Formica tables and laminated menus, is a window into a previous version of England – pre-globalisation, pre-digital, pre-colour-coded healthy food labelling. The canonical full English is fried bacon, fried eggs, fried tomato, fried mushrooms, buttered toast (possibly fried – can you see a pattern?), baked beans and sausages, served with a squirt of brown sauce and a mug of tea. Restaurants do posh versions but if the experience means more to you than the food, go for the greasy spoon!

EAT IT ! *London's family-run Electric Cafe at 258 Norwood Rd, London is a classic caff.*

69

Watch a clifftop play at the Minack Theatre

SOUTHWEST ENGLAND // Forget the Globe, the Old Vic or the National – Britain's most applause-worthy theatre is nowhere near the capital; it's 300-odd miles west on a craggy clifftop on Cornwall's coast. Created between the 1930s and 1950s by Rowena Cade, this stunning amphitheatre is cut into the cliffs above the popular beach of Porthcurno, and hosts a summer-long programme of plays, gigs and other live performances. With its epic backdrop of wheeling gulls and white-capped surf, few locations feel as intrinsically theatrical as this.

SEE IT ! *The Minack is about 9 miles southwest of Penzance. Visit any time, or see a performance from roughly May to September.*

The view across the green and pleasant South Downs from the 480ft Mt Caburn, near Lewes in East Sussex

70

Hike the rolling landscapes of the South Downs National Park

SOUTHERN ENGLAND // A 618-sq-mile swathe of undulating greenery, the UK's newest national park was a long time in the making but well worth the wait. Encompassing a huge area of classic chalk down, inhabited by thousands of sheep and hugging a ridge that runs across England's southeast, the views down to the coast are bracing, the hiking fairly easy-going. And pulling on a pair of boots is the best way to see the park, following the South Downs Way (SDW) from Eastbourne to Winchester for about five days.

Heading from Eastbourne, the first obstacle is a formidable one, the 531ft-high Beachy Head, the UK's tallest chalk cliff. Next come the Seven Sisters cliffs with their dramatic Channel vistas. Descending into pretty Cuckmere Haven (where it's said Hitler planned to kick off his invasion of Britain), the path turns inland and up into the hills where Roman villas, lost villages and deep ice-age valleys await. Hiking is just one way of seeing the park – a famous endurance event sees runners try to make it from Winchester to Eastbourne in less than 24 hours. Mountain biking is also big, as is hang-gliding.

SEE IT ! ***Trains from London serve Eastbourne and Winchester. Buses from Brighton connect other places on the SDW.***

© Adrian Woods / Alamy

71

Sample Britain's sweetest crab fresh off the boat in Cromer

EAST ANGLIA // The bustling Norfolk resort of Cromer is intrinsically bound up with the sea. A snub-nosed pier juts from broad beaches bearing fishing boats hauled high from the waves. The crustaceans landed here are so synonymous with the port that they borrow its name: Cromer Crab isn't just a local boast, it's a fishing area. And it's famously sweet-tasting. Hunt it down in the narrow lanes leading from the shore. At Davies Fish Shop, the crab is caught by its own dayboat, then boiled, cracked and dressed on-site – straight from sea to slab. Or head to the Royal National Lifeboat Institution's Henry Blogg Museum for tales of daring rescues, then up to Rocket House, an airy cafe with a balcony almost overhanging the sea and a menu packed with Cromer crab.

☛ EAT IT ! ***Trains connect Cromer with Norwich. May's Crab and Lobster Festival mixes food stalls with displays and cooking demos.***

© Rik Hamilton / Alamy

72

Plot a course for the subterranean spaces of Churchill's War Rooms

LONDON // The popular image of Winston Churchill as cigar-puffing, victory salute-giving war leader is only part of the story. To really understand the bulldog PM, you'll need to duck into the claustrophobic warren of tunnels below Whitehall, where Churchill retreated while the Blitz raged overhead, planning the operations that eventually delivered his greatest achievement.

Entering the tunnels today is a bit like time travel – indeed, the war rooms, and the passageways linking them, have been left more or less as they were in August 1945, down to the piles of papers on tables and maps of battles on the walls. Even more evocative are the cramped and humble living quarters, providing a potent impression of a man, and a nation, under siege.

☛ SEE IT ! ***The War Rooms are tucked below the anonymous-looking Clive Steps, at the end of King Charles St, near Westminster Tube.***

© Tristan Fewings / Getty Images

© LOOK Die Bildagentur / Alamy

73

Enjoy the queer goings-on at Brighton Pride

SOUTHEAST ENGLAND // The UK's biggest LGBTIQ+ shindig isn't a pride festival, it's *the* pride festival, out and proud since 1991 and still going strong. Originally held as a protest, today it's the country's largest celebration of diversity, held in the undisputed gay capital.

Even if the weather's not hot come the first week of August, the parade through the streets of the southeast's quirkiest metropolis certainly is, with all kinds of queens and queers strutting and posing to a techno beat. The event attracts almost half a million people, the highlights being the outrageous parade and the festival that takes place in Preston Park. Parties abound across Brighton with all the clubs, pubs and other gay venues getting in on the act. Pride attracts a large share of the straight population, too, who flock in their thousands to enjoy the outlandish festivities.

☛ SEE IT ! *Book your accommodation at least a year in advance for this one – some bed down in Eastbourne and commute in for the fun.*

74

Get lost in one man's hoard at Sir John Soane's Museum

LONDON // You might imagine that the man who designed the Bank of England would be a stuffy old sort, starch-collared and silver-caned, with the sense of humour of a bank ledger. Not so Sir John Soane. One of 19th-century London's pre-eminent architects, Soane knocked together three adjacent townhouses in Lincoln's Inn Fields and filled every inch of the interiors with reclaimed corbels and arches, de-framed windows and stained glass, Renaissance plaster casts, blueprints and architectural models. He even found room for a full-sized Egyptian sarcophagus.

Preserved much as Soane left it, the house is now one of London's quirkiest museums. Among the collection are paintings by Canaletto and the original of Hogarth's *Rake's Progress*. For real atmosphere, come at night for a Soane Late, when the interiors are lit by candlelight.

☛ SEE IT ! *Lincoln's Inn Fields is easy to miss, tucked away just southeast of Holborn Tube.*

Camden Lock on a warm summer's day offers a mellow respite to the area's mobbed markets and famed rock venues

75

Walk the rebel walk in countercultural Camden

LONDON // Many say punk is dead, but it's alive and kicking in Camden, where punk rockers still rage like The Clash were performing nightly at the Roundhouse. Back in the day, this was where the world's rock rebels earned their stripes: Madness; Pink Floyd; the Sex Pistols; the Ramones; even The Doors, who played their first and only UK shows at the Camden Roundhouse in 1968. Local girl Amy Winehouse pushed Camden back into the musical spotlight for a new generation before her untimely death in 2011.

There are still a few bona fide musical institutions around the Regent's Canal – Dingwalls, Koko, the Dublin Castle, as well as the Roundhouse – where you've a reasonable chance of spotting the next wave of rock 'n' rollers before they hit the big time.

Superimposed over musical Camden is tourist Camden, centred on the jam-packed canal-side markets, where theatrical fashions and band-name tees share stall space with alt souvenirs and street-food stands. Escape the madness by walking south along the Regent's Canal from Camden Lock in the direction of more tranquil London Zoo and Regent's Park.

SEE IT ! ***For a quieter back route to the markets, eschew Camden Tube and wander over from Camden Road Overground.***

© travellight / Shutterstock

© Xalbinoni / Shutterstock

76

Stride out on the famous Coast to Coast Walk

YORKSHIRE // At the risk of offending devotees of the Pennine Way and the South West Coast Path, the 190-mile Coast to Coast Walk is the long-distance walker's long-distance walk. Devised by the famous English fell-walker Alfred Wainwright (1907–91), and published as a book (*A Coast to Coast Walk*) in 1973, the route – from St Bees on the coast of Cumbria to Robin Hood's Bay in Yorkshire – has since become one of Britain's best-known and most popular hiking trails. It leads you through some of England's finest scenery, linking the national parks of the Lake District, the Yorkshire Dales and the North York Moors. It's an unofficial route – you won't find details on the National Trails website – so the waymarking is variable and inconsistent; hikers will have to use real-world navigational skills rather than painted wooden posts.

SEE IT ! ***Purists can buy the original Wainwright's Coast to Coast Walk guidebook, fully revised and updated in 2017.***

77

Gape at the vista of spectacular Malham Cove

YORKSHIRE // If you've seen the film *Harry Potter and the Deathly Hallows (Part 1)*, recall the scene where Harry and Hermione pitch up on an otherwordly plateau of gnarled and gullied stone immediately after their split with Ron. That, children, is Malham Cove. Gouged out by torrential floods issuing from melting glaciers towards the end of the last Ice Age, this vast natural amphitheatre of layered grey limestone is one of Britain's most spectacular natural features.

In spring and summer, rare peregrine falcons nest on the 260ft-high cliffs, and when they depart rock climbers reclaim their playground. If walking is more your thing, pick up a Malham Landscape Trail leaflet from the national park centre and explore the paths linking the cove to the canyon of Gordale Scar and the cascade of Janet's Foss waterfall.

SEE IT ! ***The Malham Tarn shuttle bus links Settle with Malham six times daily on Sundays and bank holidays only, Easter to October.***

78

See an ecclesiastical masterpiece at Lincoln Cathedral

MIDLANDS & THE MARCHES // The Midlands' highest-placed church (and fourth-most magnificent on this list overall) is this three-towered masterpiece, glory of Lincoln's historic quarter. Nigh on 950 years of action-packed past feature the Magna Carta, an imp instructed by Satan to wreak havoc on Earth, and 237 years as the world's tallest building: the cathedral is the country's third-biggest, too. As well as checking the cloisters and Sir Christopher Wren-designed library, don't forget to ascend the tower for astounding city panoramas.

SEE IT ! *Lincoln Cathedral sets the skyline alight in Lincoln, 38 miles northeast of Nottingham. Tower tours run from April to October.*

79

Immerse yourself in coasteering in Pembrokeshire

SOUTH WALES // Remember those childhood seaside holidays where you went off exploring along the coastline, got cut off by the tide, and got very wet? Coasteering embraces the thrill of the sea awaiting around that next headland, and plonks participants from well-trodden coastal paths into a watery cliff-base world where you belly-flop off rocks and float into sea caves, negotiating fissures, formations or stacks along the way. Pembrokeshire, just about Britain's most varied spread of coastline, is where the 'sport' originated. Sport? Great fun, anyway.

SEE IT ! *Far-western Pembrokeshire's coastline is majestically riven. Recommended local operators include Celtic Coasteering.*

80

Re-live the revolution at Ironbridge Gorge

MIDLANDS & THE MARCHES // Many places boast Industrial Revolution legacies, but the gorge around today's Unesco-listed attraction of Ironbridge was one of the first places to mass-industrialise in the 1700s. The world's first cast-iron bridge (1781) is now centrepiece of a fabulous site with five museums and an original tobacco pipe works. There's a Victorian township, where you can experience life back when Britain was the biggest global power, and an interactive museum where you can attempt to generate electricity or haul a ten-ton locomotive.

SEE IT ! *Ironbridge lies 5 miles south of Telford, although attractions fan out for several miles along the Severn Gorge.*

81

Picnic with a view on genteel Primrose Hill

LONDON // Waterloo has prime claim to the London sunset, but Primrose Hill is more refined. The graceful green space climbing behind Regent's Park has front row seats onto central London, a vantage point enjoyed over the years by locals ranging from Sylvia Plath to Jude Law.

It's perfect picnic territory (though the surrounding pastel-coloured townhouse rows offer great cafes and restaurants if you prefer), and, if you time it right, you might bump into one of Primrose Hill's resident druids, part of a cult founded here in 1792.

SEE IT ! *It's a stroll south from Chalk Farm Tube, or a steep slog north from Regent's Park. Camden Town is another approach route.*

The 18th-century neo-classical Radcliffe Camera is one of the buildings that make up Oxford's Bodleian Library

82

Feed your inner scholar at Oxford University's splendid Bodleian Library

OXFORD & THE COTSWOLDS // A medieval jewel among Oxford's dreaming spires, the fabled Bodleian library has seen such superstars as JRR Tolkien, CS Lewis, Oscar Wilde and Gertrude Bell, not to mention dozens of UK prime ministers and 50 Nobel prizewinners, scribbling away amid its antique tomes. From the majestic 17th-century quad to the intricate 15th-century, fan-vaulted Divinity School (the university's original teaching room, which morphed into the Hogwarts hospital in the Harry Potter films), it's as much an architectural marvel as a scholarly delight – and an unmissable Oxford (and UK) attraction.

The only way to explore the superbly evocative interiors is by detailed guided tour, on which you'll be allowed a glimpse of Duke Humfrey's Library, the main reading hall which dates back to 1488, as well as the imposing Convocation House and Chancellor's Court. For a peek at more of the Bodleian's treasures, don't miss nearby Weston Library.

SEE IT ! ***'Extended' tours take in the much-photographed circular Radcliffe Camera library, otherwise off limits to visitors; some even lead you through the underground Gladstone Link that connects it with the Bodleian.***

83

Dally with deer in royal Richmond Park

LONDON // Flying into the capital, you can't help but notice the abundance of green spaces below. They don't come much bigger or greener than Richmond Park, the largest of London's Royal Parks. Covering 2500 acres, this lung-restoring sprawl was founded by Charles I and used as a royal hunting range before being handed over to the populace in 1872. Today, Londoners come for the calm and chlorophyll, to glimpse the Richmond deer herd and to spot the green parakeets reputedly descended from a pair released by Jimi Hendrix in the 1960s.

☛ SEE IT ! ***Take the Tube to Richmond, then a bus to the pedestrian park gates at Petersham.***

84

Catch a wave in Newquay

SOUTHWEST ENGLAND // It might be a bit chillier than Bondi, but if you want to learn to surf in Britain, the best place to do it is the string of beaches around Newquay, on the north coast of Cornwall, which receive some of the UK's most reliable swells. Fistral is the prima donna of the town's surfing beaches, but there are lots more (including Lusty Glaze, Watergate Bay, Mawgan Porth, Crantock and Holywell Bay). Just don't even think about trying it without a wetsuit.

☛ TRY IT ! ***Newquay has good bus, train and even air connections. Numerous surf schools offer lessons for novices, as well as skills and tuning sessions for more established surfers.***

85

Follow the Banksy Trail in Bristol

SOUTHWEST ENGLAND // He's painted murals from Bethlehem to Brooklyn, but the world's most subversive street artist actually hails from Bristol, where he's said to have cut his artistic teeth as part of a guerrilla graffiti crew in the 1980s. Love him or loathe him, Banksy's celebrity has helped put the city on the map, and an official walking trail now takes in several of his artworks – including a Molotov cocktail-wielding teddy bear (*Mild Mild West*), a Vermeer spoof (*Girl with the Pierced Eardrum*) and a sexual health clinic cartoon (*Well Hung Lover*).

☛ SEE IT ! ***You can download the Banksy Trail from the Visit Bristol website.***

© Federico Zovadelli / Shutterstock

Puffins are among the plentiful birdlife that inhabit the rocky and remote Farne Islands off Northumberland

86

Go puffin-spotting on the Farne Islands

NORTHEAST ENGLAND // Nicknamed the 'clowns of the sea', endearing black and white puffins, with bright orange bills and feet, quizzical expressions and comical antics, return each year to breed and raise their pufflings on the Farne Islands – one of the best places across the UK to encounter them.

Owned by the National Trust since 1925, this rocky archipelago three miles offshore from the Northumberland coast has been classified as a national nature reserve since 1993. Of its 28 islands, you can visit three – Inner Farne, Longstone and Staple – on boat trips in season. Adorable puffins aside, birdlife that you'll likely encounter includes fulmars, Arctic terns, guillemots, razorbills, shags and eider ducks. St Cuthbert, who lived a hermit-like existence here for more than a decade before his death in 687, paved the way for conserving the islands' birds when he introduced the first-ever law of its kind in 676 to protect the eider ducks (they're often still dubbed 'Cuddy's ducks' in reference to him). On Inner Farne, you can see the 14th-century chapel dedicated to the saint. Other buildings here include a medieval pele tower (home to the reserve's rangers) and a Georgian lighthouse.

TRY IT ! ***Seahouses is the jumping-off point for (often bumpy) boat trips to the islands; wear warm, waterproof clothes and – given the prevalent birdlife – a hat.***

87

Spice up your life with a balti in Birmingham

MIDLANDS & THE MARCHES // Invented by a Pakistani chef in 1970s Birmingham, the balti launched as an east-meets-west dish where Pakistani culinary tradition fused with western tastes. It caught on like wildfire. In what is hands-down the country's curry capital, the balti blossomed into Birmingham's very own endemic spice sensation. What makes this an only-in-Birmingham thing? The dish it is prepared in, for starters: a steel receptacle in which the balti is cooked and served to retain essential flavours, originally manufactured by just one city firm. True baltis also require vegetable oil rather than ghee, dry spices besides fresh ginger and garlic and meat on the bone, not off. Fire up your taste buds by hitting the restaurant of the chef who created the dish: Adil's, in Birmingham's famous Balti Triangle. Much imitated outside the city; rarely replicated.

EAT IT ! ***The Balti Triangle, where the dish originated, is formed by Ladypool Rd, Stratford Rd and Stoney Lane.***

Pete McNeil's Top Five Places

An extreme cyclist, Pete McNeil has cycled his way across the planet, traversing the globe from the UK to New Zealand. He most recently finished as the first British rider in the Silk Road Mountain Race, a 1056-mile bikepacking race through the mountains of Kyrgyzstan.

01

FISHERFIELD FOREST, SCOTLAND – I first came across Fisherfield while racing the Highland 550. It's one of the most magical spots I've ever slept out in, and certainly has to be earned (however you approach it).

02

HOPE VALLEY, PEAK DISTRICT – This is my doorstep: a veritable adventure playground for runners, cyclists and climbers. Not only is the special landscape steeped in layers of history, but the community that ties the valley together is awesome, too.

03

LAKE DISTRICT – This is where I fell in love with the mountains. Big and wild enough for proper adventures but small enough to be accessible, to my mind it has some of the best natural mountain biking in the world.

04

HOD AND HAMBLEDON HILLS, DORSET – I grew up running, biking and playing around these Iron Age hill forts. Even going back now, the ramparts transport me to another time and tie me inextricably to the land.

05

MULL OF GALLOWAY LIGHTHOUSE, SCOTLAND – This place feels like the end of the world. A fool's errand to get to, it's surrounded by battered sea cliffs. At the end of a spindly peninsula is one of my favourite van camping spots.

88

Marvel at Mackintosh's designs for Glasgow

SOUTHERN SCOTLAND // Take an unknown youngster from a working-class family in late 19th-century Glasgow, and give him the nerve to become an architect and designer. Let that family, with 10 other children, challenge his dreams. Then watch as he transforms into a master architect, becoming a father to the international art nouveau movement.

This was the world Charles Rennie Mackintosh, Scotland's greatest designer, was born into in 1868. His architectural experiments redrew the map of Glasgow and have since become hallmarks of the city. You can see them at The Lighthouse, Scotland's helter-skelter Centre for Design and Architecture; at The Hunterian, a brick-by-brick reassemblage of the designer's home; and at the Glasgow School of Art, which was destroyed by a devastating fire in June 2018. Due to be rebuilt, it will hopefully save his masterpiece for another day.

SEE IT ! ***The Charles Rennie Mackintosh Society runs recommended guided tours.***

Urban architecture

↓

For one weekend only you get the keys to the capital's landmarks at Open House London

page 127

↓

Visit the pinnacle of 20th-century brutalist dreams at London's imposing Barbican Centre

page 131

↓

See how the post-industrial surrounds of the Baltic Triangle became Liverpool's coolest district

page 288

89

Find your rhythm at the Notting Hill Carnival

LONDON // One of the world's largest and maddest street festivals – only Rio is bigger – bass-blasting Notting Hill Carnival has blown its way into this west London neighbourhood every year since 1966. Made up of equal parts reggae, rum, Red Stripe and sometimes rain (Caribbean vibes can't change London's weather), the carnival has a reputation for chaos – perhaps not too surprising when you invite a city of eight million to a free two-day party. Still, the little ones can tag along on Sunday, known as Family Day, before a long session of dancing and sequin-spotting at the main parade on Monday. If you prefer your soulful sounds and jerk chicken sans the crowd, rock up on Saturday evening for Panorama, a just-as-energetic steel pan competition in which the country's top steel bands drum out 10-minute compositions from memory (no sheet music allowed).

TRY IT ! ***Notting Hill Carnival is held on the Sunday and Monday of the last weekend in August (the summer bank holiday).***

Right, from top: colourful drummers join the Notting Hill Carnival parade; Glasgow's House For An Art Lover, designed by Charles Rennie Mackintosh

89

88

WM

Left: a traditional wherry riverboat wends its away along the inland waters of the Norfolk Broads, the UK's largest protected wetlands

90

See the Norfolk Broads from the water

EAST ANGLIA // Water swirls around your paddle, birds flit among the reeds, your canoe glides on – and you chill out. Welcome to the Norfolk Broads, England's most beguiling stretch of inland waterway. Offering a unique opportunity to immerse yourself in nature and embark on some unforgettable human-powered, traffic-free transportation, the Norfolk Broads constitute Britain's largest protected wetlands, a largely aquatic national park where otters swim, dragonflies swoop, and marsh harriers soar. These vast wetlands were formed when the rivers Wensum, Bure, Waveney and Yare flooded gaping holes which had been dug by 12th-century crofters looking for peat. The result? One hundred and twenty-five miles of lock-free, tranquil waterways to explore.

Famously, joyfully, there's simply no point in trying to discover the Broads by car; instead, join a cruise, hire a boat or paddle your own canoe. Fleets of riverboats shuttle about on day cruises, allowing you to sit back while someone else navigates. Assorted firms hire out everything from dayboats with outboard motors to luxury cabin cruisers for week-long trips. Then it's a case of chugging from one waterside pub to the next, sampling fine food and drink and marvelling at idyllic views. Take in picturesque market towns, spot the wildlife and travel at your own pace.

But exploring by canoe, kayak or stand-up paddleboard is when the Broads really come into their own. With no motor to break the silence and better access to shallower waters, you'll be able to discover the places that the cruisers can't reach. Guided canoe trails range from half-day to three-day bushcraft camps. Or, for the ultimate tranquil experience, paddle off on your own – endless reed-edged waterways, and countless, butterflies, otters and water voles await.

SEE IT ! ***The key centres of Wroxham and Potter Heigham are reachable by bus from Norwich and Great Yarmouth, respectively.***

© Ian G Dagnall / Alamy

© Myles New / Lonely Planet

91

See the ships at Portsmouth Historic Dockyard

SOUTHERN ENGLAND // 'Rule, Britannia! Britannia, rule the waves...' So booms the national anthem, a celebration of the naval might that underpinned Britain's globetrotting and empire-building. And there are few better places to appreciate how central the role of seafaring has been in British history than the Historic Dockyard in Portsmouth, where visitors can see a flotilla of famous vessels of the past – including Henry VIII's *Mary Rose*, an imposing Victorian warship, HMS *Warrior*, and even a WWII-era submarine, HMS *Alliance*. But pride of place goes to HMS *Victory* – Nelson's flagship, from where he orchestrated victory at the Battle of Trafalgar, and breathed his last. It's a must-visit for anyone with even a passing interest in the sea: shipshape and Bristol fashion, as the saying goes.

SEE IT ! *Portsmouth is less than two hours from London. The All Attractions ticket covers all exhibits except the Mary Rose Museum.*

92

Come out of your shell at Whitstable's famous oyster festival

SOUTHEAST ENGLAND // Slurped since the Romans ruled these parts, Whitstable's meaty molluscs are one of the main reasons moneyed Londoners head to this old-world town on the north Kent coast. Local lore dictates that oysters are only eaten in months containing the letter 'r', so it comes as a surprise to some that the town's famous oyster festival, one of the southeast's top gastro events, takes place in the last week in July (actually the end of the oyster season). The festivities traditionally marked the beginning of the oyster-catchers' summer hols but have morphed into a parade and maritime-themed event. One of the (stomach-turning) highlights is the oyster-eating competition, and the whole caboodle is infused with white Downland wine and lots of Kentish ale, both Whitstable-brewed and from nearby Farnham.

SEE IT ! *Regular trains run from London to Whitstable. Buses link the town with Canterbury and other places in north and east Kent.*

The magnificent cathedral is the reason why the small settlement of St Davids has been designated city status

93

Make a pilgrimage way out west to St Davids Cathedral

SOUTH WALES // Cities don't come littler than St Davids, tucked away in a southwestern pocket of Pembrokeshire. Nor do they come with many more enchanting ecclesiastical draws than its cathedral (only just missing a podium position in this list's top religious attractions). Among Europe's most ancient Christian sites, the faithful have been flocking to St Davids since the 6th century when the eponymous saint set up a church here.

Today's cathedral, begun in 1181, sits on an aventurine-green peninsula at the city's edge. While it may seem secluded in the 21st century, this was one of the continent's key pilgrimage destinations in the 12th. Burial place of Welsh greats such as the country's one-time mightiest ruler, Rhys ap Gruffyd, its winsome Norman-Romanesque exterior, tinted purple from local stone, is a sight to behold. Inside, the nave soars in fleets of arches to an elaborate oak ceiling, while the richly adorned presbytery screen and ceiling are equally arresting. Once, two trips to St Davids were worth one to Rome for pilgrims. The building's well-preserved majesty means that for many the same holds true to this day.

SEE IT ! ***St Davids is 16 miles northwest of Haverfordwest. It is especially impressive seen during St Davids Cathedral Festival.***

© Bailey-Cooper Photography / Alamy

94

Enjoy a night of high culture at the Royal Opera House

LONDON // Plonked in the heart of London's Theatreland, Covent Garden is more associated with sequinned chorus lines and street performers than high art, but the east wall of the market square houses a premier cultural institution. The grand neoclassical Royal Opera House has lived several different lives – as the Royal Theatre in the 17th century, then later as a venue for 18th-century opera with premieres from the likes of Handel.

Today the proud home of the Royal Opera and Royal Ballet, the Royal Opera House is effortlessly elegant, and evening ballet and opera shows are world-class spectacles. Order an interval drink in the glazed, steel-canopied Paul Hamlyn Hall, built in Victorian times to house a tropical flowers and exotic fruit market that never materialised.

SEE IT ! ***Crowded Covent Garden Tube is close to the Opera House and Inigo Jones' market, but it's a more relaxing stroll from Temple.***

© Sara Melhuish / Getty Images

95

Join Dickens for seaside fun in Broadstairs

SOUTHEAST ENGLAND // At the zenith of his career, Charles Dickens chose none other than Broadstairs as his annual holiday destination. He wrote the whole of *Bleak House* in the town, in a study within a former fort perched above the beach, which later assumed the name of the famous novel. Nowadays, it's an antique-packed hotel.

But it's the sickle of sand that draws in most visitors, a gently shelving curve of rough grains protected and warmed in a tight bay by the Kentish sun. Rent a sea kayak to explore the chalk cliffs and bays of the Isle of Thanet (not an island for 400 years, despite the name). Broadstairs itself sits atop cliffs, a charming jumble of secondhand bookshops, old-fashioned bakeries and tempting fish 'n' chip joints.

SEE IT ! ***Broadstairs has direct rail services to London as well as bus connections to Canterbury. Avoid super-busy bank holidays.***

96

Walk around the Royal Crescent in Bath

SOUTHWEST ENGLAND // Since the late 18th century, the stately city of Bath has been a byword for architectural elegance. It's home to some of Britain's most beautiful Georgian buildings, designed by a visionary father-and-son duo, John Woods Elder and Younger, who were commissioned to redevelop the city in partnership with local entrepreneur Ralph Allen. Their crowning achievement is the Royal Crescent, a semicircle of 33 terraced mansions graced with Ionic columns, sash windows and architectural flourishes. While the facades all look identical, inside the owners were allowed to follow their own specifications, so none are completely alike. Most are privately owned, although No 1 has been turned into a museum illustrating the decorative tastes of Georgian high society.

SEE IT ! *You're free to wander around the Royal Crescent and its facing park. Book tickets for No 1 Royal Crescent through the website.*

97

Savour a slice of British history at Blenheim Palace

OXFORD & THE COTSWOLDS // One of the most spectacular stately homes in the UK, the birthplace of Winston Churchill (1874), a Unesco World Heritage site, base of the 12th Duke of Marlborough – need we say more? Well, yes! The extraordinary baroque beauty that is Blenheim Palace wows at every turn, from its gilded oil paintings to its soaring Great Hall, gracious state rooms and famous Blenheim Tapestries.

Built between 1705 and 1722, Blenheim was conceived by Nicholas Hawksmoor and Sir John Vanbrugh for the original Duke of Marlborough, with funds donated by Queen Anne following his triumph over the French in the 1704 Battle of Blenheim. Outside, master landscape architect Lancelot 'Capability' Brown – creator of the classic English country garden – devoted 11 years to perfecting rolling parklands.

SEE IT ! ***Blenheim is a 30-minute drive or bus trip from Oxford. Fabulous walks of up to 4.5 miles weave through the grounds.***

© Neil Setchfield / Lonely Planet

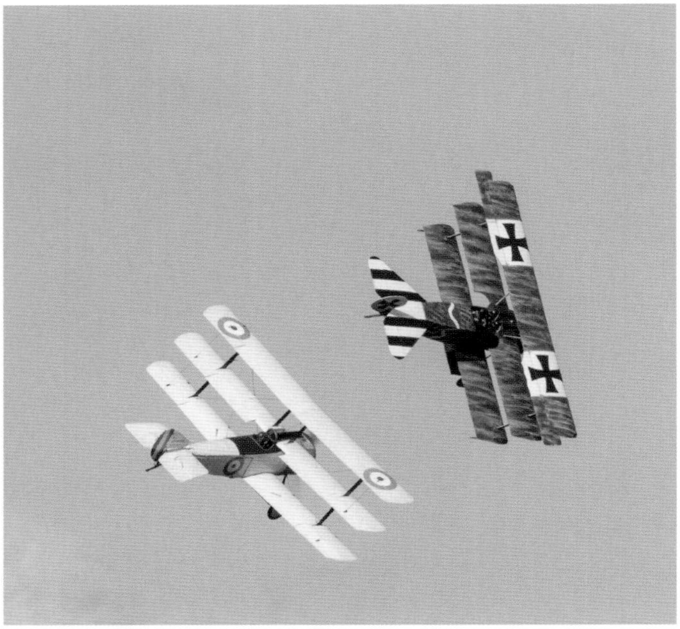

© Niall Ferguson / Alamy

98

Step into East End history at Dennis Severs' House

LONDON // The brick terraces around Brick Lane have housed a varied crowd over the centuries – French Huguenots, Ashkenazi Jews, Bengali refugees, art students, start-up techies. No location does this colourful history as much justice as Dennis Severs' House.

Reconstructed exactly as it would have been in the 18th century, right down to the smell of scones baking by an open fire, this one-time home of a Huguenot silk weaver is billed as a 'still-life drama' – an apt description for one of the most evocative experiences of old London.

☛ SEE IT ! ***Quiet little Folgate St is just north of Spitalfields Market, near Liverpool Street station. Book tickets via the website.***

99

Delight in acrobatic airborne displays at Duxford air show

EAST ANGLIA // The air thunders and the ground throbs as the world's most awe-inspiring aircraft tear up the skies. The air shows at the Imperial War Museum Duxford, Europe's biggest aviation museum, are some of Britain's best, with Spitfires, the Red Arrows and RAF Chinooks regularly streaming past the clouds. Air shows bring a carnival atmosphere, with ranks of people in deckchairs overlooking runways stacked with vintage planes and contemporary jets, and marvelling at wing-walkers on biplanes performing crazy stunts.

☛ SEE IT ! ***IWM Duxford is an hour's drive from London, 25 minutes from Cambridge. Shows take place in May, July and September.***

100–199

Willy Lott's House at Flatford in Dedham Vale was the subject of John Constable's famous 1821 painting *The Hay Wain*

100

Drink in the most romantic of English landscapes at Dedham Vale

EAST ANGLIA // Dedham Vale gives you the chance to step softly into a Constable painting. You know the ones – ancient England at its most rustic: weathered cottages, babbling rivers, yokels on horse-drawn carts. That's pretty much what you see in Constable's *The Hay Wain* (1821) and it's pretty much what you see in Dedham Vale today. This lowland on the Suffolk-Essex border overflows with languid charm, caught so beautifully by local painter John Constable, who captured its essence in romantic visions of country lanes, rambling fields and burbling creeks.

At the hamlet of Flatford you can become immersed in this serene world, and play 'spot the painting' – there's Willy Lott's House from *The Hay Wain*, there's the real-life version of *Flatford Mill*. Next door, at thatched Bridge Cottage, exhibitions outline Constable's life and work. And if all this bucolic beauty makes you want to reach for the paints, acclaimed courses are run at 15th-century Dedham Hall. Or if you'd rather reach for a pint, head to the Sun Inn, an ancient hostelry rich in heritage-chic and fine food and drink.

SEE IT ! ***The National Trust runs daily guided tours of Dedham's Constable sites between April and October. It's best to book.***

© Kev Williams / Shutterstock

© Matt Munro / Lonely Planet

101

Step into a green bubble at the Eden Project

SOUTHWEST ENGLAND // Is it an extra-terrestrial spacecraft? A madcap mega-villain's lair? No: it's Cornwall's greenhouse on steroids. Created at the bottom of a disused clay-pit outside St Austell, this complex of futuristic, bubble-shaped biomes recreates different habitats from around the globe, from tropical jungle to dry savannah. It's an eye-popping place, and educational to boot, exploring environmental issues from land use to climate change, and stocked with a cornucopia of fascinating and freaky plants – giant aloe veras, stinky rafflesia, towering palms, giant banana trees. A brilliant rooftop walkway allows you to ascend into the canopy for a bird's eye view, and a heart-in-the-mouth zip wire sends you hurtling at high speed over the biomes. Several new Eden Projects are in development around the world, but this will always be the original.

SEE IT ! *It can get very busy – beat the queues by buying tickets online or from local tourist offices. Come in winter for ice skating, and look out for live music gigs throughout the summer.*

102

See why Columbia Road is bloomin' marvellous

LONDON // London's favourite flower market still echoes with the patter of East End traders. During the week, the Victorian terraces around Bethnal Green's Columbia Rd can be almost eerily quiet, but come Sunday, there's barely breathing space for all the flower sellers and blooms. Entering one end you'll be absorbed into the crowd and whooshed along like driftwood in a storm, past riots of roses, orgies of orchids, battalions of bulbs. And all the while, stream-of-consciousness sale pitches – 'Get your anthuriums, lovely jubbly, only a fiver, when they're gone, they're gone' – provide a spirited Cockney soundtrack. Before long you'll be squirted out at the other end, arms bulging, ready to retreat to a pub or cafe. There's more to Columbia Rd than flowers, though; the side streets are dotted with shops selling art, antiques and all manner of intruiging trinkets.

SEE IT ! *Columbia Rd is an easy walk from Hoxton Overground, or you can wander through the hipster-crowded streets from Old Street Tube.*

103

Watch the sun set over Carnewas and Bedruthan Steps

SOUTHWEST ENGLAND // Thailand has its karst pillars, Scotland has the Old Man of Hoy, Australia has the Twelve Apostles – but Cornwall has Carnewas, otherwise known as the Bedruthan Steps. These huge rock towers have been carved out from the cliffs by sea erosion and landslips, and now stand like a battalion of soldiers guarding the north Cornish coast. At high tide the bases are covered, but at low tide a big sandy beach is revealed, allowing you to get up close and appreciate their stirring scale and stature.

SEE IT ! ***Bedruthan Steps is 6 miles north of Newquay, and has a small National Trust car park. Check tide times if going onto the beach.***

104

Make for Hay to find Britain's top literature festival

MID-WALES // That a tiny, out-in-the-sticks market town has come to host Britain's biggest literary festival speaks volumes about Hay-on-Wye's rise to the higher echelons of the country's cultural scene. Many volumes, actually: way before the first festival in 1988, Hay had established itself as a UK book mecca, with 20-odd bookshops still operating today. The 10-day festival, held in late May and June and described by Bill Clinton as a 'Woodstock of the mind', has attracted the world's best-known contemporary writers over its 30-year history.

SEE IT ! ***Hay-on-Wye is 20 miles west of Hereford. Tickets for the festival sell fast, so book several months in advance.***

105

Spy rare red squirrels on Brownsea Island

SOUTHWEST ENGLAND // Sadly, you don't see many red squirrels in Britain today – their huge decline results from the deadly squirrel pox virus, to which their grey cousins, introduced in the late 19th century, are mostly immune. The reds have been reduced to a few isolated pockets – including the National Trust-owned island of Brownsea, marooned in the middle of Poole Harbour. Walking the island's trails you'll have a great chance of spotting reds in the treetops – keep your eyes peeled for their tufty ears, bushy tails and fiery orange coats.

SEE IT ! ***Brownsea Island Ferries runs regular trips from Poole Quay and Sandbanks.***

© Marsha Arnold

106

Discover the Italy-meets-Wales fantasy land of Portmeirion

NORTH WALES // Best known as the setting for cult 1960s' TV series *The Prisoner*, this surreal settlement on the Gwynedd coast was the brainchild of architect Sir Clough Williams-Ellis, built in two phases between the 1920s and 1970s in Italian Riviera style. Centred around a piazza is a quirky melee of loggias, porticos, domes, turrets and even a temple, that together comprise a fake but fantastic village, lived in by no one but visited by thousands. Gorgeous gardens and a beguiling sandy beach make this a day out to remember.

SEE IT ! ***Portmeirion, 22 miles south of Caernarfon and 19 miles north of Barmouth, commands an entrance fee: get advance tickets.***

© Caron Badkin / Shutterstock

© Mark Chilvers / Lonely Planet

107

Make the pilgrimage for a pint at Ye Olde Trip to Jerusalem

MIDLANDS & THE MARCHES // Our list's highest-positioned tavern, this whitewashed edifice built into the bottom of the outcrop crowned by Nottingham Castle claims to be England's oldest inn. Established as a stop-off for Holy Land-bound pilgrims, and with Richard the Lionheart supposedly among the former clientele, the building is steeped in legend (ask about the fate that befell those attempting to clean their model galleon, now caked under layers of grime, or the pregnancy chair sat in by generations of women wanting a child). But Ye Olde Trip to Jerusalem's coolest feature is the network of caves opening directly off the rear, some used as drinking rooms or cellars. Characterful as the interior is, take a drink to the front garden courtyard if weather allows: this opens up great views of the pub and castle above.

SEE IT ! ***The pub lies below and southeast of Castle Rock, accessed from Castle Blvd or Castle Rd.***

108

Seek out street art and spirits in lively Shoreditch

LONDON // The walls of Shoreditch and Brick Lane's once-derelict warehouses and factories now moonlight as open-air canvases for street art legends, including Banksy, Space Invader and Eine, as well as a smorgasbord of artists more obscure. What's there today is almost always gone tomorrow, as new creators continually come in with their own tags, paste-ups and stencils, sometimes as official commissions from local businesses but often as 'good graffiti'.

Shoreditch is also the torchbearer of London's late-night life and home to some of the city's best bars, which like the art outdoors never stop popping up, chopping and changing. Bars range from the oddball (a drinking den with a boozy ball pit) to the strangely specific (whisky aged in and poured from a tree trunk).

SEE IT ! ***Brick Lane is at its busy best during the Sunday market. The bars are open most nights and until the wee hours at weekends.***

A 'Viking' vessel launches into the throng of Scotland's frenetic Up Helly Aa fire festival, held annually on Shetland

109

Play with fire at Up Helly Aa on Shetland

HIGHLANDS & ISLANDS // At around 7pm it begins, Lerwick harbour on Shetland falling into darkness, before waves of paraffin-doused torches light the heavens. Next, the sight of a squad of axe-wielding Vikings followed by a parade of one thousand men in fancy dress and fake bosoms works the crowd into a frenzy. You see a dragon-prow longboat burst into flames with such vivid colour and ferocity that you check to see if the alcohol you've been passed is legal.

This is a snapshot of Up Helly Aa, Europe's largest fire festival and a no-holds-barred carnival that only makes sense when you learn the backstory. It dates from the 1880s, morphing from the Victorian tradition of rolling lit tar barrels through Lerwick's streets into the all-out *Game of Thrones*-style spectacle that taps into the island's Norse heritage today. It's heaven for party animals, too – but by Odin's beard, it'll take you to a strange place. Don't be surprised to see lots of sleep-deprived Norseman stumbling around the harbour the morning after.

SEE IT ! ***Up Helly Aa takes place annually on the last Tuesday in January. Flybe flies to Shetland from Glasgow, Edinburgh, Aberdeen and Inverness. The overnight ferry takes at least 12 hours.***

Beth Tweddle's Top Five Places

Gymnast and TV pundit Beth Tweddle MBE represented Great Britain in three Olympic Games. She was the first British female gymnast to win a medal at the European Championships, World Championships and the Olympics.

01

LIVERPOOL – I spend a lot of time away, so I love being in my home town with my friends and family. Liverpool is a wonderful city to explore and you can walk around it time and time again, always discovering new things.

02

MOOR HALL RESTAURANT WITH ROOMS, AUGHTON – I love this restaurant. My husband found it and took me for my birthday for a treat. The food is amazing and the service is fantastic. I can't recommend it enough.

03

DELAMERE FOREST, CHESHIRE – I love being able to walk the dog through the forest when I go home to my parents' house, listening out for birds and watching dragonflies flit past.

04

GLASGOW – I have fond memories of visiting Glasgow for gymnastics competitions. I just love the atmosphere up there. The people are so friendly and welcoming and the city has some great shopping quarters.

05

LAKE DISTRICT – I have been to the Lake District a few times and just love exploring. We took my husband's daughter a few years ago during the summer holidays and did loads of different activities, including ghyll scrambling, walking and taking the ferry.

110

Take the (mini steam) train to Dungeness' weird and wonderful world of shingle

SOUTHEAST ENGLAND // What do a nuclear power station, Britain's best narrow gauge railway and 50 million tons of shingle have in common? Well, you'll find them all at eerie Dungeness, a pebble spit that juts out into the English Channel like a fin. Inhabited mainly by seabirds, this quiet spot is the terminus for the charming Romney, Hythe and Dymchurch Railway, with its mini steam engines and old-school stations. The bleakly beautiful garden of Prospect Cottage, the home of the late film director Derek Jarman, is another draw. And that nuclear power station? Well, it should be gone within a decade.

SEE IT ! ***Reach Dungeness by car or via the Romney, Hythe and Dymchurch Railway in summer and at weekends.***

111

Quaff quality craft-ale on Bermondsey Beer Mile

LONDON // Along a corridor of unassuming railway arches and industrial estates, sandwiched among scrap metal collectors and taxi repair garages, is the heart of London's brewery district. Now clocking in at slightly longer than its namesake distance, the Bermondsey Beer Mile is home to about 10 taprooms, some quite no-frills, plus an ever-expanding collection of craft-beer bars and bottle shops, making it an ideal afternoon ramble for hopheads. At one stop, you can even rent equipment to brew your own.

TRY IT ! ***Pace yourself: the beers are strong, and the route is long. Most taprooms are open on Saturdays only.***

112

Find green-fingered flair at the Chelsea Flower Show

LONDON // Chelsea may have a reputation for snootiness, but its famous annual flower show is a great leveller, attracting as many green-fingered window-box enthusiasts as aristocrats. The Royal Horticultural Society has been filling the grounds of the Royal Hospital Chelsea with blooms since 1913, and the pricey tickets for the May spectacle sell out quickly. The highlights for most are the fantasy gardens designed by great gardeners and the odd eccentric celebrity, opening up the world of no-expense-spared landscaping to the masses.

SEE IT ! ***The showground is a 10-minute stroll or short bus ride from Sloane Square.***

113

Celebrate May Day at Oxford's Magdalen Bridge

OXFORD & THE COTSWOLDS // 'The city of dreaming spires' celebrates its antiquity with pride each year via traditional May Day celebrations focused around Magdalen Bridge. Festivities kick off at 6am with the Magdalen College Choir singing from the top of the Great Tower, then continue around town with dancers, performers and morris dancers. Breakfast, provided by pubs and cafes, is central to the action, and much appreciated by Oxford's students, who maintain a long custom of all-night parties culminating with sunrise on the bridge.

SEE IT ! ***May Day celebrations happen on, yes, May Day (1st May). Don't forget that Magdalen is pronounced 'Maudlin'.***

© Luke MacGregor / RHS Chelsea Flower Show

114

Daydream in neon at God's Own Junkyard in Walthamstow

LONDON // Sometimes, great works of art are found not in grand galleries, but in anonymous-looking warehouses in Walthamstow. The late Chris Bracey spent 40 years assembling a luminous hoard of new and salvaged neon, from nightclub toilet signs and Soho strip bar lobby boards to beer ads and bespoke pieces for the celebrity set. If you've seen a neon-backed rock gig or stage show in the last few decades, chances are the neon made its way through God's Own Junkyard somewhere on the journey.

SEE IT ! ***It's a winding walk from Walthamstow Tube station, but the Junkyard website has directions with street photos to guide you.***

© Daniel Di Paolo

115

Find Oxonian royalty on a literary pub crawl

OXFORD & THE COTSWOLDS // What could be more classically British than tottering between old-world pubs in the footsteps of the country's literary greats? Thomas Hardy penned some of *Jude the Obscure* at the 17th-century Lamb & Flag, frequented by CS Lewis and JRR Tolkien (their discussion group, the Inklings, also supped at the Eagle & Child). The Turf Tavern has hosted Stephen Hawking, Oscar Wilde, Margaret Thatcher and Bill Clinton, while the 400-year-old Wadham College–owned King's Pub bills itself Oxford's 'brainiest pub'.

TRY IT ! ***Sleep it all off within Oxford's halls in stripped-back student rooms (book via the University Rooms website).***

116

Climb the spire of Winchester Cathedral

SOUTHERN ENGLAND // This magnificent medieval building has been inspiring pilgrims for a thousand years, and has one of the longest naves of any cathedral in Europe – a stonking 538ft, equivalent to sixteen double-decker buses parked end-to-end. Then there's the grand Gothic facade and the tomb of a literary icon (Jane Austen), but it's the soaring 150ft-high spire that draws all eyes: a sky-high pinnacle offering wraparound views of Winchester's rooftops. It's a long climb up, but so worth it.

SEE IT ! ***Winchester is just over an hour's train ride from London. The Tower and Roof Tours are very popular – book well ahead.***

© travellinglight / Alamy

© Edward Haylan / Shutterstock

117

Walk to the weather-beaten ruins of Dunstanburgh Castle

NORTHEAST ENGLAND // Looming near the kipper-famed fishing village of Craster are the ghostly ruins of Dunstanburgh Castle. It was built from 1313 as a show of strength against King Edward II by Earl Thomas of Lancaster, who was defeated en route and executed in 1322. During the Wars of the Roses, the fortress was captured by Yorkists, though left to crumble, becoming derelict by 1550. Despite its exposure to the elements, extraordinarily preserved remains include sections of the original wall and twin-towered keep.

With no road access, getting up close means taking a blustery, wave-lashed 1.5-mile walk which becomes increasingly dramatic as you approach. Or savour castle views from gastropub the Jolly Fisherman while dining on local seafood including Craster's prized kippers.

SEE IT ! ***You can also reach the castle by walking from Embleton, but plan ahead, as access can be cut off at high tide.***

118

Step onto the set of a TV drama at Castle Howard

YORKSHIRE // If you were a fan of the 2016 ITV drama *Victoria*, not to mention the 1980s' BBC series *Brideshead Revisited*, you'll go weak at the knees when you see the sets come to life here at Castle Howard. This breathtaking stately home takes 'grandeur' to a new level, being extravagantly domed, pilastered, gilded and frescoed, and set in stunningly landscaped grounds scattered with temples and follies.

When the third Earl of Carlisle decided to build a snazzy new home in 1699, he hired one of his mates, Sir John Vanbrugh, to oversee the project. Vanbrugh was a playwright who had no previous architectural experience – surely a recipe for disaster? Luckily, his second-in-command was Nicholas Hawksmoor, who had worked for Christopher Wren on St Paul's Cathedral in London, and knew what he was doing.

SEE IT ! ***Castle Howard is 15 miles northeast of York, off the A64. Weekends are busy, so try to visit on a weekday when it's quieter.***

A former Norman fortress, Leeds Castle became an opulent home for generations of royals and aristocrats

119

Follow the queens of England to Kent's Leeds Castle

SOUTHEAST ENGLAND // One of Britain's most visited historic buildings – and nowhere near Leeds – the immense, moated Leeds Castle is, for many, the world's most romantic. There has been a stone castle on this strategic lake island for over 900 years. Originally established as a Norman fortress, it has followed the fashions of the times, going from draughty fort to the comfortable Tudor-style mansion visitors see today.

In 1974 it was passed by the last owner, high-society hostess Lady Baillie, into the hands of a charitable trust. Often referred to as a 'Lady's Castle', many monarchs' wives and consorts have bustled along these splendid corridors, but the most famous was probably Catherine of Aragon – Henry VIII had the whole thing rebuilt for her in 1519.

One of Kent's unmissable sights, the exquisite period interiors and extensive, attraction-dotted grounds make for one of the county's best days out. It's a great place to bring children too; they'll love the animal enclosures, hedge maze, playgrounds, adventure golf course and little green train that takes you up to the castle.

SEE IT ! ***Bearsted train station is about 2.5 miles away, with summer shuttle buses between the castle and station. Free parking.***

The expansive and much-celebrated view from the steep escarpment of Sutton Bank in the North York Moors

120

Ramble through a purple haze of heather in the North York Moors National Park

YORKSHIRE // If one thing defines the North York Moors, it's heather. Three quarters of all the world's heather moorland is found in Britain, and this is easily the largest expanse in England. This hardy, ground-hugging, evergreen shrub dominates the high moors, covering more than a third of the national park. Red grouse, curlew and golden plover thrive amid its tangled twigs, and in summer millions upon millions of tiny mauve flowers transform the moors with a purple haze.

The moors are criss-crossed with walking trails – a total of 1400 miles of rights of way – making the park a paradise for hikers. Half a dozen long-distance trails also pass through – the 89-mile Inn Way is worth a look, starting and finishing in Helmsley and taking in no fewer than 31 country pubs along the way. The mountain-bike trails at Sutton Bank and Dalby Forest are ideal for families, while the Moors to Sea Cycle Network provides 150 miles of quiet roads, woodland tracks and bridleways for road cyclists to explore.

The region is also home to historic Rievaulx Abbey, the Kilburn White Horse hill figure and one of England's most picturesque steam railways (puffing in at #308 on this list).

SEE IT ! ***August is the best month to see the heather in full bloom.***

© Nicola Ferrari / Alamy

© Simon Stacpoole / Getty Images

121

Savour a properly English high tea at Grantchester's Orchard Tea Garden

EAST ANGLIA // Stand by (or in line) to sample the best of British high teas in the best surroundings. The tasty treats here are served up as you flop in a deckchair under mature apple trees. Think flower-filled gardens, fruit-studded orchards, clusters of tables and buzzing bees. It's all just a 3-mile riverside walk, cycle or punt from Cambridge. That proximity has made the Orchard a huge hit with generations of students. You can almost feel the presence of Brooke, Russell, Woolf and Keynes as you linger at this most beguilingly British tea stop.

☛ SEE IT ! *Book 24 hours ahead for the Orchard's famous cream teas of sandwiches, cake, scones, clotted cream and jam.*

122

Become a fan of a British obsession at a football match in Manchester

NORTHWEST ENGLAND // The world capital of football. They've been saying it for years in Manchester, but these days it's more than just local bluster. The world's most famous team (Manchester United) shares a city with the world's richest (Manchester City), with most locals either a red or a blue. Games at United's Old Trafford ground or at City's newer Etihad stadium are not just an exhibition of top-class football but a boisterous showcase of a billion-dollar global spectacle whose results are celebrated (or mourned) around the world.

☛ SEE IT ! *Old Trafford is in Salford, west of the centre, the Etihad stadium is east of the city centre; both are easily reached by tram.*

Hikers approach the summit of Corn Du, one of the four peaks of Brecon Beacons National Park

123

Stride, sup and stargaze in the Brecon Beacons National Park

MID-WALES // How do we love the Brecon Beacons? Let us count the ways... Whether it's the gold-green moorlands, illuminated by a sudden shaft of light between scudding clouds, the startling screech of a red kite as you crest a fin-shaped peak, or finding a cosy, timber-beamed pub with local ales on tap at the end of that drizzle-soaked walk, there's no denying the stark allure of this 520-sq-mile national park. Hikers, climbers, kayakers, cavers, cyclists, stargazers and lovers of single-track lane solitude and ruined medieval castles are all in their element here.

The best way to explore the park's bare, sheer-sided heights and heather-clad mountains, which bear the scars of glacial erosion, is to get out and stride. If you don't have time for the 99-mile Beacons Way, opt for an exhilarating day hike, for instance the 10-mile horseshoe ridge trail, ticking off the four peaks of Corn Du, Pen y Fan (the highest at 2906ft), Cribyn and Fan y Big. Return by night for the telescope-twitching magic of glimpsing the Milky Way in the unpolluted skies of this Dark Sky Reserve.

☛ SEE IT ! ***Abergavenny, on the park's eastern edge, has frequent trains to London. The A40 is the national park's main artery.***

© Phil Metcalfe / Alamy

© Ian G Dagnall / Alamy

124

Fall in love with rail travel aboard the Caledonian Sleeper

RAIL JOURNEY // There's something about the romance of rail travel that is only intensified by spending a night on a train, and the Caledonian Sleeper service, which runs from London to Inverness with connections to Kyle of Lochalsh, is one of the best overnighters in Britain. Boarding at Euston at 8.30pm you're lulled to sleep by the rocking of the carriage and the clickety-clack of the wheels. Morning brings another world, crossing Drumochter summit (1483ft), the highest railway line in the UK, as the train rushes into Cairngorms National Park. After a hearty breakfast, alight in the heart of the Highlands.

TRY IT ! ***Spiffy new sleeper coaches with double beds and en-suite showers make the journey all the more comfortable from 2019.***

125

Take a trip to Burgh Island on a unique sea tractor

SOUTHWEST ENGLAND // If William Heath Robinson were to design a form of public transport, chances are he'd come up with something close to Bigbury-on-Sea's bizarre sea tractor – a one-of-a-kind contraption resembling a shopping trolley perched on top of a set of Monster Truck wheels. The original was designed in 1969 by Robert Jackson (who also helped build Britain's nuclear power stations in the 1950s), and utilises a hydraulic platform that keeps its passengers above the waves as it trundles over to tidal Burgh Island. Once on dry land, they can enjoy some excellent walks and lunch at the Pilchard Inn.

SEE IT ! ***Bigbury-on-Sea is 12 miles from Salcombe, and 40 minutes' drive from Plymouth.***

An assemblage of iconic London sights as seen from Waterloo Bridge. At sunset, naturally

126

Admire Ray Davies' sunset from Waterloo Bridge

LONDON // The Kinks' biggest hit wasn't a success just because it was catchy. Millions of Londoners could relate to the experience of waiting for a date on Waterloo Bridge, with the sky turning red over Parliament, Big Ben and the Thames. Waterloo Station has been rebuilt and revamped numerous times since it opened in 1848, but Britain's busiest railway station still holds a special place in Londoners' hearts, and some 99 million journeys start or end here every single year.

As far as river crossings go, there are more beautiful bridges in the capital, but Waterloo has a prime location at the junction between Westminster and the City, with iconic views in both directions that make the most of the London sunset. Look southwest and gaze on the Houses of Parliament, framed by the London Eye and the brutalist institutions of the South Bank. Turn eastwards and you'll see St Paul's and the skyscrapers of the City, including the futuristic lines of the Cheesegrater and Norman Foster's Gherkin, with the blocky towers of Canary Wharf sneaking in far right of frame.

☛ SEE IT ! ***Waterloo is the gateway station for Waterloo Bridge, obviously! Come before or after the evening rush hour or you'll be carried away by the crowds.***

A morning mist clings to the foothills of the Cambrian Mountains, one of the most deserted areas in all of the UK

127

Wander the little-known wilderness of the Cambrian Mountains

MID-WALES // If the places on this list were rearranged by population density, from least to most crowded, the Cambrian Mountains would be jostling for number-one spot. Within Britain, it is only in far corners of Scotland's Highlands and Islands that you find fewer signs of civilisation per square mile than here. Not for nothing is this lonely tract of uplands dubbed 'Desert of Wales'. Most Brits, in fact, would struggle to name one fact about a region that has always shied away from the public eye: in the 1970s it became the only UK area ever to be proposed as a national park and then rejected, due to protests from locals. Hikers generally gravitate just south to the Brecon Beacons or north to Snowdonia, leaving this expanse in-between to the sheep and red kites.

But the Cambrians are not all nothingness. Source of the first- and fifth-longest rivers in Britain, the Severn and the Wye, the hills also host one of the country's toughest ultra-marathons, the Dragons Back Race, and harbour some evocative history, such as the legend of Wales' very own Robin Hood, Twm Siôn Cati.

SEE IT ! ***Wheels are essential. Llandovery, Tregaron, Rhyader, Builth Wells and Llanwrtyd Wells are the best access points.***

© Colin Underhill / Alamy

128

Watch world-class mix with upper-class at Henley Royal Regatta

OXFORD & THE COTSWOLDS // What do you get if you cross top-calibre sporting endeavour with champagne-fuelled frivolity? Henley Royal Regatta, a long-established event in the international rowing scene and a major fixture in the high-society calendar. For the rest of us, there's a public enclosure where we can sip Pimm's and occasionally watch some boats going up and down the river. Even for non-rowing fans, the atmosphere is sparkling and *so* traditionally English upper-crust, with some gentlemen spectators donning old-school rowing kit, including blazers and boaters. Next to the course, the pretty town of Henley-on-Thames is a favourite for London's high-rolling commuters. There's a good choice of places to stay, except in busy Regatta week, but fortunately Henley is within easy reach of London by train.

☛ SEE IT ! ***Established in 1839, Henley Royal Regatta takes place every July. Enclosure tickets start from about £25.***

© Anyka / Alamy

129

Bask on Luskentyre's bewildering beach

HIGHLANDS & ISLANDS // Sun-lovers may quibble over whether Luskentyre, with its overcast days and sea mists, is even worth the trip to Harris from the mainland. But with its memorable curve of white sand, who really cares if you leave T-shirt tanned or not? Because your profit is a swirl of shell-rich sand and water that laps the shore in shades of supernatural green and blue.

In fact, the west-facing bay neatly packages Harris' best bits in one knockout blow. To the north is An Cliseam (2621ft), the Outer Hebrides' highest mountain. In the middle distance are puffin colonies and the seal-populated Isle of Taransay. Then, south along the sand-flats, are nesting sites for migrant birds. Little changes on Luskentyre, but it still exerts a hold over all who set foot on it.

☛ SEE IT ! ***Luskentyre is located 3 miles off the A859. Park at the graveyard, then walk over the dunes.***

© Andrew Lee

© Piya Sukchit / Shutterstock

130

Look in on a Victorian hoarder at the Horniman

LONDON // Many a schoolboy has smirked at the name, but the museum founded by Victorian tea mogul Frederick John Horniman in 1901 has serious cultural credentials. For a start, there's the building: a handsome, turreted faux-castle built by Arts and Crafts master Charles Harrison Townsend, one of the best surviving examples of the style.

But the real treasures lurk inside. As the son of the world's most successful tea importer, Frederick Horniman had the opportunity and funds to travel the globe buying up curiosities, and some 30,000 of his hoarded objects form the basis of the 350,000-strong collection here. Wander past stuffed walruses and polar bears to rooms stacked with Indian sitars, veenas and tablas, and cases piled with carvings, idols and tribal masks – it's a priceless snapshot of a golden age of travel.

SEE IT ! ***Set off on foot from Forest Hill Overground station; the museum website has a video showing the route.***

131

Tour a star of the silver screen: Alnwick Castle

NORTHEAST ENGLAND // No, you're not experiencing déjà vu, Alnwick Castle's uncanny familiarity is almost certainly due to its starring role as Hogwarts School of Witchcraft and Wizardry in two Harry Potter films (kids can learn to ride a broomstick like Harry did in the Outer Bailey). Or perhaps you've seen it in *Blackadder*, *Downton Abbey* or *Transformers: The Last Knight*. 'On Location' tours take you behind the scenes or you can simply roam the 14th-century castle's dining room, guard chamber, library and staterooms, admiring a fine collection of Italian paintings including works by Titian and Canaletto.

To the east of the castle, the 4.8-hectare walled Alnwick Garden incorporates the Grand Cascade's spurting water jets and a poison garden – get a combined ticket to see them both.

SEE IT ! ***Alnwick is 35 miles north of Newcastle. Its old train station is now lovely Barter Books; Alnmouth train station is 4 miles away.***

132

Raise a world-beating dram in Speyside

NORTHEAST SCOTLAND // Spare a thought for the teetotaller. Speyside is single malt heaven and the pine-clad glens of Strathspey are rooted in whisky distilling and dram-emptying traditions. You'll discover world-beaters like Macallan and Glenlivet and find roads to smaller pot still outfits like Tamdhu and Aberlour. Beyond any measure, this is the territory of *uisge-beatha*, the Scots' water of life.

In terms of mapping a tour, a whisky triangle can be drawn north of Craigellachie, down to Huntly in the east and to Tomintoul in the south. Here, there are more concentrated distilleries than anywhere else, the focal point being Dufftown with its cooperage and seven whisky houses, including Glenfiddich and Balvenie. So, pay your respects: you're not looking at a glass of whisky, but centuries of distilling that have shaped the landscape.

☛ TRY IT ! ***Visit for the Spirit of Speyside Festival (May) and Dufftown's Speyside Whisky Festival (September to October).***

Juliet Kinsman's Top Five Places

Juliet Kinsman was founding editor of award-winning boutique hotel website Mr & Mrs Smith. She now runs Bouteco, helping travellers find the best boutique eco hotels, and is a regular guest on BBC Radio London.

01

AFTERNOON TEA AT SKETCH, LONDON – Dainty cakes and eye-candy galore await at this Mayfair spot. Book a table in the pink, David Shrigley-decked dining room and do pop to the loo and its egg-shaped cubicles.

02

WALPOLE BAY HOTEL, MARGATE – Built in 1913, this time capsule of a seaside stay is brimming with bric-a-brac, and every eccentric artefact has a story to tell, including guests' registration cards dating back to its Edwardian heyday.

03

STEEPHILL COVE, ISLE OF WIGHT – Striped deckchairs and colourful beach huts line this pebble-and-sand beach, beloved by grannies and hipster families alike. Pause at the Crab Shed for just-caught delights.

04

CHELSEA PHYSIC GARDEN, LONDON – Get a fresh-air lesson in medicinal, herbal and edible plants where the Society of Apothecaries got the botanical party started in 1673. It boasts Britain's first rock garden.

05

CASS SCULPTURE FOUNDATION, WEST SUSSEX – Walk through the woodlands of this 26-acre Sussex Downs estate founded by Wilfred and Jeanette Cass, and ogle larger-than-life sculptures by eminent artists including Tony Cragg and Antony Gormley.

©People's History Museum

133

Hail the struggle for social justice at the People's History Museum

NORTHWEST ENGLAND // The story of Manchester's radical bona fides and Britain's tortuous path to fully representative democracy are told in compelling detail at this superb museum. Inside this old Edwardian pumping station is the desk where Thomas Paine wrote *Rights of Man* in 1791; an impressive collection of hand-stitched union and political banners; and, in the city that saw the birth of the suffragette movement, a wide-ranging exhibit on the struggle for women's equality. There's a floor devoted to the campaign for equal rights since WWII, with displays on gay rights, the fight against racism and key socio-political moments such as the founding of the National Health Service, the miners' strike of 1983 and the 1990 poll tax protests that contributed to the resignation of then-prime minister Margaret Thatcher.

☛ SEE IT ! ***The museum is on Bridge St, just west of Deansgate, and is free to all visitors.***

© Michael Kiedyszko / Getty

134

Snake your way through the Honister Pass for glorious views

CUMBRIA // Not for the faint-hearted, one of Cumbria's highest passes is a narrow, perilously steep road that snakes its way through the fell (or valley) from Gatesgarth Farm, at the southern end of Buttermere, to connect with Seatoller in the Borrowdale Valley. It's a challenging drive – the 1 in 4 gradient is tough enough, and at points it turns into a single track so you'll need sharp reversing skills if you meet an oncoming car – but the reward is a stunning slice of wild Cumbrian landscape.

At the 1167ft summit of the pass is the Honister Slate Mine and the start of a popular walk up to Great Gable or Dale Head (2473ft). The pass is part of a gorgeous drive that starts in Keswick and takes in Newlands Pass, Buttermere and Crummock Water – areas not as popular as other parts of the Lake District and all the better for it.

☛ SEE IT ! ***Whether you ascend from Gatesgarth Farm or Seatoller, the ascent to the summit is 3km, with an elevation gain of 800ft.***

Boats cross the Unesco-listed Pontcysyllte Aqueduct, completed by Thomas Telford in 1805

135

Float over the Pontcysyllte Aqueduct aboard a narrowboat

NORTH WALES // Of all the waterways on Britain's unrivalled canal network, most narrowboat enthusiasts would unhesitatingly name the Llangollen Canal as one of the best stretches to chug down. Sure, there is something storybook dramatic about beginning a voyage in lazy Cheshire farmland, crossing a country border and winding up in the steep, green Welsh hills, but no narrowboater disputes the highlight here: as the canal hits Wales, it crosses Thomas Telford's engineering masterpiece, Pontcysyllte Aqueduct.

From one second (OK, minute; narrowboating is a sedate pursuit) to the next, bankside foliage transmogrifies into dizzying views over the River Dee, as a grand 18-arch bridge carries the canal for over 1000ft across the valley 126ft below. Even to gaze upon this graceful feat of construction, which underscored Telford's fame upon its completion in 1805 and gained Unesco World Heritage status in 2008, is awe-inspiring. To get to glide across it is to experience one of the finest man-made triumphs over nature.

SEE IT ! ***The aqueduct is best seen on the Llangollen Canal from Wrenbury, Cheshire. Or park in Trevor, 4 miles east, and walk.***

136

Get into birdwatching at Bempton Cliffs

YORKSHIRE // In spring and summer, the sea cliffs at Bempton witness a breathtaking wildlife spectacle. Here, where the chalk of the Yorkshire Wolds meets the pounding surf of the North Sea, crags up to 325ft in height are home to half a million seabirds – a blizzard of gannets, fulmars, guillemots, razorbills, kittiwakes and puffins – all cramming themselves on the vertiginous ledges, swooping and swirling overhead in a frenzy of feeding and breeding. The noise, movement and smell of this seabird city are almost overwhelming, as is the scenery.

SEE IT ! ***The cliffs are 4 miles north of Bridlington. For maximum bird numbers, visit between May and August.***

137

Mountain-bike top trails at Coed-y-Brenin Forest Park

NORTH WALES // Coed-y-Brenin tops the list of pedal-powered adrenaline rushes for several reasons. It was the first UK forest developed for mountain bikers, and boasts the country's first purpose-built mountain-biking trail: the rocky, corkscrewing 'Black Bull'. A range of routes from novice to ultra-advanced twist through the trees here, plus there is a bike shop, visitor centre and a cafe serving venison burgers from deer reared in the park. All this comes with a complimentary backdrop of jaw-dropping Snowdonia scenery.

TRY IT ! ***Coed-y-Brenin Forest Park is 10 miles north of Dolgellau. From here, bus 35 stops within 1.5 miles of the mountain-biking base.***

138

Walk with mixed-up dinosaurs at Crystal Palace

LONDON // Any dinosaur enthusiast worth their rock hammer knows the story of the Crystal Palace Park dinosaurs. While absurdly inaccurate by modern standards, these Victorian visions were the first depictions of flesh-on dinosaurs created anywhere, ever, so let's cut the model-makers some slack. Among the 1850s effigies is Benjamin Hawkins' and Sir Richard Owens' famous iguanodon, with its thumb spike mistakenly placed on its nose. Strolling around the park today feels like stepping inside a Victorian woodcut; out of date but all the more charming for it.

SEE IT ! ***Nearby Crystal Palace Overground and rail station were built to bring visitors to the original Victorian amusement park.***

Curious sightseers, rather than commuters, now populate the platform at the disused Aldwych station

139

Tour abandoned Aldwych, one of London's 'ghost' Tube stations

LONDON // The rainbow pattern of the London Underground map is one of the city's most iconic symbols, but since the network's creation more than 150 years ago, the system has moved and shifted in line with the city above. Changing passenger numbers and demands have led to a handful of no-longer-used 'ghost stations' around the city, the most accessible of which is Aldwych. Originally named Strand station (the sign is still emblazoned above its main bolted-up entrance), Aldwych opened to commuters in 1907. However, it was never heavily used, and closed temporarily during WWII to become a storage facility for the British Museum and a shelter for Londoners during the Blitz, before finally shutting in 1994.

Tours start in the ticket hall, complete with evocative old notices and impeccable tilework, pass the 1920s' wooden-floored lifts and head down to platform level, where a 1970s Tube carriage is parked. Aldwych might just be more popular now than when it was operational: it's been used in music videos, TV shows and films, including *Darkest Hour*, *Sherlock*, *Atonement* and *V for Vendetta*.

SEE IT ! ***Tours take place a few times a year; see the London Transport Museum website for more information on booking.***

© mauritius images / Alamy

© Loop Images Ltd / Alamy

140

Travel back in time to olde world Arundel

SOUTHEAST ENGLAND // Few places in Sussex feel as preserved in formaldehyde as the small town of Arundel. Strung up the side of a considerable slope rising from the tidal River Arun, this South Downs community has one of the most august skylines in the south, largely dominated by the Duke of Norfolk's huge castle (he still lives there but lets visitors nose around) and the town's 19th-century cathedral. The streets below are known for their Aladdin's cave antique shops – the chance to browse the brass, oak and copper-bottomed trinkets of yesteryear lures many visitors. Taking tea is also big in Arundel, with tea shops galore serving the quintessential Sussex cream tea – two scones, a pot of jam and a dish of thick clotted cream. For something stronger, local Arundel Brewery is behind some of the best ale in the region.

SEE IT ! ***Arundel can be reached by train and bus from Brighton and by train direct from London.***

141

Wander the pretty opes of Polperro

SOUTHWEST ENGLAND // In a seriously strong field of contenders, Polperro is perhaps the prettiest of Cornish fishing villages – an improbably photogenic jumble of cobbled alleyways and narrow lanes (known as 'opes' round these parts), encircling a granite harbour filled with bright blue sea. So pretty is it, you could be forgiven for thinking you've stumbled onto a set for the BBC's adaptation of *Poldark* (and in fact you'd only be half-wrong – the village has been used as a backdrop in several episodes). Once a smuggler's haunt and pilchard-fishing harbour, these days Polperro relies heavily on tourist traffic for its crust – but come dusk, once the crowds have headed back to their holiday cottages and B&Bs, you can still feel traces of the old Polperro as you wander aimlessly along the back lanes.

SEE IT ! ***Polperro is 5 miles southwest of Looe, to which it's linked by regular local buses.***

© Marius Roman / Getty Images

© Pete Seaward / Lonely Planet

142

Conquer the Cuillins on the Isle of Skye

HIGHLANDS & ISLANDS // Difficult to traverse in one go, hard to pronounce (it's 'Coo-lynn') and near-impossible to describe to those who've never been, the Isle of Skye's crowning glory is to Scotland what K2 is to the Himalayas. This belt of 17 peaks may not rival Ben Nevis for height, but in size and scale the two distinct ranges of the Black and Red Cuillin form the UK's most challenging sweep of mountains.

In general, the knife-edge massif is the domain of the hiker, but there are bonkers trail bikers, wilderness campers, scramblers and climbers, too. And what they all share is a love of off-grid adventures in inhospitable terrain. Here, midges wreak havoc, moorland is boggy and the weather rarely in tune with the forecast. But that's why it's so incomparable – and why you'll want to come back.

SEE IT ! *The best access point is from Glen Brittle, where you'll find a youth hostel and campsite.*

143

Head to Southwold for sandy toes, beer and a pier

EAST ANGLIA // For a blast of breezy British seaside charm, it's hard to beat Southwold. This charismatic Suffolk fishing port has long drawn visitors to its golden sands, cannon-dotted bluffs and brightly painted beach huts. That picturesque appeal has also attracted painters from JMW Turner to Lucian Freud and Damien Hirst.

Start your explorations at the 623ft-long Victorian pier, with its kooky collection of satirical handmade amusement machines. Amble along the promenade, admiring the squat 19th-century lighthouse, and maybe drop by the retro Electric Picture Palace to see a film – and the ascending cinema organ. But don't miss Adnams Brewery – book ahead for a tour of the high-tech kit, gin distillery and some tutored tastings. Then sample some more at the brewery's super-stylish Swan next door.

SEE IT ! *The nearest train stations are Darsham or Halesworth. July's Latitude Festival of music, dance and comedy is held nearby.*

© Andrea Calzona / Alamy Stock Photo

© Andrew Nicholson / Alamy

144

Fuel up for the scintillating Llanidloes to Machynlleth drive

NORTH WALES // If you yearn for a drive of thrilling mountain vistas, vast snaking bodies of water and gorges wheeling with red kites and precious little else, with no other motorists interrupting your view, then the mountain road between Llanidloes and Machynlleth is a must.

This is not a route to daunt drivers or thrill petrolheads – it is but 24 miles long, only briefly crests the 1300ft elevation mark and is in good nick – but the depth and texture of the summits and lake-laced valleys, with scarcely a dwelling to help grant perspective, is rarely matched on UK roads outside the Scottish Highlands.

Linger alongside the Llyn Clywedog reservoir, explore the ethereal pine forests of Hafren and save your appetite for a stop-off at the remote Star Inn at Dylife.

SEE IT ! *Llanidloes is 13 miles southwest of Newtown. Do the drive in decent weather or the best bits will be hidden in cloud.*

145

Shed light on the code breakers and computers of Bletchley Park

SOUTHERN ENGLAND // Bletchley Park is a 19th-century country house, but its fame derives from more recent times. During WWII, it was the centre of Britain's codebreaking activity, and some say it's where the war was won, or at least shortened by a couple of years. Using only basic tools, by today's standards, some of the best minds in the country cracked enemy codes, including Germany's infamous – and reputedly unbreakable – Enigma. Among the many machines invented in the 1940s as part of this vital task was 'Colossus', the world's first digital programmable computer, making Bletchley a must-visit for tech geeks as well as history buffs. Today's exhibits include the Bombe machine that helped decipher Enigma, and the recreated office of Alan Turing, the best-known of the Bletchley codebreakers.

SEE IT ! *Bletchley is just south of Milton Keynes. It has its own train station with quick links to London Euston.*

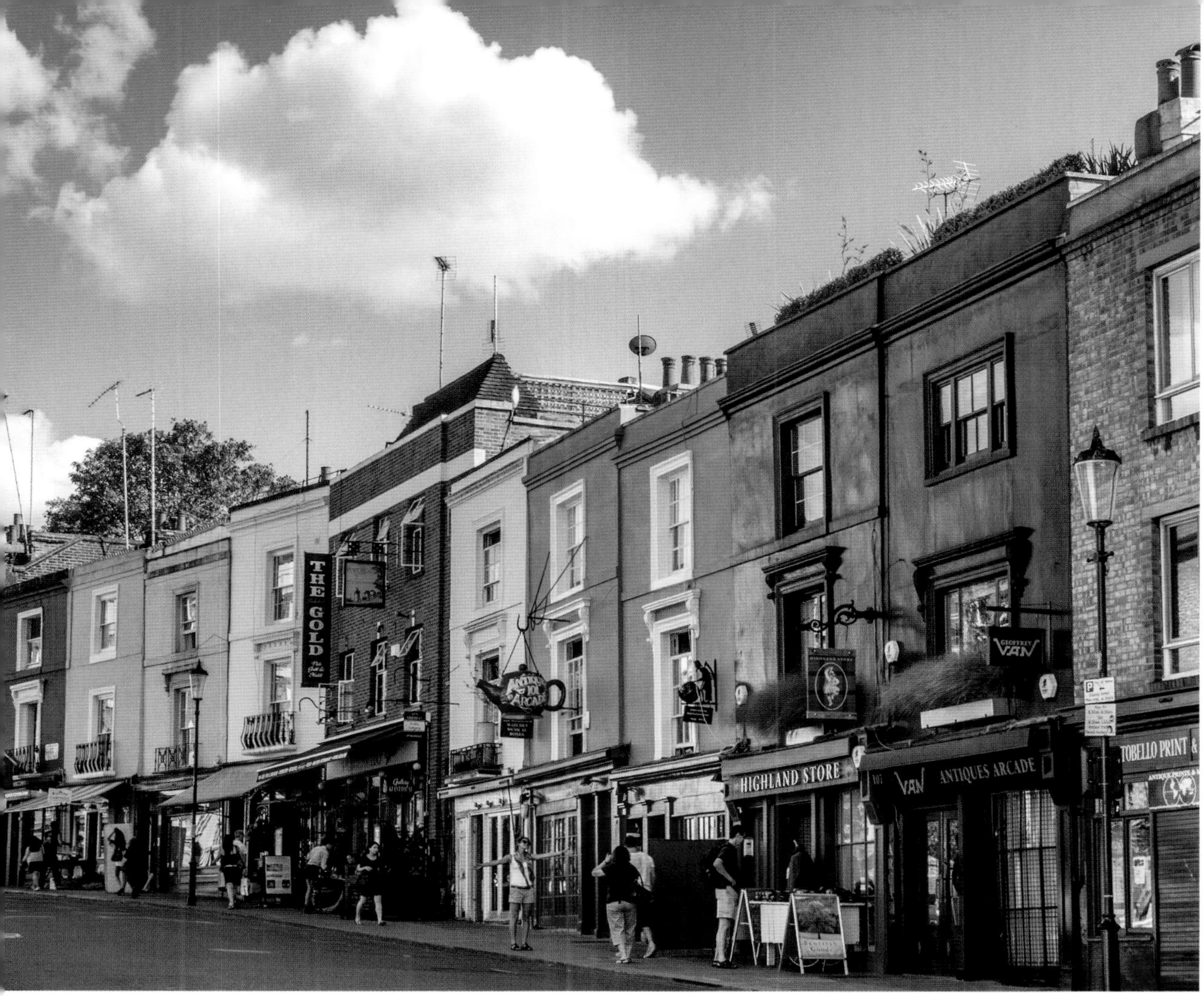

Portobello Rd in Notting Hill is a place of colourful shopfronts containing all manner of wares within

146

Seek treasure among the tat at Portobello Market

LONDON // Nowhere sums up the Notting Hill of old quite like Portobello Rd. Before the bankers and lawyers moved in, before the Julia Roberts movie, before even the boho cafes and arthouse cinemas, Portobello was a bustling Victorian produce market. During the tough years of WWII, the fruiterers and cheesemongers were joined by rag-and-bone men, hawking salvaged bric-a-brac to escape wartime poverty. Hot on their heels came the antique traders, founding the Portobello Rd Londoners know and love today.

Of course, what makes Portobello such fun is the juxtaposition between the swanky antique shops and the pavement traders selling everything from junkshop tat to neon headbands, outsized jewellery, African prints and Jamaican vinyl. Saturday is the main event, with crowds thronging through the market's five loosely defined zones, before swinging by Acklam Village Market for some globetrotting street food. Come evening, you can catch an arthouse movie, or sip a gin sling prepared using spirits from Portobello Rd's The Distillery, one of only a handful of working distilleries in central London.

SEE IT ! ***To walk Portobello's full length, head north from Notting Hill Gate Tube. Or duck in halfway from Ladbroke Grove Tube.***

The history-suffused houses of the Shambles in York date back to Medieval times

147

Let York's Shambles send a shiver down your spine

YORKSHIRE // The clanging of a death bell echoes along a dark, cobbled alley as a black-cloaked, top-hatted figure stalks menacingly towards you, silhouetted against the dim glow of the street lamps... This is the best way to experience the ambience of York's most atmospheric street: on a nightly Ghost Hunt walk, led by a guide in the guise of a Victorian doctor who begins the tour by walking the length of the Shambles, tolling a handbell.

This narrow medieval street is lined with 14th- and 15th-century Tudor buildings that overhang so much they almost meet above your head. Some are brick, some half-timbered, and some still have meathooks outside; providing a clue to the origins of the street – The Shambles takes its name from the Saxon word shamel, meaning 'slaughterhouse'. In 1862 it housed no fewer than 26 butcher shops, whose wide window shelves displayed meat and offal, while the channel in the middle of the lane made it easy to sluice blood and waste down to the drains. The butchers have long gone, making way for the souvenir shops, tea rooms and boutiques that now fill the still evocative street.

SEE IT ! ***During the day the Shambles is crammed with coach tour parties. Best to visit in the early morning or evening.***

The small St Catherine's Island just off Tenby is only linked to the mainland at low tide

148

Do be beside the seaside in the Georgian resort of Tenby

SOUTH WALES // The great British seaside is alive and kicking in Tenby, where lanes lined with Georgian mansions and houses dolled up in jolly colours slope down to gold-sand beaches. The town has all the lovable aspects of the seaside – ice cream parlours, fish 'n' chip shops, kitschy souvenirs, rollicking pubs – without overstepping the mark into rowdy and tacky territory. Peak summer season aside, when the holiday resort gets its party-going groove on, this is a place for coastal escapades and family fun, like rock-pooling, crabbing, sandcastle-building and clambering up to the scant remains of the Norman castle atop the headland.

On the south coast, Tenby is one of the few true 'resorts' in Pembrokeshire and often the first place visitors clap eyes on. There is much beauty here, too: take the boat across to nearby Caldey Island for dramatic cliffs, chances of spotting grey seals and seabirds, and to glimpse the Cistercian monastery (not open to the public), or walk across the sands to the rugged little island of St Catherine's, taking care to return before the tide comes in.

☛ SEE IT ! ***Tenby has a railway station with twice hourly connections to Swansea (1½ hours) and good coastal bus connections.***

149

See world-class art in St Ives

SOUTHWEST ENGLAND // The fishing village of St Ives may seem unlikely as a hotbed of experimental British art, but that's exactly what it was between the 1940s and '60s, when sculptor Barbara Hepworth and her husband Ben Nicholson set about founding an art colony here. Inspired by the rugged landscape and rural setting, artists such as Naum Gabo, Terry Frost, Peter Lanyon, Wilhelmina Barns-Graham and Roger Hilton flocked here to find the peace and tranquillity to pursue their own artistic visions: experimental, frequently abstract, and decidedly against the grain. St Ives has been an art hub ever since, and in 1993 received its own outpost of the renowned Tate Gallery, showcasing the work of local artists alongside other contemporary works. It's been a big success, and in 2018 opened a new extension that earned it Art Fund Museum of the Year.

☛ SEE IT ! ***The museum is open year-round from Tuesday to Sunday.***

Gillian Burke's Top Five Places

Gillian Burke is a natural history producer and voiceover artist. She has been a co-presenter of BBC nature series* Springwatch *and its spin-offs since 2017.

01

GIANNI'S ICE CREAM PARLOUR, ST DAVIDS, PEMBROKESHIRE – Visit St Davids for its seabirds and cathedral. And make sure you stop at Gianni's Ice Cream Parlour, arguably Britain's best ice cream in its smallest city.

02

SIMMER DIM ON UNST, SHETLAND – Experience the strange twilight glow of 'Simmer Dim' accompanied by a midnight summer-solstice picnic on Britain's most northerly beaches. Remember to leave nothing else but footprints.

03

TREBAH GARDEN, LIZARD PENINSULA – The beguiling trail through the subtropical garden leads to Polgwidden beach, a launch site for the D-Day landings during WWII, now a tranquil cove of crystal clear, azure waters.

04

RSPB RESERVES, FAIRBURN INGS, OLD MOOR AND ST AIDAN'S – These reserves have risen out of the ashes of post-industrial wasteland, natural gems regenerated, in part, by former miners and the local community.

05

TROYTOWN FARM CAMPSITE, ST AGNES, ISLES OF SCILLY – Wild swimming with seals off Britain's most southwesterly campsite is one of many magical moments this untamed island has to offer. One of the last outposts before the great, wide-open Atlantic Ocean.

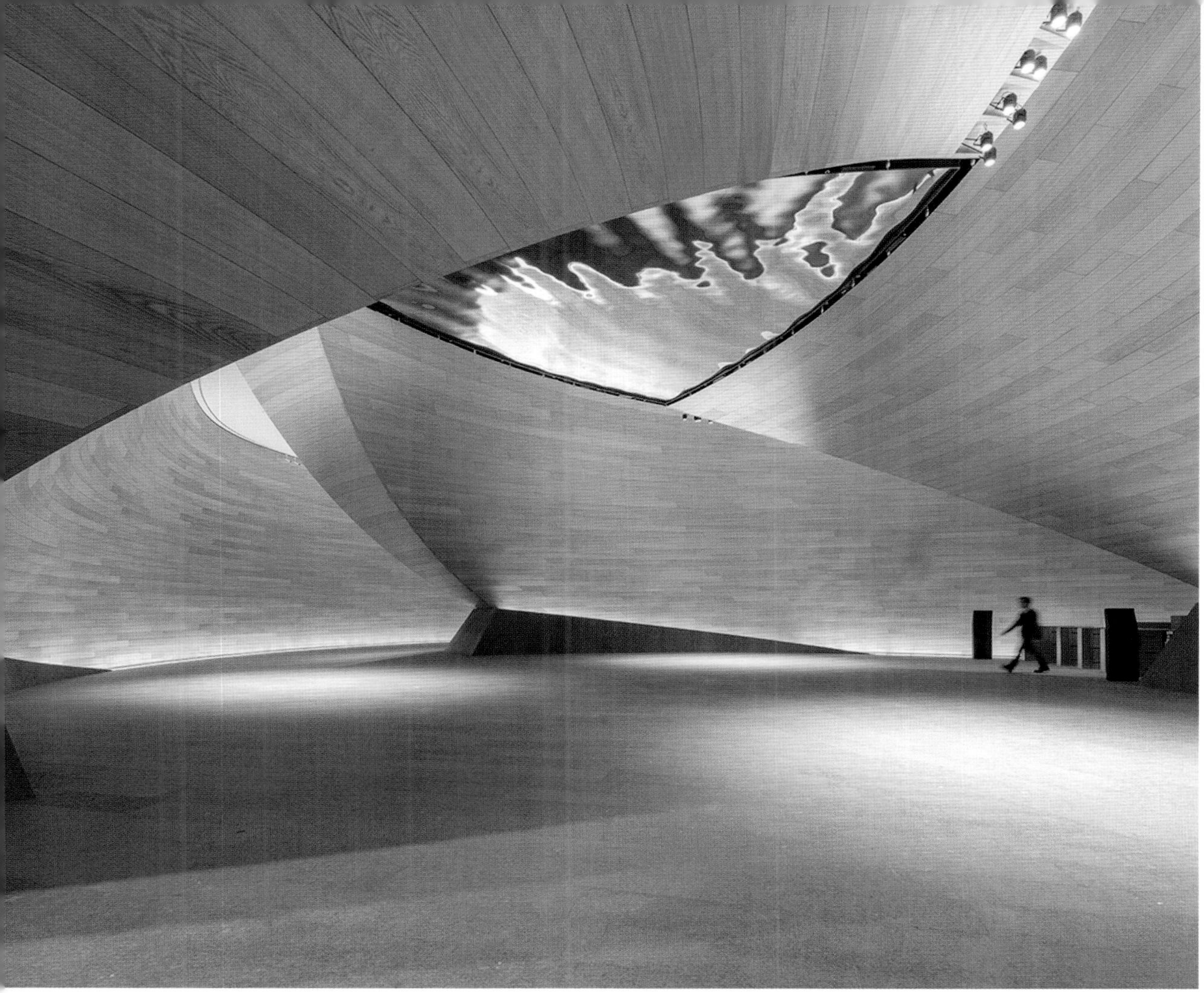

Open House enables access to buildings such as Bloomberg's European HQ, which is home to Olafur Eliasson's 'Vortex'

150

Peek behind closed doors during Open House London

LONDON // Without a doubt, Open House London is one of the city's best weekends, when more than 800 usually off-limits buildings open their doors to all. Calling itself the world's largest architecture festival and now attracting more than 250,000 Londoners and visitors, the September event started in London in 1992 and has now expanded to 35 cities on five continents. A true delight for architecture-lovers or the merely nosy, the programme includes stops in nearly every London borough, with buildings as diverse as grandiose embassies, sewage pumping stations, ancient livery halls, brutalist council estates, individuals' homes and a Masonic temple nearly lost to history.

The list varies each year, but perennial highlights include the sumptuous Victorian interiors of the Grade I-listed Foreign and Commonwealth Office, the dizzying summits of several London skyscrapers (including the Gherkin and the Cheesegrater) and even the seriously secretive prime minister's residence at 10 Downing St. Some sites are only accessible by ballot or pre-booking, so it pays to plan your route in advance.

SEE IT ! ***The buildings are scattered across the city, so get a printed guide or the app to see what's open, when and where.***

© Kiev Victor / Shutterstock

© Visit Wales / Lonely Planet

151

Watch the ships come sailing into London from Greenwich Park

LONDON // Greenwich is London's maritime history writ large, and there's no better vantage point from which to admire it than the grand park laid out for the capital's playboy monarchs, used first for hunting with hawks, then stag hunting, then promenading, before being handed over to the people.

From the lofty heights of the Royal Observatory, the wings of the Old Royal Naval College are laid out before you like an architect's plan, backed by the Thames and the skyscraper garden of Canary Wharf. In summer, the park is ideal for picnicking, so stock up en route at Greenwich Market before choosing a spot. Work off your lunch with a stroll beneath the trees, before boosting your cultural credentials with a tour of the Naval College and Maritime Museum.

SEE IT ! *North Greenwich Tube is a long hike from Greenwich, so opt for the Docklands Light Railway or mainline trains to Greenwich.*

152

Be awed by the 700-year-old defences of Beaumaris

NORTH WALES // One of the quartet of English King Edward I's North Wales castles, and with Unesco-listed status, Beaumaris was also the last, most bedazzling and biggest of the four to be built: so big, in fact, that an entire village had to be moved to make room for it.

The design of the castle was high art by the standards of 13th-century castle construction: a picture-perfect concentric stronghold consisting of a then-innovative three lines of defences, with a moated ring of 16 towers studding an outer and an inner circle of walls. Behind, in rather radiant layers, the green isle of Anglesey, the sea and then the foothills of Snowdonia help flesh out and fulfil most people's notions of a medieval fantasy fortress.

SEE IT ! *Beaumaris is on the east coast of the Isle of Anglesey. The nearest train station is 6 miles away at Llanfairpwllgwyngyll.*

The 98ft-high steel Kelpies near Falkirk were designed by Glaswegian sculptor Andy Scott

153

Cruise by canal boat to the Kelpies

CENTRAL SCOTLAND // Everything about this duo of shining silver horse heads, the largest equine sculptures in the world, sets them apart. They are momentously engineered, 98ft high, fashioned from 928 stainless steel dragon scale plates, and weigh 330 tonnes each. Impressed yet?

For those a little in the dark, Scottish mythology holds that kelpies are shape-shifting water spirits, demons with horse heads, and several Highland sea lochs burn with their legends. Now Helix Park, the lottery-funded Falkirk greenspace where the Kelpies keep watch, smoulders too. Opened in 2013, each was built as a monument to the Central Belt's horse-powered heritage during the industrial revolution.

You can discover the gigantic metalheads from the inside on a guided tour, but it's more memorable to see them from the water, cruising from the Falkirk Wheel (the world's only rotating boat lift) to the eastern gateway of the Forth and Clyde canal. More of a land lubber? Helix Park is home to cycle routes, a wetland boardwalk and towpaths, from which you can ogle the Kelpies from every angle.

SEE IT ! ***The Kelpies are located 3 miles outside Falkirk, near the Central Belt's main motorway routes.***

© The National Trust / Alamy

© Julie Priestley / Alamy

154

Sip Guinness at the Crown Liquor Saloon, Belfast

NORTHERN IRELAND // A National Trust monument that's also a pub? We like. The intricate Victorian exterior of this city-centre saloon is decorated with ornate Italian tiles and a mosaic of a crown is embedded into the pavement at the entrance. Behind swinging wooden doors, the elaborate interior features stained and cut glass, marble, ceramics, mirrors and mahogany, all atmospherically lit by gas lamps.

The bar hums with chatter at all hours of the day. Punters pack into high-sided wooden booths which invite conversation; locals swigging pints of Guinness swap stories with tourists sneaking snaps of their surroundings between sips of Bushmills whiskey. Alas, the call bells inside the snugs – once good for ordering refills – no longer work, but lining up at the magnificent bar is really no hardship.

SEE IT ! *The Crown is opposite the Europa Bus Centre and Great Victoria Street train station in Belfast, making it perfect for a pit stop.*

155

Trot and shop at the Badminton Horse Trials

OXFORD & THE COTSWOLDS // Once a year, the sleepy parkland of Badminton House comes alive with activity at the Badminton Horse Trials – a dressage, showjumping and cross-country combo that tests horses and riders on skill and endurance. Despite the 'three-day' tag, the event actually runs from Wednesday to Sunday, with warm-up events leading to dressage on the Thursday and Friday and Saturday's cross-country day, especially popular for horse fans and the general public alike. Keen spectators 'walk the course' before admiring the horses tackle sheer jumps, precipitous drops and other fearsome obstacles. If the excitement palls, you can stroll around the Shopping Village – a pop-up mall with a countryside flavour – and buy anything from local jam to a combine harvester.

SEE IT ! *Badminton is northeast of Bristol. The Horse Trials are in early May with day tickets costing between £8 and £34.*

The Barbican took 10 years to construct and was opened by Queen Elizabeth II in 1982 who declared it 'one of the modern wonders of the world'

156

See the future through 1960s eyes at the Barbican

LONDON // As architecture movements go, it would be easy to file brutalism away as a 1960s' hiccup, designed for a utopian vision of the future that never quite materialised. But wander the precincts of the Barbican – the capital's finest example of the genre – and it's hard to not feel a pang for the future that could have been.

In the minds of the Barbican's designers, high-rise living went hand in hand with a thriving community, shared spaces and an appreciation of the arts. Accordingly, their redevelopment of this former bomb site had plenty of arty spaces, balconies cascading with shrubbery and skyscraping blocks linked by 'street in the sky' walkways.

Society never quite caught up with the Barbican's grand vision, but Londoners have come to love it for its edgy art shows, arthouse cinema and cool cafe spaces. Munch a sourdough sandwich overlooking brick-lined, geometric pools, enjoy an exhibition at the Barbican Art Gallery or the Curve, then wrap up the evening with a movie or a play. Suddenly, the 1960s' vision of the future doesn't look so bad.

SEE IT ! ***Barbican is the nearest Tube station, but navigating the maze of buildings can take some skill; follow the yellow lines.***

© Hilda Weges / Shutterstock

© Ashmolean Museum, University of Oxford

157

Be inspired at the Beatles' childhood homes

NORTHWEST ENGLAND // The most famous pop musicians of the 20th century came from pretty modest backgrounds. From 1946 to 1963, John Lennon lived with his aunt Mimi and uncle George at 251 Menlove Ave, aka Mendips, a semi-detached house in the Woolton suburb of south Liverpool. His future bandmate Paul McCartney grew up in slightly less comfortable circumstances at 20 Forthlin Rd, a terraced house about a mile away. A visit to both houses is an intimate glimpse into their early lives, especially the lounge at Forthlin Rd, which is where John and Paul wrote some of the Beatles' early hits like 'Please Please Me' and 'She Loves You' (Paul later confirmed that a couple of songs were written at Mendips, including 'I'll Get You'). Both properties are now owned by the National Trust, which runs four tours each day.

SEE IT ! *Tours (www.nationaltrust.org.uk) depart from Jury's Inn Hotel on Wapping Dock and Speke Hall, another NT property.*

158

Get lost among the historical riches of Oxford's Ashmolean Museum

OXFORD & THE COTSWOLDS // Ranking second only to London's British Museum for awe-inspiring architecture and antiquities, the marvellous Ashmolean is Britain's oldest museum, founded in 1683. Blending Greek, Roman and English baroque influences, the building is one of the nation's prime examples of neoclassical architecture, and its collection sprung to life thanks to Elias Ashmole, who presented Oxford University with curiosities collected by royal naturalist John Tradescant.

Don't miss the famed 9th-century Anglo-Saxon Alfred Jewel (made for Alfred the Great), but save plenty of time for the many other world-wandering treasures – from Indian textiles, Egyptian mummies and Guy Fawkes' iron lantern, to European art from Michelangelo to van Gogh and Goya, all intelligently interwoven with Oxford history.

SEE IT ! *The Ashmolean is in Oxford's city centre. Stop for tea or modern British cuisine with city views at its rooftop restaurant.*

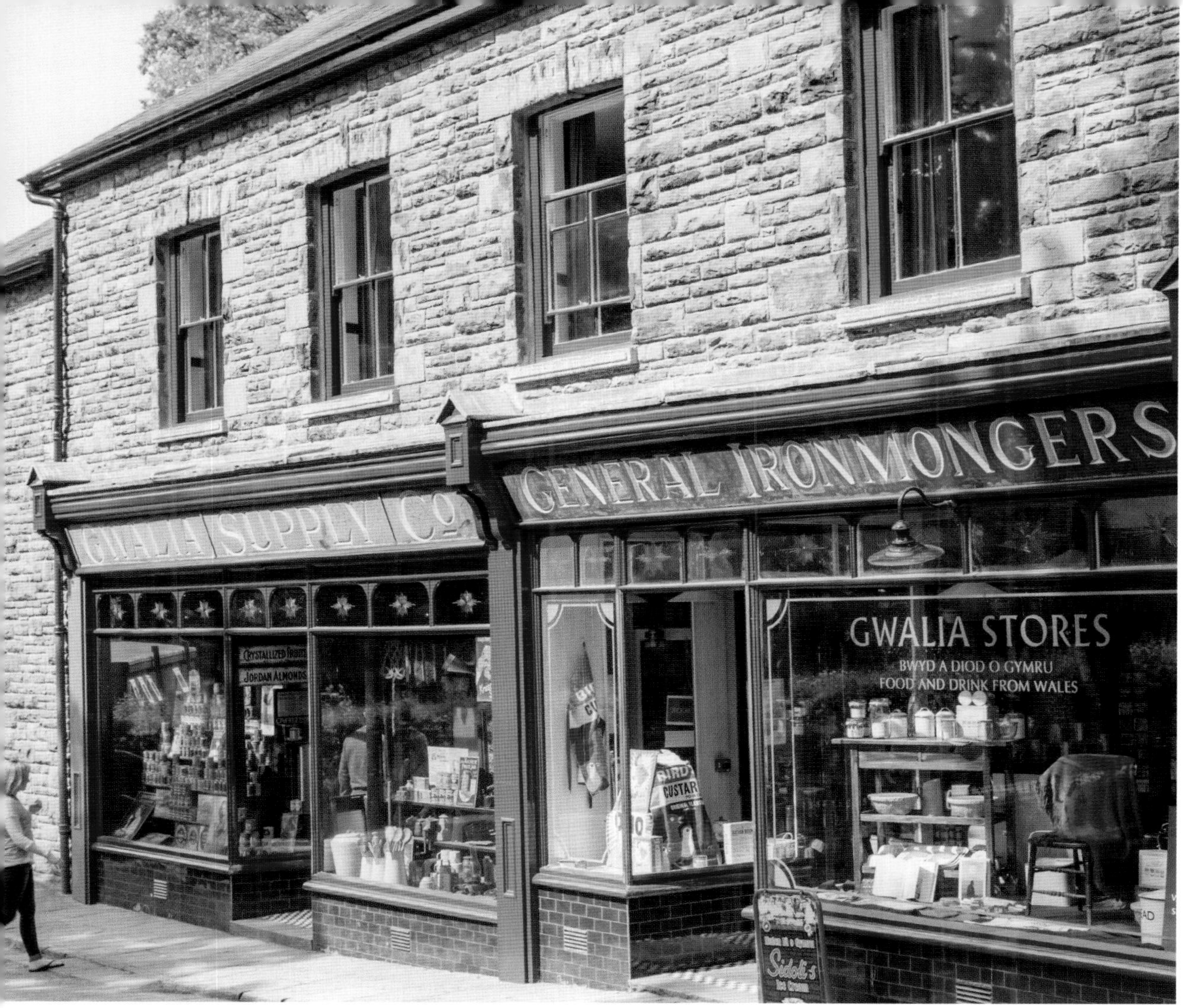

Gwalia Stores, now on display at St Fagans, is a typical Valleys general store from the 1920s

159

Go back in time at St Fagans National Museum of History

SOUTH WALES // Wales' most popular heritage attraction, sequestered within the lovingly landscaped grounds of 16th-century St Fagans Castle, preserves 40-odd original buildings taken from various locations countrywide that together depict a colourful overview of Welsh history. Buildings include Iron Age roundhouses, an 18th-century woollen mill and Unitarian chapel, and a coalmine workers' institute from 1917. Among the recent additions are a reconstruction of a Welsh prince's court based on Llywelyn the Great's Anglesey stronghold, as well as Cardiff's oldest surviving watering hole, The Vulcan, transported here brick by brick. The museum's genius is in vividly retelling the tales of the common people: through the farmhouses, workplaces and traditional craft demonstrations of times gone by.

SEE IT ! ***St Fagans is 4 miles west of Cardiff, signposted from the M4's junction 33. Easyway 32A bus runs from Cardiff's Westgate St.***

160

Inprove your world view at the WOMAD music festival

SOUTHWEST ENGLAND // All too often the same old names tend to dominate the line-ups at the UK's summer festivals. Thankfully, there's no such problem at WOMAD (or, to give it its full name, the World of Music and Dance). Founded in 1970 by Peter Gabriel, the festival is dedicated to exploring all forms of world music, regardless of geographic origin. It's wilfully, thrillingly eclectic: the kind of festival where you might find yourself grooving to desert rock, bopping to afro-beat or hopping to techno, all in the same day.

The UK WOMAD is held at Charlton Park in Wiltshire, but there are now sister events around the world, in Chile, Australia, New Zealand, Spain and Gran Canaria – proof that WOMAD really is a global gathering these days, geographically as well as musically.

SEE IT ! *The festival runs over the last weekend in July at Charlton Park, 2 miles outside Malmesbury. Tickets sell out fast, so book early.*

EXIT

161

Paddle into secluded sea caves on the Isle of Wight

SOUTHERN ENGLAND // It's only a few miles south of the Hampshire coast, but in places, the Isle of Wight's coastline feels surprisingly wild. By far the most entertaining way to explore it is by kayak, canoe or even (if your balance is up to it) stand-up paddleboard. Experienced local guides will help you find the many small coves and sea caves that pockmark the island's coastline; some of the caves are large enough to paddle into. Most day trips also include a picnic on an isolated beach.

SEE IT ! *Get to the Isle of Wight from Portsmouth, Southampton and Lymington. A full-day kayaking adventure costs from £75.*

162

Connect with your inner aristocrat at lavish Felbrigg Hall

EAST ANGLIA // It'll be the library that steals your heart at Jacobean Felbrigg Hall. The towering Gothic bookcases house 5000 leather-bound volumes; nearby sit two massive globes, one terrestrial, one celestial, which will pique your wanderlust. Felbrigg's rooms drip with gilt, door frames have more carved turrets than Hogwarts, while the great hall has stained-glass windows from a local church. In the 1700-acre estate, the walled gardens are fragrant with herbs, while ancient woods ripple with sweet chestnut, oak and ash, some bordering a lake.

SEE IT ! *In summer, drop by the nearby Victorian seaside resort of Cromer, 2 miles away, and the Queen's country estate, Sandringham.*

163

Explore Guernsey's rugged south coast cliffs on foot

CHANNEL ISLANDS // Guernsey's wonderfully diverse coastline scenery is particularly dramatic along the rugged south coast. Follow the undulating cliff paths from St Peter Port to Petit Bot Bay, peering down at pretty little coves, and you'll pass one of the loophole towers built to defend the island, as well as the Doyle Column monument. Numerous seabird nesting grounds and remains of ancient fortifications characterise Guernsey's western tip. Near the Pleinmont Peninsula, the cliffs give way to sandy bays dotted with German WWII fortifications.

SEE IT ! *In springtime, the trail section between St Peter Port and Fermain Bay is abloom with a mass of bluebells.*

© Westend61 / Getty Images

© Gary Doak / Alamy

164

Cling to the cliffs at Dunluce Castle, Co Antrim

NORTHERN IRELAND // It's hard to imagine a more romantic setting for a medieval castle than the clifftop perch occupied by the ruins of Dunluce Castle on the north Antrim coast. But keep in mind the perils of such a dramatic location: the story goes that one stormy night in 1693 the Earl of Antrim and his wife were waiting for dinner when the castle kitchen fell into the sea, taking seven servants with it. Little wonder that the castle was abandoned soon after.

The drama begins with a narrow bridge leading from the mainland courtyard across a dizzying gap to the main part of the fortress. Exploring the ruins, it's not hard to imagine the luxurious Renaissance palace that once lay within the stone walls; these days the charm lies in the ocean views from the rocky headland.

SEE IT ! *Dunluce Castle is just over 3 miles east of Portrush, a one-hour walk away along the coastal path.*

165

Indulge in a Burns Night haggis feast at Ghillie Dhu

EDINBURGH // 'Fair fa' your honest, sonsie face. Great chieftain o the puddin'-race!' So begins Robert Burns' traditional address to the national dish of Scotland, before the balloon-like pudding's animal stomach-skin is slashed with a ceremonial knife and the innards ooze out, in a moment that mixes culinary theatre with hospital drama.

Novelty aside, it's a tradition that dates back to harder times – haggis is a love-it-or-loathe-it dish made from sheep's heart, liver and lungs ground with oatmeal, suet and spices – and the pudding is now celebrated annually on 25 January, in tandem with the birth of national bard, Robert Burns. A great place to experience it is at Ghillie Dhu, Edinburgh's unabashed temple to Caledonia. You'll drink and dance, hear poetry recitals and wish you were Scottish, for a night at least.

TRY IT ! *Ghillie Dhu is in Edinburgh's West End and hosts weekly ceilidhs, whisky tastings and a week of Burns suppers each January.*

The Queen's Guards giving it full pomp and ceremony along the Mall during Trooping the Colour

166

Fly a flag for HRH at the annual Trooping the Colour

LONDON // On paper, it sounds as tacky as a toy London bus, but in real life, the spectacle of the Queen inspecting the flags of the British regiments on Horse Guards Parade stirs the same kind of nostalgia as period dramas and paintings of pomp and circumstance in the National Gallery.

In an age of smartwatches and robot vacuum cleaners, there's something reassuring about a ritual that has been unfurling with the same pantomime pageantry for close on three centuries. The quantity of polished buckles and gold brocade on display has to be seen to be believed, and the chance to see HRH in the flesh is an added perk, pulling vast crowds.

Traditionally held on the second Saturday of June, the ceremony goes back to at least 1748, but the regimental colours on display date from the earliest years of military history, when flags were flown to guide soldiers home to their regiments in the chaos of battle. Like a child's toy-soldier set blown up to full-size, the procession features 1400 marching soldiers and horsemen and 400 musicians from military bands.

☛ SEE IT ! ***Horse Guards Parade is tucked between Westminster and Charing Cross and Embankment Tube stations.***

167

Delve into Newcastle's underground history on a Victoria Tunnel tour

NORTHEAST ENGLAND // Strolling Newcastle-upon-Tyne's historic streets, taking in sights like its castle, bridges and cultural venues, you're unlikely to be thinking about what lies beneath you. Below the surface, however, there's an extraordinary tunnel that provides a fascinating insight into the city's past.

During the Industrial Revolution, Newcastle became a coal and steel powerhouse, and the 2.5 mile-long Victoria Tunnel originally opened in 1842 as a thoroughfare for wagons transporting coal to waiting ships on the Tyne. After the pits closed, it was unsuccessfully used to grow mushrooms in the 1920s and served as an air-raid shelter during WWII. Volunteers lead illuminating tours along a level, almost 2300ft-long stretch of the cramped, narrow, limestone-walled tunnel, which is a constant 12°C (54°F); you're equipped with torches (and hardhats).

☛ SEE IT ! ***Tours (book ahead!) depart from Ouseburn's the visitor centre. Wear flat, closed shoes and a washable jacket.***

Justin Francis's Top Five Places

Justin Francis is CEO and founder of specialist tour operator Responsible Travel. He sits on the UK Government's Council for Sustainable Business as an expert in eco-friendly travel and is an advocate for responsible tourism.

01

APPLECROSS PENINSULA, WESTER ROSS, SCOTLAND – Applecross is a small community with a great pub and even better views of Skye. It still feels cut off from the world, something I crave from time to time.

02

LEWES, EAST SUSSEX – My home for the past 12 years, meaning I'm still considered a blow-in. I love the ancient High Street, complete with requisite castle and brewery, but more so that the hills of the South Downs National Park rise at the end of every street.

03

NORFOLK COAST – A wild and ancient place where salt marshes, curlews and skeins of winter geese mark the landscape. The pretty villages of Cley and Blakeney are favourites, as are the pines and beach at Holkham.

04

THE NEW FOREST – In this misnamed forest (created 1079) I like to side track off the trails and get lost. The sky-high redwoods of the big tree walk are the next best thing to California's Sequoia National Park.

05

LONDON – I like the old parts of London and shops like Lock & Co in St James's, the world's oldest hat shop. The backstreets of Shoreditch and Hoxton are where I'm inspired by new ideas and brands, and the V&A is an absolute wonder.

168

Sip a crisp white at Sharpham

SOUTHWEST ENGLAND // We all know Britain knows how to make good beer – but wine? You must have had one too many. Well, maybe not, according to oenophiles: over the past few decades, the UK's winemakers have learned how to hold their own against their European neighbours, their wines even trumping champagne in recent awards and garnering plaudits normally reserved for their mainland Europe neighbours.

Nowhere has earned a more stellar reputation than Sharpham, a renowned vineyard on the banks of the River Dart. It's known for its crisp whites and champagne-style bubblies, which are well suited to the area's chalky soils and temperate climate, and have scooped top awards at some of the world's most prestigious wine fairs. You can take a tour of the vines, then head to the on-site cafe for a tasting session – ideally accompanied by a few chunks of the estate's homemade cheeses. On a warm summer day, it all feels convincingly continental – so who are we to quibble?

©Tim Cuff / Alamy

☛ TRY IT ! ***Sharpham Wine & Cheese is 3 miles from Totnes in Devon.***

169

Enjoy kedgeree with the Bentley set at the luxurious Wolseley

LONDON // Well-heeled Mayfair residents used to test-drive the latest luxury saloons from Bentley Motors at 160 Piccadilly. Today, it's the creamy kedgeree – a colonial-era concoction of smoked haddock, poached eggs, rice and Madras curry spices – that pulls punters in. This brunchtime classic has become a firm favourite at the restaurant that now occupies the old showroom, the Wolseley. What makes it so special? Well, apart from the sumptuous setting, it's the house use of full-flavoured curry pastes instead of dry spices.

☛ EAT IT ! ***Green Park Tube is only a few minutes away. Breakfast starts from 7am weekdays and 8am at weekends.***

170

Uncork the little-known world of Hampshire wine

SOUTHERN ENGLAND // Hampshire is more synonymous with Britain's illustrious maritime and literary history than growing grapes, but in fact the county produces excellent whites, mostly from champagne grapes, which have even outgunned their French counterparts at international wine events. Several guided wine routes run through the county – one even passes through the New Forest – but book well in advance as they are madly popular. If you can't get on a tour, Winchester hosts Hampshire's November wine festival.

☛ SEE IT ! ***For booking details and an overview of Hampshire's wine attractions, log on to the Visit Hampshire website.***

Looking west from the Black Mountains peak of Sugar Loaf, which rises to 1955ft above Abergavenny

171

Trek through the barren upland borderlands of the Black Mountains

MID-WALES // The famously charming towns and villages along the Black Mountains' base (Abergavenny and Crickhowell in the south, Talgarth in the west and Hay-on-Wye in the north) are as close as most people get to this formidable England–Wales frontier. Some might make it out to Wales' oldest pub, the Skirrid Mountain Inn, or to stunningly located Llanthony Priory with its lonely tavern secreted nearby. Some may even climb one of the mountains' better-known peaks, such as idiosyncratic Sugar Loaf at the southern end of the range.

But to really acquaint yourself with this rugged ridge you have to hike the length of it, from Abergavenny to Hay-on-Wye: 25-odd miles of savagely beautiful roof-of-Britain tramping, with a different country either side of you and an exposed brown plateau descending into a luxuriant palette of valley greens all around. Bisected by trails from the Offa's Dyke path to the Beacons Way and the Marches Way, this is terrain to leave everyone from fairweather hikers to hillwalkers properly dewy-eyed.

TRY IT ! ***South to north, the range roughly follows the Offa's Dyke trail, from Pandy near Abergavenny to Hay-on-Wye.***

172

Sip gin under the arches at Maltby Street Market

LONDON // London loves its railway arches, home to everything from vintners and food markets to nightclubs and S&M dungeons. Lively Maltby Street Market falls into the former camp – an appealing gaggle of food vendors, cocktail bars and gourmet coffee places, tucked into a row of Bermondsey arches beneath strands of fluttering bunting. The selection of world food on offer is particularly good – think South African-style peri-peri burgers, Taiwanese waffles and raclette, best washed down with a drink prepared with locally distilled London gin.

TRY IT ! *Walk south along Tower Bridge Rd from the South Bank, and turn left onto Tanner St just after the railway bridge.*

173

Bring binoculars for a twitch at London Wetland Centre

LONDON // The stretch of the Thames through the City of London has more stand-up landmarks than Monument Valley, but peace and quiet? No. For that, you'll need to head west past Putney, where a tree-shaded towpath follows the banks of a long loop in the river. The highlight here is the London Wetland Centre, sprawling across four reclaimed Victorian reservoirs and teeming with uncommon London visitors such as gadwalls, bitterns, lapwings, sparrowhawks, kingfishers and grebes – a playground for birdwatchers and tranquillity-seekers.

SEE IT ! *This rare piece of urban wilderness is a little inaccessible – from Barnes Bridge railway station, jump on the 209 bus.*

174

Turn the 'Key to England' at Dover Castle

SOUTHEAST ENGLAND // Standing sentinel over the narrowest stretch of the English Channel, Dover Castle is often called the 'Key to England' due to its defensive role in the country's past. Once meant to deter foreigners, the castle now draws visitors from across the globe, who come to explore the tall keep, Roman lighthouse and chalk-hewn wartime tunnels. These subterranean spaces, brought to life by a captivating AV exhibition, evocatively tell the story of the castle's role in the 1940 Dunkirk evacuations.

SEE IT ! *Take the coach or train from London and Canterbury, or local buses from nearby towns. Ferries dock just below the castle.*

© nagelestock / Alamy

© Anthony Chappel-Ross

175

Recreate a TV classic as you puff your way up Gold Hill

SOUTHWEST ENGLAND // If you watched British TV in the 1970s or '80s, you will almost certainly have seen the advert that made this cobbled street in Shaftesbury nationally famous. Made for a well-known bread company (and directed by a youthful Ridley Scott, no less), it depicted a young lad wheeling his bike up the steep slope, against a quintessentially English backdrop of thatched cottages and rolling countryside. Forty years on, Gold Hill looks much as it did in the ad: the cobbles and cottages are still there, as is the formidable incline. If you want to re-enact the scene, you'll need to bring your own flat cap, short trousers, loaves of bread and boneshaker bicycle – not forgetting, of course, a brass band to play the second movement from Dvořák's Symphony No 9 as you trudge wearily uphill.

SEE IT ! ***Gold Hill is in the middle of the village of Shaftesbury in Dorset.***

176

Voyage back to the Viking age at York's Jorvik Centre

YORKSHIRE // Ever wondered what a Viking smelt like? This entertaining reconstruction of Jorvik – the Viking village that predated York and gave it its name – does a great job of recreating the sights, sounds and, yes, smells of the 10th-century settlement discovered here in the 1970s. A 'time-capsule' monorail transports you through a series of tableaux, from muddy streets and timber houses to workshops and even primitive toilets, all based on hard archaeological evidence.

At the end is a gorgeously designed exhibition gallery, built following the devastating floods of 2015, which showcases 1000-year-old artefacts recovered from the site, from jewellery and socks to pans and padlocks. Look out for the Lloyds Bank coprolite, a fossilised human poo that's an eye-watering nine inches long and half a pound in weight.

SEE IT ! ***You can reduce time waiting in line by booking timed-entry tickets online; there is almost always a queue to get in.***

Cape Wrath marks the most northwesterly point of mainland UK

177

Test your limits on Cape Wrath

HIGHLANDS & ISLANDS // Breathe it all in, slowly. You're standing at the most extreme point on the British mainland, with no land between you and the Arctic. The Orkney Islands play peekaboo through unpredictable clouds to the northeast and the outline to the west reveals the Outer Hebrides. The name itself is the giveaway – Cape Wrath wrings pure poetry out of the landscape.

Here are just a few reasons why the peninsula holds a special place in the hearts and minds of all those who make the long, arduous journey there. In summer, birdwatchers gawp at colonies of puffins nesting in the cliffs, while walkers endure the final stages of the Cape Wrath Trail – an unofficial long-distance walk from Fort William over extreme terrain. But for many, the draw is the lighthouse, the most remote in Britain and built in 1828 atop pink-hued cliffs by master architect Robert Stevenson. As totems go, it's a memorable monument to man's ability and desire to tame the world's wildest places.

SEE IT ! ***Getting to Cape Wrath is a challenge. There is only one road, separated from the main road network by the Kyle of Durness. Take the passenger ferry, then the minibus to complete the 11-mile journey.***

© Gavin Dronfield / Alamy

© Stephen Dorey / Alamy

178

Hop, swing or jump into the cool pool waters of Eskdale

CUMBRIA // There's nothing quite like jumping into a pool of cool water on a hot summer's day, and Eskdale has two of Cumbria's best-loved spots for a wild swim. Stanley Gill Force was a major tourist destination for Victorians, but its gorgeous falls, tumbling 20m into a deep plunge pool, are nowhere near as popular today – which means the bridge jumps and rope swings will be all yours to enjoy.

The wonderfully named Tongue Pot, two miles upriver from the bottom of Hardknott Pass, is much more popular. This long, crystal-clear pool beneath a roaring waterfall has a pebble beach on one side and a sheer cliff on the other – the perfect jumping spot if you can handle the 5m drop. The shallower Kail Pot above the waterfall is another option if you fancy something a little more relaxing.

☛ TRY IT ! ***Stanley Gill Force is a 0.5-mile walk from Beckfoot Station; for Tongue Pot, park beyond the Woolpack Inn in Boot.***

179

Be swept away by the Roman mosaic floors of Fishbourne Palace

SOUTHEAST ENGLAND // The largest Roman villa ever discovered in Britain, Fishbourne Palace is a must-see for any archaeology buff or Roman Empire enthusiast.

Found in classic style by unsuspecting workmen in the 1960s, the site dates back to just a few decades after the Roman invasion. But this is no dull pile of Roman landfill – the almost 2000-year-old floor mosaics are some of the best-preserved north of the Alps and represent a high point in Britain's Roman heritage. The spectacular floor depicts Cupid riding a dolphin flanked by various animals, the colours so vibrant it looks as though it was laid last week. The scale model in the museum shows just what a vast complex this was – whoever built the place must have been an Empire bigwig.

☛ SEE IT ! ***Fishbourne is 1.5 miles west of Chichester – a 35-minute walk or short ride on bus 700 from Chichester Cathedral.***

© Keith Douglas / Alamy

180

Re-live the Age of Steam in miniature on La'al Ratty

CUMBRIA // A contender for England's most beautiful rail journey is the 7-mile chug aboard La'al Ratty ('old railway' in the local West Cumbrian dialect), the miniature steam train that runs between the old Roman port of Ravenglass and the village of Dalegarth, at the far end of the beautiful Eskdale Valley.

The 15in, narrow gauge railway track was laid to ferry iron ore mined in the valley to the coast, but today it is one of the Lake District's most popular family-friendly experiences. Most of the 40-minute, seven-stop journey takes place in the shadow of the Scafell Range, home to England's tallest mountains. It's a hop-on, hop-off service, allowing you to explore from any of the stops, and there's a ticket that includes a visit to the historic (and, some say, haunted) Muncaster Castle.

☛ SEE IT ! ***The Furness and Cumbrian Coast railway lines loop 120 miles from Lancaster to Carlisle, stopping at Ravenglass.***

© John Henshall / Alamy

181

Commune with the ancients at Avebury stone circles

SOUTHWEST ENGLAND // While the hordes head for Stonehenge, wiser sightseers head 25 miles north to Avebury. Yes it lacks Stonehenge's distinctive trilithons, but Avebury is actually bigger – way bigger, in fact, with a diameter of 1142ft, making it the largest stone circle in Britain (so big, half the village sits inside it). But apart from its size, the great thing about Avebury is that you're free to wander at will around the stones, with none of the access restrictions you'll encounter at Stonehenge. As such, it's possible to get really close to the menhirs – and appreciate the effort required to quarry them, shape them, move them and raise them. Maybe, given its scale, Avebury may even have been more important than Stonehenge – a tantalising question to which we'll never know the answer.

☛ SEE IT ! ***Buses run from Swindon and Devizes to Avebury. It's owned by English Heritage and is free to visit.***

© Philip Bird / Shutterstock

© Daniel Di Paolo

182

Stop the clock in the medieval gem of Sandwich

SOUTHEAST ENGLAND // The twisted lanes of half-timbered Tudor houses within the old walls of Sandwich constitute what must be England's most perfectly preserved medieval town. But the time-warped feel of this quaint former port doesn't stop there; the local cinema is frozen in the 1930s, the garage deals more in classic cars than modern motors. The town's museum tells Sandwich's unique tale, from England's fourth city (incredible to imagine today) and vital Cinque Port to silted up backwater. Its prize possession is a genuine original of the Magna Carta, recently found (in typical English style) in a drawer in the town's archives. When you've had your fill of history, hop aboard the river taxi for a trip on the River Stour – a pod of seals basks on the mudflats where the waters slide sluggishly into the Channel.

SEE IT ! ***Sandwich enjoys direct rail connections to London and Canterbury and is linked by local bus to a few nearby towns.***

183

Insert a token at the Novelty Automation homemade arcade

LONDON // London might be miles from the sea, but a Victorian-style pier-side arcade is closer than you'd think. The brainchild of Tim Hunkin, an engineer turned artist turned Channel 4 TV presenter, the wacky homemade consoles at Novelty Automation will test your wits and earn you the badge of next-level adulting. The zany selection includes seeing who gets what in the 'race to separate' divorce game, building your own reactor ('free edible nuclear waste every time!'), papping celebrities with a drone then scrambling to get the photos to your tabloid editor before the deadline, and using a crane and magnets to sneak 5p coins up past the skyscrapers of the City of London without being spotted by regulators: one glance and your profits rain back to the ground.

SEE IT ! ***The nearest Tube station is Holborn. The arcade is open late on the first Thursday of every month.***

184

Drop in on the Lady of the Lake at Llyn-y-Fan Fach

MID-WALES // All alone in the Black Mountain range in the Brecon Beacons National Park's western reaches, Llyn-y-Fan Fach is well hidden and worth finding. Stark peaks sweep abruptly down to this petrol-blue lake, steeped in the legend of the Lady of the Lake, which appears in the medieval Welsh folk epic, *The Mabinogion*. Traipse the 4-mile trail along the sheep-grazed valley, following the river upstream to the lake, ridge and high moors beyond, and the landscape feels brutal, primordially beautiful, even – especially when the mists descend.

SEE IT ! ***Set your GPS to Llanddeusant (just south of the A40 via Llangadog), then follow the road to the car park just beyond Blaenau.***

185

Bliss out by yourself on sublime Barafundle Bay

SOUTH WALES // There's something special about a beach that can only be reached on foot over clifftops and through dunes. Barafundle Bay, a crescent of flour-soft, pale golden sand shelving into glass-clear turquoise, is pinch-yourself pretty – and unsurprisingly often crops up on lists of Britain's best beaches. While just a half-hour's amble from the car park at Stackpole Quay, it feels a million miles away. Dodge summer weekends and you might get these National Trust sands all to yourself. Pack a picnic and be sure to check tide times.

SEE IT ! ***Park at Stackpole Quay, just south of the village of Stackpole, a few miles' south of the main A477 road to Pembroke.***

186

Indulge your inner romantic at Newstead Abbey

MIDLANDS & THE MARCHES // An Augustinian priory built in 1170, and converted into a sumptuous residence after the Dissolution of the Monasteries, Newstead Abbey later became home to the Baron Byrons. It's best-known as the abode of Baron No 6, George Gordon, one of England's most gifted poets. Like his predecessors, Byron acquired expensive tastes: think landscapes by Tillemans, a Great Hall purportedly panelled from a single oak, and 300-acre grounds with a monument to Byron's hound taking pride of place.

SEE IT ! ***Buses from Nottingham's Victoria bus station regularly run the 12 miles north to Newstead Abbey's gates.***

© Steven Bramall / Alamy

187

Ride the Ffestiniog & Welsh Highland Railways through Snowdonia

NORTH WALES // This is the leisurely way to see Snowdonia: atop a story-steeped set of rails on a vintage steam train, between inland slate-mining town Blaenau Ffestiniog and seaside Caernarfon, under the nose of some of Britain's best mountain scenery. This 40-mile chug alights at spots so scenically remote you need to pinch yourself to accept they are linked by locomotive: places like Tan-y-Bwlch, a lovely lake above Blaenau Ffestiniog, picturesque Beddgelert and Rhyd Ddu, below a popular trail up to Snowdon. Vistas of water extending tendrils around glaciated peaks are unforgettable, but the tricky topography this route negotiates makes the line's very existence pretty stunning.

The railway's history is an animated one, too: construction milestones were celebrated by wayward canon-firing, and the Blaenau Ffestiniog–Porthmadog and Porthmadog–Caernarfon branches were once bitter arch-rivals. These days, they are connected by a single amicable platform changeover.

☛ SEE IT ! ***Start at Blaenau Ffestiniog, encircled by sheer slate workings, and finish by mighty Caernarfon Castle. Book ahead.***

Huw Stephens' Top Five Places

Huw Stephens is a Welsh radio presenter on BBC Radio 1 and BBC Radio Cymru. He is a champion of new music and runs his own live-music nights in London, as well as hosting a weekly BBC Introducing Radio 1 podcast.

01

SPILLERS RECORDS, CARDIFF – Now located in Morgan Arcade, Spillers Records is an essential stop. I always pop in there to see what's on offer. It's been a constant since I was growing up in Cardiff.

02

PEMBROKESHIRE – A walk along any part of Wales' coastline is truly energising. In west Wales, Pembrokeshire always takes my breath away. From Cemaes Head to Milford Haven, it's simply stunning.

03

CASTLE ARCADE, CARDIFF – I love wandering around Cardiff's Victorian arcades. They're full of the independent shops that give the city its unique character and are one thing that hasn't changed since my childhood.

04

CARDIGAN – The town has a really special vibe right now. New independents such as Pizzatipi at fforest (a pop-up stone-baked pizza restaurant) and Bara Menyn (an artisan cafe) are making it a hotspot for foodies.

05

TAFF TRAIL, CARDIFF – From where I live I can cycle into the centre of Cardiff on the Taff Trail. After following the riverside path through Bute Park, I call into Pettigrew Tea Rooms in the old Victorian gatehouse.

© John Michaels / Alamy

188

Muse on mind-bending works of modern art at BALTIC

NORTHEAST ENGLAND // With a whopping 28,000 sq ft of exhibition space, BALTIC is the largest dedicated contemporary art institution anywhere in the UK. This 1950s' former grain store has hosted headlining shows and installations by some of the art scene's biggest names since 2002. Expect the unexpected: there's no permanent collection, but instead a constantly rotating array of edgy, innovative exhibitions, along with artists-in-residence, a performance space and a cinema. Best of all, entry is free.

Definitely don't miss the view from the 4th-floor outdoor viewing platform and the 5th-floor glassed-in viewing deck, which both have panoramas of the River Tyne's iconic bridges. Views also extend from the rooftop restaurant, and there's a bar too.

SEE IT ! *Cross the Tyne from Newcastle via the Millennium Bridge to BALTIC, located on Gateshead Quays in Gateshead.*

© Radharc Images / Alamy

189

Get loud and proud in Manchester's Gay Village

NORTHWEST ENGLAND // Manchester's vibrant LGBTIQ+ culture is centred on and around Canal St. From old-fashioned tea rooms and rustic little pubs to drag-queen shows and high-octane club nights, the Gay Village caters to all tastes and persuasions throughout the week – Wednesday night for example is 'Butterflies' – with venues like Napoleons, New York New York and Bandit, Mugger and Thief hosting nights that are especially popular with the trans community.

Celebrations are held year-round (including the Great British Bear Bash in May, and Sparkle, the national transgender celebration weekend in July), but the main event is Manchester Pride, held over three days on the last weekend in August. There's music, a huge parade and, on the last night, a moving candlelit vigil for all victims of HIV.

SEE IT ! *Canal St runs alongside the Rochdale Canal, just south of Chinatown in the middle of the city.*

190

Find yesterday and today on South Harris

HIGHLANDS & ISLANDS // To visit this sand-fringed hunk of land, located across a narrow isthmus from North Harris, is to encounter another time – a place that marries yesterday with today. And what a privilege it is. The croft-dotted landscape of naked hillocks, isolated coves and wild-swimming nooks is one that has changed little in the past century. There's a choice of some of Britain's finest beaches (including #129 on this list, Luskentyre), plus the kind of turquoise sea you'd expect to find in the Caribbean. The modern touch comes from sugar-kelp-infused gin produced by the Isle of Harris Distillery in Tarbert and the catwalk glamour of Harris Tweed showrooms in Drinishader and Grosebay. The handwoven fabric is in the island's DNA, and the Hebrides is the only place where it's legally allowed to be made.

SEE IT ! ***There is one road around the island, giving a choice of driving east or west. A car or camper van is recommended.***

191

Recreate Swallows and Amazons on Derwent Water

CUMBRIA // The largest of the four islands in Derwent Water, St Herbert's is named after the saint who brought Christianity to the area in AD 685. Looking for a bit of spiritual r 'n' r, Herbert retreated to the 4-acre island where he built a small cell and lived off fishing. The remains of his hermitage can still be seen at the northern end of the island, which you can reach via canoe.

St Herbert's featured as the fictional Owl Island in Beatrix Potter's *The Tale of Squirrel Nutkin* (1903), where Nutkin, Twinkleberry and their cousins go to gather nuts. It also appears in the 2016 film version of Arthur Ransome's *Swallows and Amazons*, chronicling the adventures of the Walker children's Lake District holiday. Whether you're a squirrel, a hermit or a Walker, pack a lunch and let your imagination fly.

☛ SEE IT ! ***You can hire canoes at the marina in Keswick, the Nichol End Marina in Portinscale, or at the southern end of the lake.***

© Angus McComiskey / Alamy

Runners pass the Cutty Sark in Greenwich, some seven miles into the London Marathon

192

Chase the pace of Olympic athletes at the London Marathon

LONDON // Taking part in the London Marathon is pretty high up on the list of must-dos for the peripatetic long-distance runner. The distance is exactly as advertised, but the route it follows offers a sightseeing tour of London, looping from Blackheath around the Isle of Dogs and slicing through the City and Westminster before finally spilling out onto the Mall.

Every year, some 40,000 runners compete, from international superstars such as Mo Farah and Paula Radcliffe to ordinary Londoners happy to beat four hours, and charity runners dressed as rhinos, storm troopers and kids' TV characters. The two hours three minutes set by Kenyan Eliud Kipchoge in 2016 is the time to beat, but perhaps more realistic is topping Lloyd Scott's five days and eight hours, set in 2002 while wearing a deep-sea diving suit. The biggest challenge, however, will be getting a place, with competition tight for the public ballot. However you get in, you can rely on the vocal support of tens of thousands of spectators, particularly at the start in Greenwich and finish in Westminster.

SEE IT ! *There are different start points, all in and around Greenwich, for different categories of runner.*

193

Soul-search on a journey to Sandwood Bay

HIGHLANDS & ISLANDS // In Britain's extreme northwest, a remote tract of paradise exists that presents a prehistoric twist on a day at the seaside. You can't drive to it, there's little public transport, and it's accessed only by a 5-mile trudge across bleak moorland. On approach, you'll think there's nothing to see here, but then the dunes fall away to reveal an empty belt of golden sand and Am Buachaille, a sensation-bending sea stack buffeted by cliffs. In the silence, with not another soul in sight, time will seem to stop.

SEE IT ! ***Parking is available in Blairmore near Kinlochbervie. Beach access is via a well-used path.***

194

Spot puffins and seals on Rathlin Island, Co Antrim

NORTHERN IRELAND // Imagine catching a ferry across a 6-mile stretch of ocean to a tiny, inhabited island, where seals bask on rocks in a postcard-pretty harbour. Hiking trails snake around the island and no destination is more than an hour and a half's walk away. No doubt you'll head to the West Light Seabird Centre, an unusual upside-down lighthouse built into the cliff. From here, hatching chicks can be spotted on nearby sea stacks, one of the UK's most important breeding grounds for puffins and other seabirds.

SEE IT ! ***Daily ferries run from Ballycastle. Only residents can take their car but nowhere on Rathlin is more than 3.7 miles from the pier.***

© Lucasz Pajor / Shutterstock

195

Drop in on a monarch at Buckingham Palace

LONDON // Did you know that the British monarch lives in the home of a former courtier? When the phenomenally wealthy Duke of Buckingham had this lavish pile built, the sovereign was still splitting time between Kew Palace and Kensington. King George III saw the potential of a central London pad and snapped up the mansion for the princely sum of £21,000 (property website Zoopla recently valued the palace at £935 million, to put that into a modern context).

Today, people come to either gawk at the guards – and potentially any royals in residence – through the main gates, or to admire the lavish collection of royal artworks and treasures in the Queen's Gallery and state rooms, which open annually to the public from July to September while HRH takes her summer holiday.

SEE IT ! ***Green Park Tube is closest to Buckingham Palace, but the grandest approach is on foot along the Mall, from Trafalgar Square.***

© Tim Gainey / Alamy

196

Learn a barrel-load of history at Hook Norton Brewery

OXFORD & THE COTSWOLDS // For foreign visitors, British beer can be a shock. A warm, flat and expensive shock. But delve deeper, and you'll find that traditional beer is all about subtle flavours; it doesn't need to be chilled or fizzed to make it palatable, and there's a surprisingly wide range of tastes and aromas. To learn more, visit Hook Norton Brewery, where good honest ale has been produced since 1849. The process has hardly changed since then, with some machinery still steam-powered and casks delivered to nearby pubs on a dray, pulled by giant English shire horses. Take a guided tour around the fantastical brewery building, complete with turrets, towers and half-timbered overhanging gantries, admire the mix of old and modern techniques and tools, and come out knowing your grist mill from your mash tun.

SEE IT ! ***Brewery tours (from £15) must be booked in advance. Drink it! Hook Norton beer is sold in pubs across the Cotswolds.***

197

Get spooked in Glasgow's Necropolis

SOUTHERN SCOTLAND // Glasgow is the perfect city to wander in, a description that can equally be applied to strolling its graveyards. The highlight is the Dickensian Necropolis, a Victorian-era cemetery that anchors a vast hilltop plot east of St Mungo's Cathedral. From top to toe, it's layered with architectural tombs, memorial columns and elaborate tributes to the merchants, bankers and provosts who helped the city prosper. Surrounded by the ghosts of 50,000-odd graves, a meditative wander can become nothing short of a personal awakening.

SEE IT ! ***The Necropolis opens from 7am to 4.30pm daily. Guided tours can be booked with the Friends of the Necropolis.***

198

Sample Scotch egg perfection at Fortnum & Mason

LONDON // Surely there's no great science to making a Scotch egg? Sausage meat encasing a boiled egg, rolled in breadcrumbs. The version served up in London's most regal department store, however, is something else entirely. For one thing, Fortnum & Mason has a claim to having invented the snack, in 1738, taking the name from the Scots guards stationed around Wellington Barracks, who reputedly developed a taste for the treat. Some historians however point out conspicuous similarities to the traditional Indian dish *nargisi kofta*.

EAT IT ! ***Green Park and Piccadilly Tube stations bookend the interesting part of Piccadilly, with Fortnum's midway along the strip.***

Designed by Kengo Kuma, the first V&A museum outside London opened in Dundee in late 2018

199

Be dazzled by design at the V&A Dundee

NORTHEAST SCOTLAND // On first glance, the look of Scotland's first design museum – and only the second outpost of London's incomparable V&A – is beyond inscrutable. The hull-shaped, concrete-slab design by Japanese architect Kengo Kuma has been described as a conversation between nature and the sea. It's been talked up as a nod to Dundee's maritime heritage, in the form of a futuristic galleon. And spoken of as a mirror image of the cliffs found further along the North Sea coast.

Whatever your take, the collection of the waterfront museum claims as many talking points. Amid the touring exhibitions, there are 300 genre-hopping exhibits – from an elephant sculpture to a pair of wellington boots and a chunk of the Titanic. The perfect restoration of Charles Rennie Mackintosh's Oak Room, the nucleus of a Glasgow tea room lost to view for nearly 50 years, is a bona fide breath-taker. The relentless industry on show provides a shot of inspiration, but the overarching mission is far grander – the hope is it will help transform Dundee's waterfront into a global design hotspot.

SEE IT ! ***Having only opened in 2018, the V&A is packed at weekends. Avoid the crowds by visiting on a weekday.***

200–299

200

Battle stations! All aboard the Belfast!

LONDON // There's something slightly surreal about seeing a fully armed battleship parked up across the river from the Tower of London. In fact, HMS *Belfast* last saw action during the Korean War, but this Town Class cruiser still looks tooled up and ready for combat.

With its grey camo paint job, the battleship fits in remarkably well with the Portland stone colour scheme of the city of London. It's part of the Imperial War Museum family, and the interiors throng with school groups and sightseers indulging wartime Boys' Own fantasies.

SEE IT ! *HMS* **Belfast** *is moored on the south bank of the Thames, just yards from London Bridge station.*

201

Take a cab around Belfast with a Black Taxi Tour

NORTHERN IRELAND // Belfast's fractious history can be hard to grasp. If only there was a friendly local who could show you around and explain what's what. Hopping in a black taxi for a driver-guided tour gives you just that, helping you dig beneath the surface to get a better understanding of the city's troubled past and hopeful present. Murals on the gable walls of terraces have traditionally staked out sectarian territory, commemorated historical events and glorified terrorist groups. Take them in and hear their stories – all from the comfort of a cab.

SEE IT ! *Tours are offered by numerous taxi companies and local cabbies. Drivers will pick you up anywhere in Belfast city centre.*

202

Footsteps and fantasy in the Forest of Dean

SOUTHWEST ENGLAND // Wedged between England and Wales, part of the former but with traits of the latter, the Forest of Dean is a rich area, ideal for easy strolls or serious hiking. Tranquil paths lead past ancient oaks, while the Offa's Dyke National Trail skirts the western edge. The heart of the forest is Puzzlewood, a maze of moss-covered trees, weird rock formations, tangled vines, twisted roots and rickety bridges. It reputedly inspired Mirkwood in Tolkien's *The Lord of the Rings*; more recently, it's starred in *Dr Who*, Star Wars and Harry Potter.

SEE IT ! *Monmouth is a handy gateway for Dean exploration. Puzzlewood is open weekends spring and autumn, daily in summer.*

203

Go down to the farm at Riverford Field Kitchen

SOUTHWEST ENGLAND // In a world where everyone is becoming more conscious of what they eat (and just as importantly, where it comes from), Riverford stands out as a shining example to all. Founded by eco-pioneer and organic farmer Guy Singh-Watson in the 1990s, this trailblazing, all-organic farm established one of the UK's first farm-to-plate 'food box' schemes, delivering fresh produce directly to customers across the UK. Riverford has gone from strength to strength, and now delivers around 45,000 food boxes every week. It also has its own fantastic barn bistro serving home-grown seasonal produce and daily-changing dishes to hungry diners, which has become one of the most coveted destinations for visitors to Totnes. Or pick up picnic ingredients or take-home goodies from the on-site farm shop. The farm hit the headlines in 2018 when Singh-Watson handed the business to its employees, opting for a co-operative structure rather than selling out to big business.

SEE IT ! ***Riverford Farm is 10 miles northwest of Totnes. It's popular (especially for Sunday lunch) so book well ahead.***

Levison Wood's Top Five Places

British explorer, writer and Leica Camera ambassador Levison Wood is known for his walking expeditions in Africa, Asia and Central America. His latest book, **Arabia: A Journey Through the Heart of the Middle East**, ***is out now.***

01

CASTLETON AND DOVEDALE, PEAK DISTRICT – Amid unspoilt countryside, the village of Castleton and valley of Dovedale (a National Nature Reserve with ancient ash woodland) are perfect for long walks.

02

KNOYDART PENINSULA – Walking from Mallaig to Inverie on the wild Knoydart Peninsula is a fantastic way to see the western Highlands of Scotland. Be sure to pay a visit to The Old Forge in Inverie, the most remote pub on mainland Britain.

03

ARUNDEL CASTLE, WEST SUSSEX – This restored medieval castle overlooking the River Arun is filled with 1000 years of history. Stroll outside the grounds and you'll find lots of lovely antique shops to explore, too.

04

ST BRIDES BAY, PEMBROKESHIRE – Britain's best-kept coastline secret (until now!) is scattered with beautiful empty beaches and quaint fishing villages. Take a ferry to Skomer island to see thousands of puffins nesting.

05

BATTERSEA PARK, LONDON – This 200-acre green space in central London is a must-visit and is always bustling with people and pets. Sit on a bench, or just lie on the grass here and watch the world go by.

Plunging through fire on Alton Towers' Wicker Man rollercoaster, which welcomed its first victims in 2018

204

Adrenaline rush around the 10 rollercoasters of Alton Towers

MIDLANDS & THE MARCHES // The UK's largest theme park, Staffordshire's Alton Towers has been smashing ride records since it opened, and is forever upping its game. A resort incorporating 850 acres of hotels and lodges, restaurants, a water park, spa and mini-golf course, it is the theme park's 10 rollercoasters for which Alton Towers is renowned. A favourite is The Smiler, which has 14 inversions, the most of any coaster worldwide, while Oblivion is the world's original dive coaster. Added in 2018, the Wicker Man was the first wooden rollercoaster to be built in Britain for over 20 years, and is where thrill seekers hurtle towards sacrifice amid a six-storey flaming effigy. Just another run-of-the-mill family day out, then.

SEE IT ! ***Alton Towers has a variety of passes and deals for accommodation and attractions available on its website.***

Visitors explore the ruins of Cornwall's Tintagel Castle where, according to legend, King Arthur was born

205

Seek out King Arthur at Tintagel Castle

SOUTHWEST ENGLAND // Teetering on the edge of crumbling Cornish cliffs, this ruined fortress is surrounded by myths and legends. It's said to be the birthplace of the legendary English warrior, protector and nation-builder, King Arthur. Never mind the fact that the castle was largely built during the 13th century, long after Arthur (if he even existed) was said to have lived – if anywhere seems suited to mythic origins, Tintagel is certainly it. The castle is separated into two sections: one on the mainland, another on a rocky tower accessed via a steep cliff-side staircase (although a controversial plan to link the two via a footbridge is underway). Visit at low tide and clamber down to Merlin's Cave, where the wizard is said to have cooked up his spells.

SEE IT ! ***The Castle is a short, steep walk down from Tintagel in north Cornwall. Come in midwinter for the full windswept glory.***

© Andrew Montgomery / Lonely Planet

© Marco Prati / Shutterstock

206

Hike a little bit of history along the Pennine Way

YORKSHIRE // Whether you meander for a mile or two or gird your loins to tackle the whole 268 miles of it, the Pennine Way will leave its mark. Mud, wind, rain, steep hills and sheer distance provide the challenge; scenic views, remote pubs like the Tan Hill Inn (#406 on this list) and a glowing sense of achievement are among the many rewards.

Britain's first long-distance trail had its origins in the 1930s when the public were routinely denied entry to private land, including the wild and windswept moors of the Peak District and the Pennines. A coalition of ramblers, youth hostellers and progressive politicians fought hard to open up these privately owned lands, finally pushing through the National Parks and Access to the Countryside Act in 1949, followed in 1965 by the opening of the Pennine Way.

TRY IT ! ***To experience the Pennine Way in a day, hike the 9-mile round trip from Dufton to the scenic highlight of High Cup Nick.***

207

Push all the right buttons at the Science Museum

LONDON // The third great Kensington museum, alongside the Natural History and the V&A, the Science Museum is the place to take tech-obsessed kids who might be fired up by the sight of genuine space-mission capsules, airplane cockpits and the first train to run on rails. Whereas its neighbours are all architectural splendour, the Science Museum serves up geek-and-proud science behind its refined stone facade. Halls are stacked with groundbreaking technology and most exhibits have a lever to pull, button to press or screen to interact with, transforming this to a supersized playroom. There are definite must-sees – Crick & Watson's DNA model, Amy Johnson's plane, the Black Arrow space rocket, an undetonated WWII V2 flying bomb – but almost anyone will get a buzz out of most of the assembled tech on display.

SEE IT ! ***South Kensington Tube is the jumping-off point for the Kensington museums; just follow the crowds to Exhibition Rd.***

© Angel Villalba / Getty

© Ian Dagnall / Alamy

208

Visit a medieval crime scene in Canterbury Cathedral

SOUTHEAST ENGLAND // England's most important place of worship and mothership of the Protestant Church, Canterbury Cathedral once drew pilgrims by the million who came to visit a famously bloodstained spot – it was here in 1170 that Archbishop Thomas Becket was put to the sword by hitmen sent by King Henry II. Today it's tourists who make the 21st-century pilgrimage. The striking altar that marks the place where Becket was murdered is just one feature of a church packed with monuments and tombs, including that of Edward the Black Prince.

SEE IT ! ***Canterbury is linked to London by coach and train and local bus routes radiate out to all parts of Kent.***

209

Pretend you're an extra (or even a star) in Downton Abbey

SOUTHERN ENGLAND // Turreted Highclere Castle is the family seat of the Earl of Canarvon – but you'll know it better as the backdrop for the blockbuster TV series *Downton Abbey*, Julian Fellowes' upstairs-downstairs tale of life in aristocratic England. Fans will spot numerous locations around the house – the great hall, drawing room, library, dining room and several bedrooms have all been showcased on screen, as has the estate's glorious, 1000-acre landscaped park, designed by none other than Lancelot 'Capability' Brown.

SEE IT ! ***Highclere is about 6 miles south of Newbury. Pre-book tickets online, or risk it on the day – though tours sometimes sell out.***

210

Meander along stone walls in the Mourne Mountains

NORTHERN IRELAND // These rolling mountains – dotted with grazing sheep, pretty white cottages, slabs of grey granite and patches of purple heather – offer peaceful hiking trails and breathtaking views of the Irish Sea. The Mournes' beauty is the stuff of poetry: Irish writer William Percy French based the lyrics of a folk song on his longing to be 'where the Mountains of Mourne sweep down to the sea'. Follow the spectacular, drystone Mourne Wall across the summits of 15 surrounding peaks, including the highest, Slieve Donard (2790ft).

SEE IT ! ***Hiking trails in the Mournes are easily accessed from the seaside town of Newcastle.***

211

Re-live the monastic heyday of Devenish Island

NORTHERN IRELAND // These days it's a peaceful haven, but Devenish Island was once a bustling centre of learning and craftsmanship. In its prime, it was home to a thriving community of up to 1000 monks, and was a place where architectural techniques were developed.

The largest of several holy islands on Lower Lough Erne, Devenish is dominated by a superb 12th-century round tower; nearby lie the remains of an Augustinian monastery, founded in the 6th century, an unusual 15th-century high cross and some fascinating old gravestones.

SEE IT ! ***The Island is accessed by boat. From July–October ferries run from Trory Jetty, or book water taxis at Enniskillen tourist office.***

212

Splash into some riverside adventures at Symonds Yat

SOUTHWEST ENGLAND // The village of Symonds Yat sits astride the meandering River Wye, flanked by steep wooded hills. The landscape is dramatic without being overwhelming, so it's no surprise the term 'picturesque' was coined here. Enjoy your own vistas by hiking or climbing up Symonds Yat Rock for wraparound views across the valley; with luck you'll spot the resident peregrine falcons. Take to the water in a canoe for a different vantage point, or rent a bike and explore riverside trails, then reward your endeavours at the historic local pub.

SEE IT ! ***Rather than negotiate the narrow lanes by car, approach on foot and cross the river on the quirky hand-pulled ferry.***

© stocker1970 / Shutterstock

213

Discover Sutton Hoo: England's Valley of the Kings

EAST ANGLIA // In the pantheon of archaeological discoveries, haunting, ethereal Sutton Hoo looms large. Here, in 1939, archaeologists discovered the ship burial of an Anglo-Saxon king surrounded by his treasures – including finely worked precious metals, weapons and a helmet of interlocking panels, covered in elaborate designs. The 263 finds thrillingly transformed the way we see the 'Dark Ages', revealing a previously unrecognised depth of culture, trade and skill.

Today, no fewer than 18 burial mounds sit in sandy heathland. A £4 million project is transforming the site, so you'll eventually be able to climb a 55ft viewing tower and retrace what may have been the burial ship's processional route. Looking into the eye sockets of the replica helmet of Rædwald, King of the East Angles, feels like staring straight into the past.

☛ SEE IT ! ***The nearest train station is just over a mile away at Melton.***

Robin Sheppard's Top Five Places

Robin Sheppard is the founder of Bespoke Hotels, the UK's largest independent hotel group. He is also Hotel Sector Champion for the Office for Disability Issues, and is a tireless campaigner for awareness around accessible travel.

01

STOURHEAD, WILTSHIRE – Capability Brown's finest bit of parkland, especially if they bring back the fête champêtre for some competitive picnicking. Lurk behind the giant rhubarb trees for a late afternoon Earl Grey tea.

02

DAYMER BAY, NORTH CORNWALL – Best explored after a zesty seafood lunch at Nathan Outlaw's restaurant The Mariners, enjoying a gentle zephyr of a breeze off the Camel estuary, while getting the sand between your toes.

03

ALDEBURGH, SUFFOLK – Gaze out at this pretty coastal town from the Wentworth Hotel dining room after a fine claret and watch the huge Suffolk skies, all plump and pink atop the copper pebbles of the raised beach.

04

BERMONDSEY SQUARE – Walk down the coolest street in England for a greasy spoon breakfast at the Friday market in front of Bermondsey Square Hotel and watch all the stallholders haggle away with shoppers.

05

HOTEL GOTHAM, MANCHESTER – The terrace at Brass, the top-floor member's bar at Hotel Gotham, is fantastic. Settle in for Lady Didsbury cocktails and views of Old Trafford, the Etihad stadium and Strangeways prison.

214

Promenade around Wales' greatest Welsh-built fortress, Powis Castle

MID-WALES // Out of an astonishing Italianate terraced garden whose colours are especially radiant in autumn looms Powis Castle, its red gritstone circular towers and turrets rendering it easily the finest castle raised by a Welshman in Wales.

The circumstances of the construction were hardly cause for national pride, with Owain ap Gruffydd ap Gwenwynwyn, last hereditary prince of once-mighty Powys, permitted to build only because of his subservience to English King Edward I, but the results are impressive all the same.

Neither is the beauty confined to the outside. The property's 18th-century owner, Robert Clive, amassed one of the most extensive collections of Indian and Bangladeshi artefacts ever seen in Britain. Displayed throughout the castle, it appropriated spoils of war from Indian ruler Tipu Sultan and includes an exquisite jewelled tiger's head, besides lavish painting, and sculpture.

SEE IT ! ***Powis Castle lies on the edge of Welshpool, with a railway station on the Shrewsbury–Aberyswyth line.***

The verdant terraced gardens at Powis Castle are another of the medieval fortress's draws

© ad_vaughan / Getty images

The International Slavery Museum is situated in Albert Dock, close to where slave trading ships were constructed in Liverpool

215

Learn about history's horrors at the International Slavery Museum, Liverpool

NORTHWEST ENGLAND // The unimaginable horrors of slavery are explained in sometimes uncomfortable detail at this superb museum, opened on Slavery Remembrance Day in 2007 at Liverpool's Albert Dock.

The museum's location is telling, sited as it is yards away from the dry docks where slave trading ships were fitted out in a city which grew wealthy trading human beings during the second half of the 18th century. Through a series of compelling multimedia exhibits and gruesome artefacts (including original shackles, chains and barbaric instruments used to keep rebellious slaves in tow), the story of the slave trade is revealed.

This includes a captain's diary, which carefully details the slaver's experience of packing his ship with slaves in West Africa and sailing them across the dreaded Atlantic 'Middle Passage' before selling the ones that survived in the West Indies for rum, sugar, tobacco and cotton. He then returned to Liverpool and sold his wares for huge profit.

The museum also takes an uncompromising look at racism in all its guises, leaving visitors in no doubt as to its destructive ugliness.

☛ SEE IT ! ***The museum shares an old warehouse on Albert Dock with the equally compelling Merseyside Maritime Museum.***

216

Step back in time at Dickensian-style New Lanark

SOUTHERN SCOTLAND // Back at the start of the 18th century, New Lanark was booming. Cotton mill wheels turned, machinery buzzed night and day, and workers clogged the Dickensian streets of this thriving, River Clyde-set factory village. The mood is somewhat different today, with the Unesco World Heritage site turned into a curious peek back in time. There are painstakingly restored houses, a working mill, a utopian workplace nursery – the first in the world – and a motorised pod ride to help you dig deeper into the past.

SEE IT ! *New Lanark is a one-hour drive from Glasgow and Edinburgh. Public transport is available from nearby Lanark.*

217

Channel your inner Braveheart at Stirling Castle

CENTRAL SCOTLAND // Figuring out how would-be invaders might have scaled the spine-tingling crags of this 16th-century castle is hard work. Every fortified stone seems to float above the Forth Valley, while each step along Castle Hill reveals arrow-slit windows and cannon ports, from where soldiers would take shots at battle-scarred knights. The history steals your breath, but reaching the crenellated battlements is just the beginning. Beyond the nooks of the Great Hall there's a palace where a who's who of Scottish royalty plotted wars – and ate crumpets.

SEE IT ! *Free guided tours begin on the hour from the Lower Square.*

218

See the changing colours of Old Aberdeen

NORTHEAST SCOTLAND // Few places sparkle like Old Aberdeen. Lying on a latitude north of Moscow, the ever-variegated weather brings the kind of sights for which smartphones were invented. When the sun shines, the granite of this time-worn quarter shimmers silver. Start at 15th-century St Machar's Cathedral, the world's only medieval granite church, then seek out the stocky Renaissance spire of King's College. Delve deeper to find beautifully preserved lanes and college buildings that demand as much of your time. Wow doesn't begin to cover it.

SEE IT ! *Old Aberdeen is 10 minutes from the centre. Buses leave regularly from Union Square station.*

Many rooms in the Brontë Parsonage Museum are as they were when the three literary sisters were writing their novels

219

Pay literary homage at the Brontë Parsonage Museum

YORKSHIRE // The year 2018 marked the 200th anniversary of the birth of novelist Emily Brontë, creator of *Wuthering Heights*, an undisputed classic of English literature. It was also the 40th anniversary of the release of Kate Bush's number-one hit single of the same name, inspired by Emily's novel. And this modest parsonage in the quaint West Yorkshire village of Haworth is where it all started.

Emily and her sisters Charlotte (author of *Jane Eyre*) and Anne (author of *The Tenant of Wildfell Hall*) lived here from 1820 until their deaths, and the house has been preserved exactly as it would have appeared then.

Most of the three sisters' creative writing was done in the dining room, and the table here is scattered with original notebooks, papers and pens. It makes the hairs on the back of your neck stand up to realise that this is the very table, in the very room, in which *Wuthering Heights* was written.

Following a visit to the museum, you can hike across the moors via four carved stones installed in 2018 – one for each sister and one for the family as a whole. Emily's stone bears a poem written, fittingly, by Kate Bush.

SEE IT ! ***Arrive via the Keighley & Worth Valley Railway, a heritage line used in the making of* The Railway Children *TV series.***

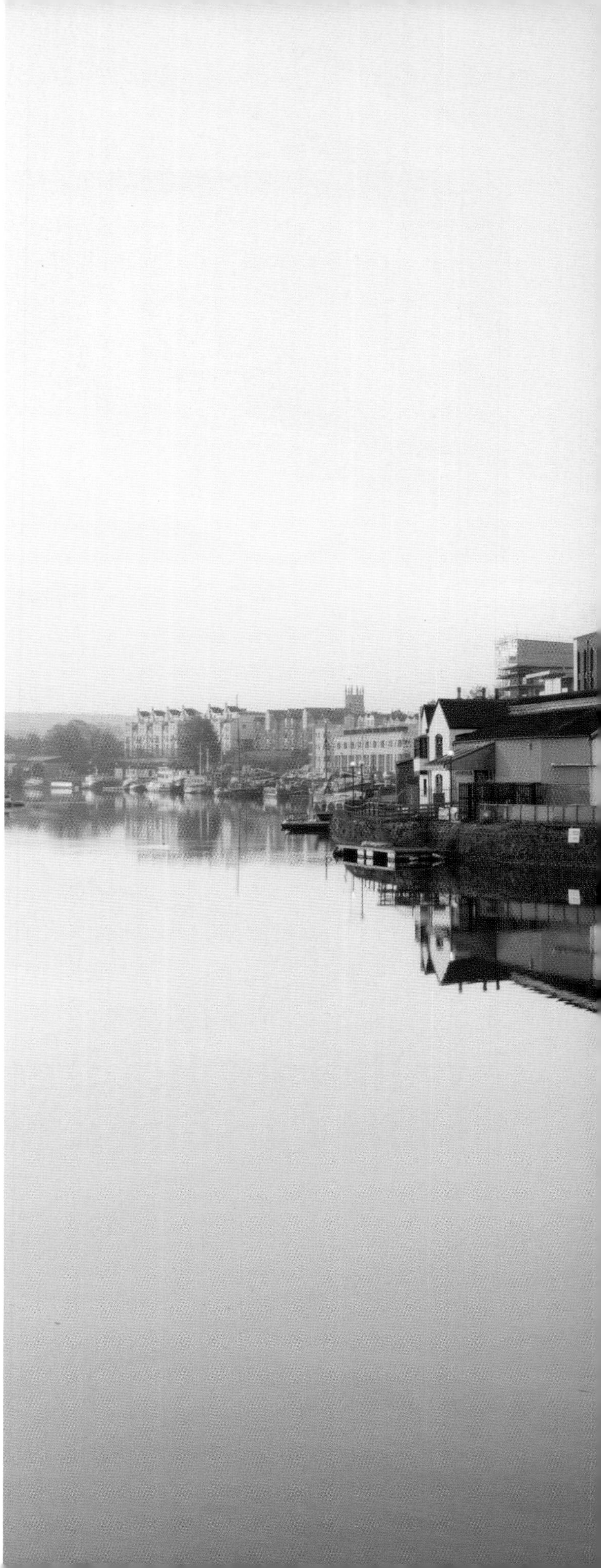

220

Climb aboard the SS *Great Britain* in Bristol

SOUTHWEST ENGLAND // Along with railway-creating, tunnel-boring and bridge-raising, Isambard Kingdom Brunel was also a serial shipbuilder, designing a series of pioneering steamships. One, the 322ft-long SS *Great Britain*, was the first screw-propellered steamship ever built and once steamed from Bristol to New York in just 14 days – the Victorian equivalent of Concorde. Restored to its former glory, the ship now sits grandly on Bristol's dockside; explore the galley and dining saloon, peer into the surgeon's rooms and descend to view the iron hull up close.

SEE IT ! *The SS* Great Britain *is moored on Bristol's harbour near the M Shed Museum.*

© James Osmond / Alamy

BRUNEL'S ss GREAT BRITAIN

The magnificent Reading Room at the John Rylands Library is enough to distract the most devoted bibliophile

221

Get bookish in the John Rylands Library

NORTHWEST ENGLAND // The term 'library' doesn't quite do justice to Basil Champneys' stunning Victorian Gothic building, commissioned in 1890 by Enriqueta Rylands in memory of her husband John, Manchester's first multi-millionaire. Enriqueta's tribute was a philanthropic gift to the city, made up of Champneys' genius and incorporating 43,000 books that belonged to the 2nd Earl Spencer and cost Rylands the sum of £210,000.

The library collection includes 4000 incunabula, as books printed before 1501 were called, as well as a Gutenberg Bible, the earliest extant New Testament text and the country's second-largest assemblage of works by Britain's first printer, William Caxton. But the real star is perhaps the building itself, especially the Reading Room, which features remarkable stained-glass windows and high-vaulted ceilings.

SEE IT ! ***The free-to-enter library is in central Manchester. Thirty-minute tours take place at 3pm on Wednesdays and Fridays.***

Dusk falls as the teams play on in front of a full house at the Oval, one of English cricket's most famous grounds

222

Watch T20 wickets tumble at the Kia Oval

LONDON // If a test series is a pint of English bitter, T20 cricket is a shotglass of tequila with salt around the rim – while a test match can stretch on for days, a T20 match can last as little as three hours, with wickets falling fast and sixes scored with joyous abandon. In other words, a perfect bite-sized introduction to the gentleman's game. And where better to see a match than the Kia Oval, where the first ever game of international test cricket was played in 1880? This landmark cricket ground has seen more overs than WG Grace, as well as being briefly requisitioned as a prisoner-of-war camp.

The most sought-after tickets are for T20 international matches. Easier to come by are seats for the rather uncricketly named Vitality Blast, the domestic T20 competition in England and Wales. Either way, expect plenty of fan support alongside the thwack of leather on willow.

SEE IT ! *Oval has its own Tube station, just a short walk from the cricket ground.*

223

Stroll along the world's longest pier at Southend

EAST ANGLIA // Stretching out into the Thames Estuary, the monumental iron and wood construction of Southend Pier is the Big Daddy of all piers – at 1.341 miles, it's the longest in the world. Standing at its entrance, the sweeping walk can seem daunting. But soon you're far from land, buffeted by the wind and experiencing the curious sensation of walking high above the waves. About half an hour's stroll leads to the restored pier head and a cafe, sun deck and lifeboat station. Hopping aboard the Pier Railway saves the long slog back.

SEE IT ! ***Trains run on the hour and half hour from the shore end; at quarter past and quarter to from the pier head.***

224

Admire a grand social experiment in Titus Salt's Saltaire

YORKSHIRE // You've got to hand it to Titus Salt. Industrial baron, philanthropist and teetotaller, he built what was, in the 1850s, the biggest factory in the world, and surrounded it with a village designed not only to house his workers, but also to instil a sense of community and moral rectitude. He called it Saltaire, combining his name with that of the local River Aire, and it's now a Unesco World Heritage site, with rows of honey-coloured cottages surrounding the vast factory building – Salts Mill – which houses an exhibition of David Hockney's art.

SEE IT ! ***Saltaire is roughly 13 miles west of Leeds and is easily reached by train.***

225

Take a sip of the Herefordshire & Wye Valley Cider Route

MIDLANDS & THE MARCHES // Over half of the UK's cider is produced in Herefordshire, which yields apples for twenty-odd cider producers across almost a thousand orchards. Lovely Hereford is at the core of this boozy regional reconnoitre, where Bulmers, the world's biggest cider mill, is located, and where a cider museum gives a good grounding in all things apple-related. For more, scrump your way out to northwestern Herefordshire's historic black-and-white villages, or along the River Wye in pursuit of sixteen cider-themed attractions.

SEE IT ! ***Ledbury and Pembridge cycle routes (on Herefordshire Cider Route's website) allow exploration of several cider attractions.***

© Richard Childs / Alamy

© Nik Taylor / Alamy

226

Hike 3000 million years of history on Stac Pollaidh

HIGHLANDS & ISLANDS // Just a quick glance at this sugarloaf of Torridonian sandstone reveals a mountaintop packed with the greatest hits of northwest Scotland. Alongside the weathered gullies leading to the 2000ft summit, 'Stac Polly' (as it's pronounced) offers the photo op of unparalleled views over the Summer Isles and the distinctively shaped mountains, lochans and treeless hills of Assynt – the stars of the surrounding Unesco-worthy North West Highlands Geopark.

The vertiginous summit can be tackled as part of a tough scramble up a steeply pitched path (1.5 miles), but a gentler clockwise ridge and circuit below it is equally rewarding, taking in the profiles of dramatic neighbours Cul Mor and Suilven, and crossing a rocky plateau that dates back some 3000 million years.

TRY IT ! *Drive 10 miles north of Ullapool on the A835 to Drumrunie before turning off to follow Loch Lurgainn.*

227

Cycle through the magical world of the (not so) New Forest

SOUTHERN ENGLAND // Two important facts about the New Forest: 1) it's not new (it was established as a royal hunting reserve in 1079), and 2) it's not a forest (more like an open heath dotted with the occasional tree or copse). But that doesn't mean the New Forest isn't worth visiting: a national park since 2005, it's a bewitching place.

With a largely flat landscape, and a 100-mile network of signposted trails, it's ideal for exploring by bike: hire the right one for you from a wide selection in Brockenhurst or at the New Forest Centre in Lymington, and as you pedal between sleepy, traditional villages such as Burley, Brockenhurst, Beaulieu and Lymington, keep your eyes peeled for wild deer and ponies wandering through the foliage, not to mention all manner of birdlife.

SEE IT ! *The New Forest's gateway is Brockenhurst, which has a railway station with regular connections to London via Winchester.*

Urquhart Castle on the banks of Loch Ness, where a mythical beastie stalks the deep

228

Search for monsters at Loch Ness

HIGHLANDS & ISLANDS // 'Look!' screams the boatman with urgency, as he thrusts a finger out across the water. Hazy sunlight is casting shadows across the loch's surface, the gloom underscored by the sound of waves gently lapping against the vessel's hull. But further away, where the loch fades to black, a roll of water emerges, then another, then another – could these really be signs of the mythical Loch Ness monster below the water?

Whether you're sceptical or not, there is a correct way to hunt monsters on Scotland's second largest loch and it starts with taking a boat from Drumnadrochit, located halfway up the loch's west bank. Out on the water, the monster fantasy is aided by toothy Urquhart Castle and the undulating hills, your camera primed for the prospect – no matter how slim – of snapping the world's most famous humpbacked creature. Back on shore, the Loch Ness Visitor Centre delivers a kitsch and kooky appraisal of the natural history and legend of Nessie. To enjoy it fully, park your suspicions – there's magic in the water if you only know where to look for it.

SEE IT ! ***Drumnadrochit is 15 miles south of Inverness. Several companies offer hourly, half-day and full-day cruises.***

© John Bracegirdle / Alamy

© Helen Hotson / Alamy

229

Lord it up on a road trip through Royal Deeside

HIGHLANDS & ISLANDS // En route to the River Dee Valley, it's clear the heather-clad hills have pedigree. Past visitors range from Queen Victoria, who fell for it so much that Prince Albert bought the Balmoral Estate for her in 1852, to Her Majesty the Queen, who maintains the estate as a Scottish holiday home. It teems with wonderful places to stay, eat and explore – from the Prince Charles–backed Rothesay Rooms restaurant in Ballater to the swit-swoo Fife Arms in Braemar, first built in the wake of Victoria's annual visits.

SEE IT ! *Balmoral is open from April to July. The estate is 50 miles east of Aberdeen and 100 miles north of Edinburgh.*

230

Step back in time in handsome Rye

SOUTHEAST ENGLAND // Arguably the most seductive town in southern England, Rye is a chocolate-box perfect little place of cobbled streets, crooked Tudor facades, yesteryear shops and lashings of clotted cream to go with all the tea. Perched high on a promontory that was once lapped by the sea, the Cinque Port is crowned by the Church of St Mary, boasting England's oldest working church clock. Descending from the church is Mermaid St, one of the country's most attractive with its pebbles, oddly named houses and some very charismatic hotels.

SEE IT ! *Take the train from London, changing in Ashford. Buses running between Dover and Hastings stop in Rye.*

Isambard Kingdom Brunel's posthumous Clifton Suspension Bridge sits 331ft above the Avon Gorge

231

Cross the Clifton Suspension Bridge

SOUTHWEST ENGLAND // Perhaps the most visionary engineer of the Victorian era, Isambard Kingdom Brunel created a host of industrial landmarks that transformed the British landscape. He was the mastermind of the Great Western Railway, built numerous stations and tunnels, and designed two of the southwest's most important bridges – the Royal Albert Bridge over the River Tamar between Cornwall and Devon, and the Clifton Suspension Bridge, a 1352ft-long, 331ft-high wonder spanning the River Avon in Bristol.

Brunel won the contract to build the latter in 1830, while still in his mid-twenties. Construction began that year, was halted by the Bristol Riots, then restarted in 1836, but it was another 28 years before the bridge opened to traffic in 1864. Tragically, Brunel never lived to see its completion, having died five years earlier. The bridge is famous for a spectacularly improbable suicide attempt in 1885, when young barmaid Sarah Ann Henley jumped off it, only to be saved by her copious petticoats acting as an impromptu parachute. You'll learn lots more historical nuggets like this on one of the free guided tours.

SEE IT ! ***The bridge's Visitor Centre runs free tours at 3pm on weekends and bank holidays from Easter to October.***

© shoults / Alamy Stock Photo

232

Ride some of Wales' wildest waves along Hell's Mouth Beach

NORTH WALES // The name of this tempestuous 3-mile-wide bay out on a lovely limb of the Llŷn Peninsula is the most telling insight into its nature: sailors, for whom the waters were perilous when storms gathered, christened it thus. Stretching between the towering headlands of Mynydd Rhiw and Mynydd Cilan, where precipitous exposed cliffs help whip up the waves, Hell's Mouth has no shelter its entire length.

What brought woe for sailors, though, brings exhilaration for surfers. The bay is right up there with some of Wales' very best breaks, and swells can usher in 8ft waves. The reefs off the northern end of the beach lure the surfers, but the dune-backed sands are beautiful walking terrain regardless.

SEE IT ! *Hell's Mouth Beach is near Llanengan, 21 miles southwest of Porthmadog. Bus 18 runs daily (weekdays) from Pwllheli.*

© Deatonphotos / Shutterstock

233

Enjoy the state-of-the-art Library of Birmingham

MIDLANDS & THE MARCHES // The bedazzling answer to anyone who says libraries are losing their relevance, this Francine Houben-designed architectural masterpiece is an instrumental part of Birmingham's 20-year plan to transform its inner-city districts. Resembling a giant stack of glittering gifts, the building – Europe's largest public library and cultural space – features a spiralling atrium interior, subterranean amphitheatre, and a lift shooting you up to a 7th-floor roof garden with views out over the city centre. Some phenomenal collections are housed here, including the world's most important collection of Industrial Revolution texts and Britain's biggest and best body of Shakespearean works, the latter contained within John Henry Chamberlain's reassembled Shakespeare Memorial Room from 1884.

SEE IT ! *The library is 15 minutes' walk west of New Street station, itself revamped as part of the 'Big City Plan' to regenerate Birmingham.*

© Robert Falconer / Alamy

© Ian Dagnall / Alamy

234

Ride elegantly on the Watercress Line in Hampshire

SOUTHERN ENGLAND // There's just something about the puff of the engine, the toot of the horn, the clatter of the track – and the sense that on board a steam train you're slipping back into a more elegant age of rail travel, when sky-high prices, impenetrable timetables and byzantine fare structures were still just a twinkle in a malevolent ticket inspector's eye. And when it comes to the pleasures of steam, few trains top Hampshire's Watercress Line, aka the Mid-Hants Railway – a heritage beauty that puffs its way between Alton and Alresford. With its racing-green livery, the line gets its name from the days when it carried Hampshire-grown watercress to the London markets. Nowadays, its cargo is sightseers and steam enthusiasts come to ride the rails, admire the scenery, and enjoy cute stations like Ropley and Medstead.

TRY IT ! ***The Watercress Line is about seven miles from Winchester. You can ride in either direction from Alresford or Alton.***

235

Re-live British history at Beamish Open-Air Museum

NORTHEAST ENGLAND // History lessons don't have to be dry or dull, as this open-air museum proves. Beamish pulls you into the day-to-day life of northeast England during the 1820s, 1900s and 1940s through brilliant hands-on attractions. They include going down a mine (at the industry's peak in 1913, Durham's 304 mines employed 165,246 men and boys), rattling aboard a vintage trolleybus, tram or steam train, and visiting a working farm. Even more immersive experiences (which cost extra) include blacksmithing, operating a steamroller, learning traditional baking methods and driving a tram or train. What's more, Beamish is expanding to add a 1950s town with a relocated cinema, recreated police station and bowling green, and replicated semi-detached houses, promising a glimpse of mid-20th-century life.

SEE IT ! ***Beamish is 9 miles northwest of Durham; if you're coming by bus, it's quicker to take one from Newcastle, 10 miles north.***

© Adrian Beasley / Getty

236

Go head over heels at Blackpool Pleasure Beach

NORTHWEST ENGLAND // Britain's most popular amusement park by far is the 16-hectare Pleasure Beach just south of Blackpool's South Pier. The park draws over 7 million thrill seekers a year, who come to test their stomachs on its collection of 10 rollercoasters, four of which are 'woodies' – antique wooden coasters including the Big Dipper (at 235ft still the tallest in the country) and the perennially popular Grand National. Newer rides offer a more high-tech thrill: Icon is the UK's first double-launch coaster, propelling riders 88ft skyward at 53mph, while Infusion is the first suspended looping coaster completely over water.

When you're done with having your insides pulled this way and that, you can reset in the park's champagne and oyster bar, one of a host of food outlets offering respite from the barrage of lights and noise.

☛ SEE IT ! *Book online for the best choice of saver tickets, including a selection of 'speedy' passes that let you skip the queues.*

© Jon Sparks / Alamy

237

Bike or hike – or swing – through Grizedale Forest

CUMBRIA // A 9.4-sq-mile forest straddling the hills between Coniston Water and Esthwaite Water, Grizedale's carpet of conifers is home to walking and cycling trails as well as a branch of the Go Ape woodland assault course, where you can zip and swing between the trees.

This is a modern edition of an ancient forest, replanted over the past hundred years or so after major deforestation in the 19th century due to logging and mining. Still, as you walk or bike your way through the trees it feels as though you're following well-worn tracks through a dale whose Old Norse name means 'valley of the pigs'.

The nine walking trails and seven cycling tracks cater to different levels of expertise; all offer encounters with more than 40 outdoor sculptures designed and created by a series of international artists.

☛ SEE IT ! *Grizedale Mountain Bikes rents out bikes and supplies trail maps; for more information visit the Forestry England website.*

238

Seek summer sun, sounds and slides at Victoria Park

LONDON // Looking like a miniature Regent's Park, Victoria Park is an unusually grand civic space on the borders of Hackney and Tower Hamlets. Younger Londoners love it for its live music events and cafes, but families come for its ponds and playgrounds – including, some would say, the best set of kids' slides in London. The park is intersected by Grove Rd, which runs up to genteel Victoria Park village, and on both sides there's water, greenery and vintage London history, including salvaged pieces of the original London Bridge, demolished in 1830.

SEE IT ! *The park is a short walk from Hackney Wick or Cambridge Heath overgrounds, or a 15 minute-walk from Bethnal Green Tube.*

239

Splash into the surf in revamped Scarborough

YORKSHIRE // Why would Scarborough make it onto a list like this? Surely it's an old-fashioned place, conjuring up images of traditional seaside holidays with saucy postcards, sand-laden sandwiches and kiss-me-quick hats? But this most retro of resorts is fast reinventing itself for the 21st century. Along with revamped versions of old-school attractions that include a redeveloped Victorian spa and Edwardian pleasure gardens, there's a state-of-the-art water park, a small but growing number of good restaurants, and a burgeoning surf scene.

SEE IT ! *Scarborough Surf School is based at Cayton Bay, 3 miles south of the town centre.*

240

Get a taste for bonkers Britain at its cheese-rolling best

OXFORD & THE COTSWOLDS // If you like odd customs, you'll love the annual Cheese Rolling at Cooper's Hill in Gloucestershire. The rules are simple: a large disc of cheese (Double Gloucester, naturally) is rolled down a steep hill, followed by contestants. First person down wins the cheese. Running is impossible on the precipitous slope; most participants slide and tumble to the bottom. Fancy dress is optional, madness obligatory, and injuries frequent. Even spectators are not safe, as contestants can bounce off course. You have been warned.

SEE IT ! *Cooper's Hill is near Gloucester. The cheese rolling, these days with a foam replica, takes place on the late May bank holiday.*

© Robert Harding / Alamy

© Gerard Puigmal / Getty

241

Rock down to Electric Avenue and Brixton Village

LONDON // Brixton Market had a buzz about it as early as the 1950s, when the first of the Windrush generation upped sticks from the Caribbean and relocated to the surrounding Victorian terraces. While central London was still starch-collared and stiff-upper-lipped, Brixton was the place to come for urban sounds and narcotic indulgences, a reputation that still persists, despite controversial gentrification.

Looking at vibrant, mixed Brixton today, it's hard to believe that race riots scarred the streets in the 1980s, inspiring Eddy Grant's groundbreaking reggae hit, 'Electric Avenue'. These days, people come for the hipster playground of Brixton Village, a cluster of shops and world-food cafes in the 1930s Granville Arcade. They also come for the nightlife – the Effra Social is a prime spot for multigenerational jams.

SEE IT ! *Brixton Tube is the beating heart of Brixton, just minutes from Electric Avenue, the Ritzy and Brixton Village.*

© David Cabrera / Getty

242

Marvel at medieval masonry in Norwich Cathedral

EAST ANGLIA // Work started on Norwich Cathedral in 1096, resulting in a soaring, barbed 315ft spire and, fast-forward to today, one of the most complete Norman cathedrals in England. It's the interior that really catches your breath – both the sheer size of the nave and the superb Gothic rib vaulting. Among the spidery stonework are 1200 mesmerising, ornate ceiling bosses – more than any other cathedral in the Christian world. Together they represent one of the finest achievements of English medieval masonry. You can study equally exquisite carved bosses in even closer detail in the cathedral's extensive, two-storey cloisters. These serene spaces, started in 1297, are unique in England. As the sun sculpts slanting shadows you can almost sense the 100 monks who lived here, and the masons who chiselled the stone.

SEE IT ! *Norwich has good rail and bus connections. Do a guided tour of the cathedral, or come for evensong, held Sundays to Fridays.*

© Dave Porter / Alamy

© David Graham / Shutterstock

243

Brave the Iron Way at Honister Slate Mine and Via Ferrata

CUMBRIA // A visit to Britain's last working slate mine mightn't seem all that inviting at first, but you'll not have seen one in such a gorgeous setting, atop a snaking road that wiggles its way through Borrowdale to Honister Pass and the mine. They've been splitting slate here for over 300 years, and while the processes have remained the same (give or take a machine or two), the mine has diversified so as to offer visitors more than just tours in the dark bowels of the mountain.

The most thrilling of the new activities is the walk along the Via Ferrata - the 'iron way' - an exhilarating climb utilising a vertigo-inducing system of clifftop ropes and ladders once used by the slate miners. Real daredevils can try their luck with the Infinity Bridge – a high-wire crossing above a 600m-high gorge.

SEE IT ! *Bus 77/77A crosses Honister Pass from Keswick and Buttermere; an all-day pass for all activities costs from £55.*

244

Be knocked out by the spread and scale of the Angel of the North

NORTHEAST ENGLAND // If you're travelling to Newcastle by motorway, you literally can't miss the Angel of the North: the outsized sculpture stands 66ft high and has a 177ft wingspan. It's estimated that it's seen by one person every second, equalling 33 million views every year.

Built over a former coal mine in 1998 as a beacon of the area's mining heritage and transition from heavy industry to high-tech, the rust-coloured steel form weighs 229 tons above ground, with a counterweight of 550 tons extending below ground, allowing it to withstand winds in excess of 100mph. Artist Sir Antony Gormley based the frame on a plaster cast of his own body, and the 3.5-degree tilt of the outstretched wings evoke a reassuring embrace that's especially noticeable when you're directly beneath it.

SEE IT ! *Buses from Newcastle stop by the sculpture, which has a car park at its base.*

245

Circle London on the Capital Ring walk

LONDON // Stepping its way through Zones 3 and 4, the 78 mile-long Capital Ring path encounters a surprising amount of greenery as it loops its way around London. With some eight million people and counting, London might not be an obvious rambler's paradise, but parts of the Capital Ring are utterly charming. Highlights abound in the city limits, from the art deco grandeur of Eltham Palace and the wilds of Wimbledon Common to deer-filled Richmond Park and the soaring Wharncliffe Viaduct.

SEE IT ! ***The Capital Ring is divided into 15 sections, making the start and end points more accessible on public transport.***

246

Go underground at London's Postal Museum

LONDON // A museum devoted to the postal service might not sound like a top crowd-pleaser, but Clerkenwell's Postal Museum has hidden depths – specifically the Mail Rail, a miniature underground railway once used to transport millions of missives beneath the city streets.

There's a hint of a James Bond baddie's lair about the tiny train, which can just accommodate sitting passengers as it zips between high-tech visual displays and the ghost platforms that once thronged with posties hard at work sorting mailbags or relaxing with games of darts.

SEE IT ! ***Mt Pleasant's postal depot is in a bit of a transport black spot; jump on a bus at Farringdon, the nearest Tube station.***

247

Open the doors to Churchill's Chartwell home

SOUTHEAST ENGLAND // A popular National Trust property, this muscular, brick-built manor house near the Kentish town of Westerham belonged to one Winston Churchill. A day wandering through Chartwell's rooms offers an absorbing insight into the cigar-chomping former prime minister, how he lived, his artistic flair and even his self-doubt. From 1922 until his death in 1965, Britain's wartime leader would retreat here during tough times (though the family lived elsewhere during WWII), painting, writing and composing his rousing speeches.

SEE IT ! ***Trains run from London to Oxted and Sevenoaks (both 6 miles away), and Edenbridge (4 miles away), but driving is easiest.***

© Miles Willis

248

Stroll along literary shores on Chesil Beach

SOUTHWEST ENGLAND // Pebbles, pebbles and more pebbles pretty much sums up Chesil Beach – except that until you've seen it, you just can't appreciate its brain-befuddling scale. At 650ft wide and 18 miles long, the beach stretches out along the south coast of Dorset, a gigantic pebble barrier extending from the Isle of Portland to the village of Chiswell. A notorious shipwreck site, it's also (as far as we know) the only beach to have given its name to a Booker Prize-nominated novel, *On Chesil Beach* by Ian McEwan – essential beach reading.

☛ SEE IT ! ***The beach can be accessed at several points between Portland and Chiswell.***

© Graham Custance / Getty

© Milosz Maslanka / Shutterstock

249

Grab some enriching resort time at Aberystwyth

MID-WALES // Aberystwyth is an enigma: a bright and breezy seaside resort, and yet arguably also one of Wales' most sophisticated cultural centres, where amusement arcades and souvenir shops seem perfectly at home with state-of-the-art creative hubs and refined restaurants. But the setting – handsome candy-coloured townhouses hogging scant low-lying ground between a striking string of hills – guarantees the town is a puzzle people will be happy to hang around to crack.

Aberystwyth has ancient foundations, as its castle and the hill fort to the south testify, but also some cultural sights of formidable clout, such as the National Library of Wales, and Wales' largest arts centre. Offset by a beach and a buzzing dining and nightlife scene, it's small wonder the place is a big hit.

☛ SEE IT ! ***Aberystwyth, the largest settlement in mid-Wales, is at the end of the Cambrian Railway Line from Shrewsbury.***

© G. Wright / Getty

250

Turn those fingers green at Sissinghurst Castle Garden

SOUTHEAST ENGLAND // Denied her ancestral home at nearby Knole through inheritance laws, poet and writer Vita Sackville-West and her husband, writer and diplomat Harold Nicolson, purchased an estate at Sissinghurst in 1930. Accompanying the mainly 16th-century brick buildings was 450 acres of land, and it was on this dilapidated patch of 'slovenly disorder' (as Sackville-West described it) that the couple proceeded to create a world-class garden.

After three years of clearing Sackville-West put together a team of gardeners and began the planting according to a design by her husband, with input from close friend and architect Edwin Lutyens, who collaborated with horticulturalist and designer Gertrude Jekyll. The gardens have matured into arguably the finest in south England.

☛ SEE IT ! ***Local buses run from Maidstone and Hawkhurst to Staplehurst train station, 5 miles from the gardens.***

© Craig Easton / Lonely Planet

© Josh Harrison / Alamy

251

Enjoy precious isolation on the Knoydart peninsula

HIGHLANDS & ISLANDS // Not for nothing is the Knoydart peninsula called 'Britain's last great wilderness' – the world feels more alive here, wilder and vast. What's kept it so pristine – so secret – is that there is no direct road access, with visitors relying on the ferry ride from Mallaig, or a knee-crunching 16-mile hike over rarely visited moorland.

Once checked in, Knoydart reveals itself slowly; from the crest of a quartz-topped Munro, from horseback or mountain bike, or while waist-deep in Inverie River angling for trout. There are catches, of course: first you need to earn the right to enjoy such spectacular wilderness by undertaking the journey, and the midges are fierce. But it's a place that becomes more intimate, more quickly – as though each footstep to a summit, or paddle turn to the shore, is already a prized memory.

☛ SEE IT ! ***Ferries run three to four times daily from Mallaig (the journey is 30 minutes).***

252

Be part of the Tour de Yorkshire cycling spectacular

YORKSHIRE // When the 101st Tour de France decided to stage its Grand Départ in Yorkshire in 2014, more than 2.5 million people turned up to line the roads. Yellow-painted bicycles appeared in villages across the county (in honour of the race leader's yellow jersey), along with sheep dyed green (for the top sprinter's green jersey) and pubs painted white with red polka dots (the colours of the King of the Mountains). Such was Yorkshire's enthusiasm for cycle racing that it was decided to create the county's own annual event, the Tour de Yorkshire.

Yorkshire has a vast network of country lanes that are perfect for road cyclists, and the TdY follows a 350- to 400-mile route, broken into stages that are raced on four consecutive days. Crowds of 2.8 million can be expected, and the atmosphere is electric.

☛ SEE IT ! ***The Tour takes place in early May. Spectators can watch the race for free anywhere along the route.***

253

Reach for the sky in Skye on the top of Sgurr na Stri

HIGHLANDS & ISLANDS // On paper, this 1620ft-high viewpoint – a mere vignette in comparison to other Isle of Skye peaks – doesn't seem so remarkable. The footpath leaves from a car lay-by, and wriggles up a long slope. Towards the end, it turns into a tiring scramble. However, once breathless at the top, the outlook reveals one of Britain's most stunning views, with a mind-blowing take on Loch Coruisk and the Cuillins. If a visit to Skye can teach you one thing, it's that there's no such thing as a bad day in the hills.

☛ SEE IT ! *The walk starts from the Sligachan Hotel (15 miles), or you can charter a boat from Elgol.*

254

Sit back and take in the Settle-Carlisle Railway grandeur

RAIL JOURNEY // As you rattle across the spectacular Ribblehead Viaduct in the heart of the Yorkshire Dales National Park, you'll realise why this is one of Britain's great scenic railway journeys. The view from the train window takes in the gnarled limestone crags of Ingleborough and the heathery slopes of Blea Moor before a series of tunnels and inclines lead to the highest railway summit in England at Ais Gill (1169ft above sea level). Completed in 1875, the line runs for 72 miles from Settle in Yorkshire to Carlisle, near the Scottish border.

☛ SEE IT ! *Diesel trains run eight times a day, but check out the vintage steam trains that offer special tours.*

255

Risk vertigo crossing Sark's amazing land bridge, La Coupée

CHANNEL ISLANDS // This precariously narrow land bridge connects Big Sark to Little Sark, where you'll find an excellent restaurant, La Sablonnerie, as well as ancient dolmen. La Coupée has a sheer drop to one side, and steep steps descending to the splendid La Grande Grève beach, whose white sand and clear cerulean waters would not look out of place in the Caribbean. Crossing La Coupée used to be a heroic feat, with locals crawling across on windy days, before protective railings were installed in 1900.

☛ SEE IT ! *Horse and buggy tours of Sark include La Coupée as a highlight. Combine the crossing with a trip to Little Sark's Venus Pool.*

256

Hike and hack in the Cotswolds' pretty Slaughters

OXFORD & THE COTSWOLDS // You'll find the tiny twin villages of Upper and Lower Slaughter nestling among rolling hills. Despite the macabre-sounding names, this is 'chocolate-box' England at its most bucolic: muted-yellow cottages, grassy banks, and time-worn stone bridges crossing the gently flowing River Eye. It's an ideal spot for a relaxed stroll – the villages are linked by a riverside path – or you can saddle up for a different perspective. Horses can be hired from various stables, and a hack is an appropriately rustic way to enjoy the Cotswold countryside.

☛ SEE IT ! *For walkers, the Slaughters sit on the Wardens' Way, a long-distance path. For riders, hacks cost £40 per hour.*

257

Escape civilisation on Herm, the smallest of the Channel Islands

CHANNEL ISLANDS // Hilly, green and fringed by some of the Channel Islands' most spectacular beaches, tiny Herm is completely traffic-free and feels like a step back in time. Whether you're a camper looking to kick back for a while, a beach buff in search of pristine sand and tropical-looking (but chilly) teal waters, a keen birdwatcher, or a historian come to wander amid Neolithic tombs, your needs will be met on this sub-1-sq-mile island.

Herm has worn many hats through millennia of human habitation: a home for seafaring hunter-gatherers and Neolithic farmers, a refuge for monks, a pirate hideaway, a hunting reserve for aristocracy, a granite quarry, and present-day Ramsar wildlife refuge. Take the loop trail around the island to make the most of it, meandering through pine groves, past clifftop puffin nesting sites, and lingering on the white-sand sweep of Shell Beach.

☛ SEE IT ! ***Fast ferries run from St Peter Port, Guernsey. May or September offer good weather without the summer crowds.***

Lizzie Carr's Top Five Places

In 2016 activist, author and adventurer Lizzie Carr became the first person to solo paddleboard the length of England's waterways unsupported. She continues to fight to rid the world of single-use plastic with her Plastic Patrol campaign.

01

ISLES OF SCILLY – This is the first place I ever put a paddle in the water and immediately fell in love with SUP. Sandy beaches, clear blue waters and a peppering of tiny islands make it the perfect location to explore by water.

02

RIVER TRENT – Find tranquil waters in England's landlocked Nottinghamshire as you meander downstream from Farndon through open farmland, rolling hillsides and even sandy bays perfect for picnics.

03

CRESTWELL RIVER, PEMBROKESHIRE – Hidden in the Pembrokeshire Coast National Park, this is dubbed the world's secret waterway. You can paddle through creeks and quarries and it's like a little watery maze.

04

RIVER CAM, CAMBRIDGE – Cambridge is unrivalled when it comes to history and beauty. You've got these incredible bridges and as you paddle below them it's fascinating to see them from the water.

05

ULLSWATER, LAKE DISTRICT – This is where Wordsworth was inspired to write: 'I wandered lonely as a cloud'. You have views of Helvellyn, the third-highest mountain in England, and the pace of life is slow.

© Jon Arnold / Alamy

258

Fall in love with Lavenham, a magic medieval village

EAST ANGLIA // Lavenham casts a magical, medieval spell. Its 15th-century buildings number around three hundred and fan out from the centre, leaning and lurching to dramatic effect. The result is bewitching – an array of beautifully preserved, half-timbered, pargeted and thatched houses, many virtually untouched since the 1400s.

Start in the triangular Market Place, dominated by an early 16th-century guildhall that's home to a local museum. A few steps away sits caramel-coloured, 14th-century Little Hall, where another careful restoration leaves you feeling like you've stepped back in time. Next make a beeline for the magnificently medieval Swan Inn, replete with a latticework of ancient wood. Finally, head to the Airmen's Bar to see the wall bearing the signatures of US pilots based nearby during WWII.

☛ SEE IT ! *Lavenham makes a nice trip from Bury St Edmunds, which has a ruined abbey, a cathedral and a tempting brewery.*

© Paul Quayle / Alamy Stock Photo

259

Admire an awesome view at every turn at Rhossili Bay

SOUTH WALES // Picking the best beach in Wales might seem like mission impossible, but Rhossili Bay could well be it. This three-mile scoop of sand at the Gower's western tip is quite something, backed by dunes where skylarks trill, pummelled by Atlantic surf, and flanked by the heather-flecked heaths of Rhossili Down, from where you can glimpse the outline of Devon on clear days.

The views from Worm's Head peninsula are spirit-lifting, the picnic spots plentiful, and on cloudless days, the pastel-washed sunsets really are worth lingering for. Stride out on the bracing, dog-friendly, 5-mile circular walk and look out for the wishbones of the Helvetica shipwreck at low tide. Finish up with a pint on the terrace at the highly perched Worm's Head Hotel.

☛ SEE IT ! *From Swansea it's an 18-mile drive to Rhossili via the A4118, B4271 and B4247. There's a car park above the bay.*

© Alistair Dick / Getty

260

Peel back layers of history at Bamburgh Castle

NORTHEAST ENGLAND // Looking like the ultimate castle you'd hope to build at the beach, Bamburgh Castle sits atop a basalt outcrop that archaeologists believe humans have visited since 10,000 BC. Today's castle is thought to have been built by Henry II around an 11th-century Norman keep, and was the first English castle to fall during the Wars of the Roses in 1464. Industrialist Lord Armstrong (whose country retreat, Cragside, is #441 on this list) restored it in the late 19th century, and his descendants still live in what is one of the UK's largest inhabited castles.

Inside, palatial staterooms are stuffed with treasures, including 15th-century furniture and ceramics. The neo-Gothic Kings Hall, with its lofty teak-beamed ceiling, and a museum showcasing Lord Armstrong's innovations from armoury to military aircraft, are knockouts.

SEE IT ! *Berwick-upon-Tweed, 19 miles north of Bamburgh, is the nearest main town, reached by bus in under an hour.*

261

Branch out at the National Botanic Garden of Wales

SOUTH WALES // Spreading across a 560-acre Regency Park developed by Sir William Paxton, the National Botanic Garden of Wales commands sensational views across the hills and Towy Valley. Its centrepiece is the Norman Foster-designed Great Glasshouse, the world's largest single-span glasshouse, presenting a thrilling floral romp through California, Australia, the Canaries, Chile, South Africa and the Mediterranean.

And there's more: a double-walled garden showcasing the evolution of flowering plants, an apothecary's garden of healing herbs, a Welsh apple orchard full of uncommon varieties, a bee garden with a behind-the-hive window, a bird of prey centre, and a glasshouse aflutter with rare butterflies. Hands down one of Britain's most phenomenal gardens, it's wholly deserving of a full day's exploration.

SEE IT ! *The garden is a 10-minute drive from the M4 and two minutes from the A48 in Carmarthenshire.*

262

Stargaze in Northumberland National Park

NORTHEAST ENGLAND // True wilderness is a rarity in the UK, which makes this gloriously remote national park (England's least populated) even more special. And dark – its minimal light pollution saw the International Dark Skies Association award the area dark-sky status in 2013. Take in the celestial splendour of shooting stars, comets and constellations at around a dozen dedicated stargazing sites throughout the national park, or get an even closer look at two observatories, Battlesteads Dark Sky Observatory and nearby Kielder Observatory.

SEE IT ! ***Transport is limited in this far-flung area; to do it justice, you'll need your own wheels.***

263

Ramble in Knole, one of England's largest stately homes

SOUTHEAST ENGLAND // Occupying four acres of the Kent Weald, Knole is a monster of a manor house, a 17th-century Kentish ragstone hulk containing hundreds of rooms, many open to visitors, and a priceless art collection including works by Van Dyck and Gainsborough.

Knole is part-owned by the National Trust but the Sackville family still occupy some of it. The best-known member of that dynasty was, of course, writer and poet Vita Sackville-West, who created the elegant gardens at Sissinghurst (#250 on our list).

SEE IT ! ***Sevenoaks is just over half an hour from London by train. The manor is 30 minutes on foot from the station.***

264

Step back into Saxon history at Escomb's village church

NORTHEAST ENGLAND // Little Escomb Church has history in spades. On the northern exterior wall, an upside-down inscription 'LEG VI' (Sixth Legion) and a groove made by a chariot provide clues to its age: the stones used in its construction came from the nearby Roman fort at Binchester (Vinovia to the Romans), and the church is estimated to date to c.670–675. On the southern wall, a sundial is also believed to date from the 7th century. Restorations in the 19th and 20th centuries notwithstanding, this remains the UK's oldest complete Saxon church.

SEE IT ! ***Escomb is 3 miles west of Bishop Auckland, and 14 miles southwest of Durham. There are guided tours during the summer.***

© Harry Green / Alamy

© Steve Vidler / Alamy

© Premierlight Images / Alamy

265

Beware the wicked witch who lurks in the caves of Wookey Hole

SOUTHWEST ENGLAND // Once upon a time, the caves around Wookey Hole were said to be the lair of a wicked witch, who was turned to stone by a plucky local priest. And if you squint a bit, there is at least one rock formation which could (just about) be said to resemble the profile of a petrified hag.

Witches aside, the caves are famous for their impressive array of stalactites and stalagmites, which festoon every inch of the limestone walls, and are either (depending on your point of view) enhanced or ruined by the addition of electric lighting. It's kitsch on overdrive, with attractions ranging from animatronic dinosaurs to a mirror maze, penny arcade and pirate adventure golf. Best to just embrace it – if you're lucky, you might even bump into the witch herself.

☛ SEE IT ! *Wookey Hole is 3 miles northwest of Wells. A day ticket costs £19, but there's 15% off if you book online.*

266

Find sophistication as well as seaside tranquillity at The Mumbles

SOUTH WALES // One of the highest-ranking city districts on this list, The Mumbles is Swansea's and Wales' most well-to-do neighbourhood. Once synonymous with the legendary 'Mumbles Mile' pub crawl, the area is now renowned for its fine restaurants and shops, thanks to developments like oceanfront Oyster Wharf.

Fanning out around 12th-century Oystermouth Castle and culminating in the pretty promontory of Mumbles Head, with its Victorian pier, lighthouse, bays and beaches, the area is remarkably fetching given it all lies within the second-largest city in Wales. Hungry? You're spoilt for choice, but grabbing a fresh fish dish from Gower Seafood Hut and moseying along the prom to find your own al fresco dining spot might be the most quintessentially Mumbles thing to do.

☛ SEE IT ! *Swansea, served by regular trains from London, is 40 miles along the coast from Cardiff. Buses run from central Swansea.*

267

Get your posh on at the Oxford & Cambridge Boat Race

LONDON // This could be one of the world's most predictable races – there are only two competitors, Oxford and Cambridge universities, and one of them wins every year. But people come mainly for the atmosphere and a glimpse of the rarefied lifestyles enjoyed by students at England's two most prestigious seats of learning.

This posh boy's grudge match takes place on the broad curve of the Thames between Putney and Mortlake in late March or early April, attracting mobs of spectators and the occasional protester. Bring some cucumber sandwiches and make a day of it.

☛ SEE IT ! ***Putney Bridge Tube is just yards from the start line. To see the finish live, take an overground train to Mortlake.***

David Lindo's Top Five Places

David Lindo, otherwise known as The Urban Birder, promotes the appreciation and conservation of the birds that share our city lives. He is the author of How to be an Urban Birder *and an ambassador for Leica Sports Optics.*

01

WORMWOOD SCRUBS, WEST LONDON – This 183-acre park is an unexpected inner-city ornithological paradise. It is also the venue that gave birth to The Urban Birder and inspired my love of spotting birds in the city.

02

BARONS HAUGH RSPB RESERVE, MOTHERWELL – Motherwell is not the most picturesque city in the world but this nature reserve is beautiful, with architecturally striking hides and a surprising array of birds.

03

LOCHINDORB, STRATHSPEY – I love this large loch. I always feel that there is something decidedly rare about to be uncovered among the common sandpipers and loafing greylag geese. One day.

04

LOWESTOFT, SUFFOLK – Set on the most easterly point of the UK this town is an exciting place to be in the autumn when migrating birds are passing through. Anything can and has turned up here.

05

HARTLEPOOL HEAD – Announcement: Hartlepool is an urban birding nirvana! I want to buy a house on the headland and spend my days walking around staring into people's gardens looking for birds.

© MH Country / Alamy

268

Revisit old England at the Weald & Downland Living Museum

SOUTHEAST ENGLAND // Open-air museums are a tricky proposition in inclement Britain, but the Weald & Downland Living Museum near Chichester in West Sussex pulls it off. Each of the fifty or so buildings here, representing over 800 years of the southeast's architectural past, were once threatened with the wrecking ball. Instead, they've been painstakingly dismantled and resurrected here – the ticket office, for instance, was moved from Folkestone to make way for the Channel Tunnel. Each of the buildings is brought to life with demonstrations of often defunct trades and crafts. You can also get hands-on, trying your hand at weaving or cooking according to old Sussex recipes. Over the summer, the museum runs living history events on everything from medieval medicine to rare local animal breeds in a family-friendly way.

☛ SEE IT ! *Singleton is around 6 miles north of Chichester, a journey of 20 minutes from the city centre by bus.*

269

Enter the realm of the bizarre at Hawkstone Park Follies

MIDLANDS & THE MARCHES // The brainchild of successive generations of the aptly named Hill family, this undulating estate of woods and sandstone cliffs was developed during the 18th century into a pleasure garden fantasy land. Hawkstone Park's follies are a one-of-a-kind experience: an extravagant, eccentric expanse of Gothic arches, grottos and gardens, plus arresting geological features, all fashioned into points of interest with liberal amounts of romantic-era sensibility. The park's creators clearly cared deeply about their vision without taking themselves too seriously: check the tongue-in-cheek names of park features and the story about the real hermit once stationed in the Hermitage for visitors' amusement. Oh, and the point? Not much, besides providing guests with some playful entertainment.

☛ SEE IT ! *Get a respite from the foolish fun of the follies at the park's upscale hotel, Hawkstone Park. It's all 13 miles north of Shrewsbury.*

270

Walk the gilded decks of the Royal Yacht Britannia

EDINBURGH // Masterminded in a shipyard in Glasgow, the irony isn't lost that the final resting place of the former floating palace of Queen Elizabeth II is in Edinburgh. After it was decommissioned in 1997, Britannia was permanently anchored in Leith, not Clydebank. You'll come for the interiors – the five decks range from swanky State Apartments, where kings, queens and world leaders were wined and dined, to the steam-powered Engine Room. To lord it up like a royal, feast on a cream tea at the Royal Deck Tea Room.

SEE IT ! ***The Royal Yacht welcomes 400,000 visitors a year. Avoid the crowds with a midweek visit.***

© Hemis / Alamy Stock Photo

271

Commune with the sunrise on Glastonbury Tor

SOUTHWEST ENGLAND // Ask a local on Glastonbury's high street what lies under the legendary hill just outside town, and you'll get all sorts of answers. Some say it's the Isle of Avalon, where King Arthur sleeps until his nation calls again. Others that it's a mystical nexus where ley lines meet. A few maintain it's the home of Arawn or Gwyn ap Nudd, the faerie king of the Celtic underworld. One thing's for sure: Glastonbury Tor provides a knockout view over the Somerset Levels, especially at sunrise, when the land is cloaked in a blanket of silver, swirling mist.

SEE IT ! ***Walk to the tor from the centre of Glastonbury; the main trail starts on Well House Lane.***

© Radomir Rezny / Shutterstock

© Alamy Stock Photo

272

Drift through East London on the Regent's Canal

LONDON // When it comes to canals, London may not be Venice, or even Birmingham, but the snaking course of the Regent's Canal is still a much-loved back route from the capital's western suburbs to the East End. Indeed, plenty of narrowboat-living Londoners call it home, and thousands more jog or commute along its towpaths every day.

Walking east from Angel, you pass hip little coffee bars, bohemian art projects and a string of cheerful waterside boozers. Along the way, you can veer off at Broadway Market for superior eats, Kingsland Rd for top-notch Vietnamese, or Victoria Park for lungfuls of clean(ish) air.

Most narrowboat tours operate from Camden, but the London Canal Museum runs trips through the spooky Islington Tunnel in summer, and you can watch boats navigating the locks and channels year-round.

TRY IT ! ***For the trip east, pick up the Regent's Canal at Angel Tube. Return via Haggerston or Cambridge Heath Overground stations.***

© Banana Pancake / Alamy

273

Spot wild choughs on the cliffs above Kynance Cove

SOUTHWEST ENGLAND // Even in a place as scenery-spoiled as Cornwall, Kynance really takes some beating. A perfect little cove, edged by black cliffs, grassy headlands and rugged islands, it's famous for the brilliant, blazing blue of its waters: on a warm summer's day, this is as near as Cornwall gets to the Mediterranean, and a favourite hang-out for sunbathers and swimmers (the beach cafe is a cracker, too). But there's another reason to make the journey here. The cliffs above Kynance are a great spot to spy wild choughs – a close cousin of the crow that's distinguished by its bright orange beak and legs, and features on Cornwall's official coat-of-arms. Careful conservation has gradually helped chough numbers recover from the threat of extinction – and several nesting pairs now call Kynance home.

SEE IT ! ***National Trust-owned Kynance Cove is on the remote Lizard Peninsula: look for signs a couple of miles before Lizard Point.***

A competitor gets into the swing of the hammer-throwing contest at the Braemar Gathering

274

Dance a Highland fling at the Braemar Gathering

HIGHLANDS & ISLANDS // Whoosh! A hammer whizzes through the air, scaring the bejesus out of a buzzard circling above. Whish! A hum murmurs around the grounds as a stone is released with a neck-cracking spin. Whirl! A caber, a rough-trimmed tree trunk, hurtles skyward, before crash landing in the dirt.

Hammers. Putting the Stone. Tossing the Caber. These are some of the perplexing, hoof-it-the-hard-way events at the Braemar Gathering, a Highland Games where Celtic wits and willpower are tested in the wilds of the Cairngorms. Forgive the hyperbole, but this is Scotland's own Olympics, time-honoured since 1832 and dazzling spectators with more bagpipe reels than most Scots can fit in a lifetime.

It's not just the tug o' war, track races and dances jigged over heavy-handed claymore swords that attract visitors to the one-day event (held on the first Saturday in September). They come for the gorgeous River Dee setting, too. The amount of tartan on display is arguably unforgivable, but it's easy to get swept up in the festive atmosphere – in these parts, they know a thing or two about having a good time.

☛ SEE IT ! ***Braemar is 59 miles east of Aberdeen and 93 miles north of Edinburgh.***

© Richard Hilsden / Alamy

275

See the suburbs turn wild in Leicester's Bradgate Park

MIDLANDS & THE MARCHES // For what is essentially a city park, a couple of miles northwest of Leicester's suburbs, Bradgate Park is nothing short of spectacular. Equivalent to New York's Central Park in size, the scale of this tract of heathland, a designated SSSI (Site of Special Scientific Interest) with a 500-strong herd of wild deer, extensive woodlands, a river and a reservoir, not to mention a ruined Elizabethan mansion and an 18th-century folly, plonks it firmly in the premier league of the UK's urban green spaces.

SEE IT ! ***Leave your car in the Newtown Linford car park, 5 miles northwest of Leicester on the south side of Bradgate Park.***

© Hufton + Crow / Alamy

276

Mix a gin martini to lift the spirits at Laverstoke Mill

SOUTHERN ENGLAND // Laverstoke Mill in Hampshire is the home of Bombay Sapphire, the premium gin brand distinguished by its bright blue bottles. There's been a mill on this site since at least AD 903, and more recently it's been converted by the cutting-edge designer Thomas Heatherwick into a model of modern-meets-old industrial architecture. But for connoisseurs, it's the gin that matters – and there's a range of spirit-based experiences on offer, from self-guided tours to tutored tastings, distillery visits and cocktail masterclasses.

SEE IT ! ***The distillery is between Andover and Basingstoke. A shuttle bus runs from the train stations at Overton and Micheldever.***

277

Journey into myth at Fingal's Cave on Staffa

HIGHLANDS & ISLANDS // From a distance, Fingal's Cave looks as if it's been plumbed from the depths of the earth. At first, you're met by a 230ft cathedral of stone, then a cliff face of fractured columns shaped like a church organ. What follows is a one-two punch of sea spray and blast of cool air as your boat bounces past the cave's entrance. It's a puzzle of mind-bending symmetry, and after landing you follow the causeway deep into the cave's mouth, a magical journey that's inspired Wordsworth, Keats, Verne and Scott.

☛ SEE IT ! ***Trips can be arranged from Oban or Mull, with several companies offering combined tours of Staffa and Iona.***

© Lebrecht Music & Arts / Alamy

278

Sample treasures of France at the Wallace Collection

LONDON // This stunning small museum was the private home of Sir Richard Wallace, whose family was one of the biggest buyers of French treasures from the *ancien régime* in the revolutionary sales held after the fall of Louis XVI. Accordingly, the bijou stately home is stuffed to the rafters with paintings by the likes of Titian, Rembrandt and Delacroix, alongside snuffboxes, bronzes, and one of the best collections of arms and armour in the country, including extravagantly decorated weaponry that Wallace purchased for a song from the Louvre's fleeing director.

☛ SEE IT ! ***The Wallace is on Manchester Sq, north of Bond St Tube; turn into the backstreets of Marylebone by the side of Selfridges.***

© Courtesy of the Wallace Collection

© eye35.pix / Alamy

279

Get a taste for the Cotswolds in Stow-on-the-Wold

OXFORD & THE COTSWOLDS // Strategically perched on the Roman Fosse Way, at the junction of a mere six roads, little, enterprising Stow-on-the-Wold pulls together the key calling cards of the classic Cotswolds market town: a grand square, a twice-monthly market, a medieval church (whose door is rumoured to have inspired that of JRR Tolkien's Moria in *Lord of the Rings*), the odd boutique hotel, and a smattering of galleries, tea rooms, local-produce shops and just-rustic-enough, curl-up-by-the-fire pubs.

Wandering between tall-walled alleys once used to funnel sheep and ogling handsome Cotswold-stone buildings overflowing with flowerpots, you'll feel fully immersed in the Cotswolds lifestyle. Make time to feast on home-baked cakes and linger over a cuppa, before heading out for a hike over the softly rolling hills of the northern Cotswolds. For the ultimate chic Cotswolds scene, head four miles east to Daylesford: deli, cafe, nursery, spa and cookery school all rolled into one.

SEE IT ! ***Stow-on-the-Wold is 4 miles southwest of Moreton-in-Marsh, which has good train connections.***

© Philip Kieran / Alamy

280

Find watery wonder at Fountains Abbey & Studley Royal

YORKSHIRE // Every garden should have a water feature. But few can approach the scale and spectacle of Studley Royal. Its 800 acres of perfectly groomed lawns and neatly trimmed woodland are adorned with a succession of landscaped lakes, canals, streams and cascades so vast that the picturesque ruins of 12th-century Fountains Abbey – one of Europe's largest Cistercian foundations – is reduced to the status of a garden ornament. Built in the 18th century by a disgraced politician following his expulsion from parliament, the park gained Unesco World Heritage status in 1986 due partly to meeting the test of 'being a masterpiece of human creative genius'.

This masterpiece is best explored on foot by hiking one of the many trails that link the abbey ruins to neoclassical follies such as the Temple of Piety, the spooky Serpentine Tunnel, and the gorgeous St Mary's Church, designed by William Burgess (look out for his trademark mouse carved into the stone).

SEE IT ! ***Fountains Abbey and Studley Royal lie 4 miles west of Ripon. The park is huge; devote a full day to a visit.***

281

Feed feathered friends at Slimbridge Wetland Centre

OXFORD & THE COTSWOLDS // Slimbridge is the perfect stopover for birds migrating from Greenland, Russia or elsewhere in the Arctic. So for birdwatchers, it's the perfect spot to see winged wildlife, especially waders and water-lovers, from grebes and plovers to spoonbills and avocets, as well as the reserve's famous Bewick's swans. Even if you're not an ornithologist, Slimbridge is still entertaining and (shh, whisper it) educational for kids and adults alike. Who can fail to enjoy hand-feeding the ducks, admiring the pelicans, and playing a game of flamingo bingo?

☛ SEE IT ! ***Slimbridge is on the River Severn floodplain west of the Cotswolds. The nearest town is Dursley.***

282

Have a medieval retail experience in Chester Rows

NORTHWEST ENGLAND // Chester's most attractive feature is the cruciform Rows, the two-level half-timbered galleries along the four streets that fan out from the Central Cross. Although galleries with shops were common in the Middle Ages, the Chester Rows are unique in the world for their assumed Roman origin, split-level construction and relatively intact appearance – even if only a handful (like the Three Old Arches in Bridge St) have survived Tudor and Victorian refurbishment. They house a fine array of independently owned shops.

☛ SEE IT ! ***The Rows are reached by steps along Watergate St, Northgate St, Eastgate St and Bridge St.***

283

Be captivated by the quirkiness of Hebden Bridge

YORKSHIRE // Eat your heart out Hoxton. West Yorkshire's Hebden Bridge was a haven of hipsterdom long before the modern-day 'hipster' was a thing. This attractive former factory town, set along the narrow banks of the River Calder and the Rochdale Canal, offers its resident academics, artists, environmentalists and sizeable gay community a a quirky bohemian vibe thanks to an appealing range of vintage shops, pottery studios, organic and vegan cafes, and secondhand bookshops. And don't miss an evening at the Trades Club, a classic live-music venue.

☛ SEE IT ! ***The road to Hebden Bridge suffers badly from traffic congestion – better to take the train from Leeds.***

© Christina Bollen / Alamy

The walls and ramparts of Corfe Castle in Dorset were all but destroyed in the 17th century

284

Re-live the Civil War at Corfe Castle

SOUTHWEST ENGLAND // Whether seen at sunrise or sunset, in high summer or the depths of midwinter, the crumbling silhouette of Corfe Castle looks like a scene from a Turner painting: a moody, tumbledown ruin perched on a grassy hilltop above its eponymous village, perfectly framed against a panorama of sea and sky.

It's also a fascinating slice of history: originally built during the 11th century, the castle was besieged several times during the English Civil War, before being blown to smithereens by Parliamentarian forces in 1645 (aristocratic owners the Bankes subsequently moved to Kingston Lacy nearby). It's been a romantic ruin ever since, and though only a few walls and the remains of the central keep now stand, lovingly maintained by the National Trust, it all feels convincingly medieval. Close your eyes and you could almost imagine you've walked out onto the set of *Monty Python & the Holy Grail* – though last time we visited, the Knights Who Say Ni must have been off on their tea break. Nevertheless, it makes a cracking picture and a memorable day out.

SEE IT ! ***There are buses from Poole, Wareham and Swanage, and the Swanage Steam Railway stops in the village.***

285

Find poetry at the Wordsworth Museum, Grasmere

CUMBRIA // The unofficial HQ of the British Romantic movement in the first decade of the 19th century was this creeper-clad cottage where poet William Wordsworth lived with his wife, sister and three children. The house is (roughly) as Wordsworth would have known it, and it is full of his personal belongings, including his chaise longue and writing desk, as well as a trove of other objects like his passport and spectacles. The museum next door houses one of the country's best collections relating to the Romantics and includes a stack of original manuscripts.

☛ SEE IT ! *The National Trust is closing the house and museum until 2020 for repairs. Check the website for details of its phased reopening.*

286

Find your inner Flopsy at Hill Top, Lake District

CUMBRIA // Beatrix Potter's idyllic farmhouse (think climbing ivy, thick walls and lots of Potter memorabilia) stars in some of her best-loved tales, including those of Samuel Whiskers, Tom Kitten, Pigling Bland and Jemima Puddle-Duck, while the kitchen garden made an appearance in Peter Rabbit. She bequeathed the house to the National Trust before her death, on condition that they maintain it exactly as it was. As a result, Hill Top is one of the Lake District's most popular museums, with regular queues of Potter fans waiting patiently to get a peek.

☛ SEE IT ! *The house is in the village of Near Sawrey, 2 miles south of Hawkshead.*

287

Season a perfect English day with a ploughman's lunch

SOUTHERN ENGLAND // Pick the right day in spring or summer, when the sun is out, the air is fragrant with blooming flowers and birds flit through the hedgerows, and if you're at a rural English pub, waiting for a ploughman's lunch to be delivered to your outside table, count yourself blessed. A ploughman's lunch in its simplest form comprises a hunk of bread, a chunk of cheddar cheese, pickle and salad. Add a pint of local ale and settle down at an outside table to absorb the sights and smells of the archetypal English summer.

☛ EAT IT ! *The 17th-century Harrow Inn is between Steep and Sheet in northeast Hampshire, close to the cricket ground and tennis club.*

288

Recharge to the sea's symphony at Aldeburgh

EAST ANGLIA // To the left and right, Aldeburgh's shingle beach runs as far as the eye can see; the sea fills the space in between. In this expansive place, the elements are hard to ignore but switching off is easy. Behind you, pastel-coloured houses and fresh fish kiosks line the shore; quaint streets are filled with galleries and independent stores. Wander north on the beach to Maggi Hambling's *Scallop*, two 13ft-high steel shells featuring lines from an opera by local hero Benjamin Britten. Finish with the best fish supper in town at the Fish & Chip Shop.

☛ SEE IT ! ***Visit in June to experience a prestigious classical music event: the Aldeburgh Festival, founded by Benjamin Britten in 1948.***

© Kimjanel / Shutterstock

289

Dive into the World Bog Snorkelling Championships

MID-WALES // Some 34 years ago, deep in the muddy, rain-lashed, sheep-dotted moors of mid-Wales, folk looked across the bleak, sodden land and came up with a cunning plan to liven things up: the World Bog Snorkelling Championships was conceived.

In Llanwrtyd Wells, on the last Sunday in August, you can grease up, slap on a snorkel, fancy-dress outfit and novelty hat and plunge into a tea-coloured bog, along with hundreds of equally bonkers bog snorkellers from all over the world.

☛ SEE IT ! ***Llanwrtyd Wells is north of the Brecon Beacons on the A483, and has a railway station on the Heart of Wales Line.***

290

Take a snap of an archetypal castle at Bodiam

SOUTHEAST ENGLAND // Just like a child's drawing of a castle, Bodiam in East Sussex is a turreted stone stronghold with a keep and corner towers surrounded by a kitschy moat. This fantastically photogenic fortress was built in the 14th century to defend the south from French menace, but passed from the last owner Lord Curzon to the National Trust in 1925. It was Curzon who carried out extensive renovation to the structure, the castle's turrets and crenellations returned to their original glory using local stone.

☛ SEE IT ! ***Local buses run between Hastings and Hawkhurst. In summer, a steam railway operates from Tenterden to Bodiam.***

One brave soul negotiates the rope bridge that sways 100ft above the Co Antrim coastline

291

Test your nerve on the Carrick-a-Rede Rope Bridge, Co Antrim

NORTHERN IRELAND // It takes some nerve to take the first tentative steps across the swaying rope bridge that spans the 65ft chasm between the mainland sea cliffs and the small rocky island of Carrick-a-Rede. The wind whistles through the knotted rope lengths that hold up the bridge, while gaps between the wooden slats reveal dark water almost 100ft below. Dare to look down and you might spot basking sharks, dolphins and porpoises.

The narrow rope bridge was first erected more than 350 years ago by fishermen, who used it to cross to the island to catch Atlantic salmon. Declining fish stocks mean these days the bridge is used only by thrill seekers; the last salmon was caught here in 2002. An atmospheric former fisherman's cottage on the island has been preserved and is open some weekends.

The island lies at the end of a mile-long walk via a rocky coastal path through windswept grasslands, with steps descending down to the bridge. Once on Carrick-a-Rede, peer over the cliffs and look out for seabirds before fortifying yourself for the return trip. Vertigo sufferers need not apply.

SEE IT ! ***The footpath to the bridge is near Ballintoy on the north Antrim coast road. Buses run from Ballycastle and Coleraine.***

© Dan Bridge / Getty

© Carly Jane / Alamy

292

Get spooked in one of the Magnificent Seven cemeteries

LONDON // Within just 50 years of the start of the 19th century, London's population had more than doubled, and deceased residents were being unceremoniously buried in small, past-capacity parish churchyards. Inspired by the Père Lachaise cemetery in Paris, British entrepreneurs used land on what was then the outskirts of suburban London to create seven private cemeteries: Kensal Green, West Norwood, Highgate, Abney Park, Nunhead, Brompton and Tower Hamlets. Today, these spaces are part burial ground, part nature reserve, having been left to flourish undisturbed. Highgate is the jewel in the crown; no expense was spared in constructing the gargantuan mausoleums along Egyptian Avenue. The eastern grounds, resting place of Karl Marx, Douglas Adams and other well-known names, can be explored by candlelight on All Saints' Day.

SEE IT ! *Each of the cemeteries offers its own guided walks, events and open days, so check their respective websites before you visit.*

293

Dine out in the capital at 3am at Duck & Waffle

LONDON // Forget the city that never sleeps – London is often at home and making a cup of tea by midnight. Few places beyond greasy takeaways welcome the ultra-late-night crowd, which makes it such a treat that Duck & Waffle, one of the capital's finest restaurants, never closes its doors. Perched on the 40th floor of the Heron Tower, the restaurant has commanding views across the entire city – eye up the neighbouring skyscrapers and admire the twinkling lights through the floor-to-ceiling windows. Don't miss Duck & Waffle's namesake dish, an American-style waffle topped with a succulent confit duck leg and a fried duck egg, all ready to be doused in mustard maple syrup. There's nothing more delightfully indulgent than raising a toast with a champagne cocktail as you watch the sun awaken the city far below.

EAT IT ! *The nearest Tube station is Liverpool Street. It's worth booking a table in advance, no matter when you plan to visit.*

294

Mountain-bike the hard way on the 7stanes network

SOUTHERN SCOTLAND // It's too late to turn back as your mountain bike rollercoasters downhill, past swathes of pine and over obstacles. All that remains now is one final descent, taking you through a wooded chicane of sweeping bends, before you're slapped in the face with pure exhilaration. Sound tempting? This is the routine at Glentress, the mountain-biking centre near Peebles, and a highlight of the 7stanes network of seven centres spread from the Borders to Dumfries and Galloway. Biking novice? The instructors will shape you up in no time.

TRY IT ! *The 7stanes centres include Mabie, Forest of Ae, Dalbeattie, Glentrool, Glentress, Newcastleton and Kirroughtree.*

© Chris Strickland / Alamy

295

Flinch at The Old Operating Theatre & Herb Garret Museum

LONDON // Anyone who has ever seen an old Hammer movie will feel a frisson of recognition on visiting the Old Operating Theatre & Herb Garret Museum. In the 19th century, trainee medics squeezed through narrow doors to watch the surgeon's art, live and spurting, in an operating theatre that's precisely the kind of place that would have inspired a young Victor Frankenstein. The adjacent herb garret is likely where he would have carried out his forbidden experiments; hung with medicinal herbs, it's one of the most atmospheric spaces in London.

SEE IT ! *The Old Operating Theatre is tucked around the back of London Bridge station.*

© Doug McKinlay / Lonely Planet

296

Meet the authors at Cheltenham's yearly literary extravaganza

OXFORD & THE COTSWOLDS // Each October, about 1000 authors, scholars and other creatives descend on the 18th-century spa town of Cheltenham for its 10-day booktastic literature festival, which in recent years has hosted events with luminaries such as David Attenborough, Hillary Clinton, Chimamanda Ngozi Adichie (*below*), Philip Pullman, Jacqueline Wilson, Michael Morpurgo and Darcey Bussell – to name just a few in the star-studded line-up. Celebrating its 70th birthday in 2019, it is one of the world's oldest literary festivals (and the UK's original).

SEE IT ! ***Cheltenham has good train connections with many towns and cities. It's around two and a half hours' drive from London.***

© Courtesy of the Cheltenham Literary Festival

297

Shop till you drop in Brighton's North Laine

SOUTHEAST ENGLAND // In the market for some vegetarian shoes, a retro wedding dress, a chocolate broomstick... You'll find these and much, much more in Brighton's North Laine. Hundreds of independent shops line the narrow streets of this part of the city – highlights include junk shop Snoopers Paradise, crammed with quality secondhand paraphernalia, the Beyond Retro vintage clothes market, and Jump the Gun, a gentleman's tailor specialising in mod attire. The North Laine is also home to some popular, veggie-friendly places to eat.

SEE IT ! ***Brighton has frequent train connections with London and towns in the southeast. Weekday mornings are best for shopping.***

© Simon Dack / Alamy

298

Feel like a Cockney with pie and mash at an F Cooke shop

LONDON // The story of pie and mash is the story of working-class London. Inhabitants of East End tenements would fuel their labours with stodgy meat pies, drowned in eel jelly gravy made from the eels from the Thames. One of just a handful of original London pie shops still in business, with outlets in Hoxton and Broadway Market, F Cooke is an institution, beloved of East End pensioners, market traders and the odd foodie outsider. These days, the 'liquor' is less eel-y than it used to be, but the pies are as solid as ever, and we mean that in a good way.

EAT IT ! *F Cooke is a piece of old London, clinging on in hipster Hoxton; walk there from Old Street Tube or Hoxton Overground.*

© Alamy Stock Photo

© Alamy Stock Photo

299

Get into training at York's National Railway Museum

YORKSHIRE // York's National Railway Museum is the biggest in the world, and full of stuff that will fascinate even if your eyes don't mist over at the thought of a 4-6-2 A1 Pacific class thundering into a tunnel. Highlights include the gorgeously streamlined Mallard, holder of the world speed record for a steam locomotive (set in 1938 at 126mph); and the world-famous Flying Scotsman, the first steam engine to break the 100mph barrier. Extend your visit with a trip to York Minster, appropriately connected to the museum by a tourist road train.

SEE IT ! *The museum is only five minutes' walk west of York train station.*

300–399

300

Patrol the ramparts of Unesco-listed Caernarfon Castle

NORTH WALES // Cited as Europe's best example of 13th-century military architecture, Caernarfon Castle dwarfs the surrounding town with its Brobdingnagian ring of uniquely polygonal towers thrusting heftily into the Menai Strait. If the fortress dimensions seem intimidating today, imagine how much more so they would have appeared when English King Edward I erected them in 1283. The monarch intended the design to emulate the mighty walls of Constantinople and drum home to the locals that England now ruled the roost in Wales.

SEE IT ! *Visit in summer via the beautiful Ffestiniog & Welsh Highland Railway from Porthmadog.*

© PayPal / Getty Images

© Chris Hepburn / Getty Images

301

Explore the historic Albert Dock, Liverpool

NORTHWEST ENGLAND // Liverpool's waterfront is a Unesco World Heritage site, and at its heart is Albert Dock, ringed on three sides by rust-red columns and handsome five-storey warehouses that once served the world's busiest port. The stevedores are long gone but some of the warehouses now house many of the city's best museums, including the International Slavery Museum, the Merseyside Maritime Museum, the Beatles Story and the northern branch of the Tate art gallery. Between them are a mix of cafes and restaurants, a boutique bakery and a couple of pop-up shops.

Immediately north of the dock on Pier Head is the impressive Museum of Liverpool, an eye-catching building but one that doesn't hold a candle to the city's architectural showstoppers a little further north. The Three Graces is the collective name given to the trio of Edwardian buildings that have dominated Pier Head since the turn of the 20th century, when the city was still a major maritime force: the Port of Liverpool, the Cunard and the Royal Liver buildings – with the last topped by the Liver Bird that is the city's symbol.

SEE IT ! *The Albert Dock is at the western edge of the city centre, about 500 yards from the huge Liverpool ONE shopping centre.*

Live life in the slow lane on the Kennet and Avon Canal at Bathampton in Somerset

302

Ride the Avon Ring by narrowboat

MIDLANDS & THE MARCHES // A canal is a staple of any self-respecting best-of-British tour – given the UK has one of the most historic and extensive canal systems in the world – and the Avon Ring is the network's most popular round trip. In the heart of the area that gave us the Industrial Revolution, the Avon Ring and its four constituent waterways of rivers Avon and Severn, the Worcester and Birmingham Canal and the Stratford-upon-Avon Canal, were always at the centre of canal technology, and a highlight of the voyage is navigating Britain's longest flight of locks (30 all-told!) at Tardebigge.

The drama heightens still further with the chug into the winsome, timber-framed town of Stratford-upon-Avon, birthplace of William Shakespeare, where you can moor at Bancroft Basin, across the park from the town's two famous theatres. The historic destinations of Worcester, with its grand cathedral, and Tewkesbury, with its abbey, plus dozens of picturesque villages and country pubs in-between, help make up this memorable 109-mile, 129-lock run, and present the Midlands in their utmost glory.

TRY IT ! ***Several firms on the Avon Ring hire out narrowboats; try Calcutt Boats, a day's cruise from Stratford-upon-Avon.***

303

Hike and cycle through the Ribble Valley

NORTHWEST ENGLAND // Occupying much of northern Lancashire, the Ribble Valley is all rolling hills and a huge, grouse-filled moorland known as the Forest of Bowland, from ancient days when it was a royal hunting ground. Collectively known as 'Little Switzerland', the Ribble Valley and its collection of handsome market towns and villages (home to some of the northwest's best restaurants and places to stay) is an Arcadian antidote to the concrete spread in the south of the county… and one of the region's most popular walking and cycling spots.

SEE IT ! ***Buses from Preston and Blackburn run to Clitheroe Interchange, and there are regular trains from Manchester.***

304

Sharpen your wits at the Derwent Pencil Museum, Keswick

CUMBRIA // A pencil museum, you say? Well, Keswick is where the first graphite pencil was invented in the 17th century, so it's fitting that there should be a museum to mark such an important breakthrough. Besides learning about the history of the humble pencil (which is neither dull nor pointless) you can feast your eyes on one of the world's largest (26ft), gawp at the Queen's diamond-encrusted Jubilee pencil and examine the collection of WWII writing tools, complete with secret maps hidden inside. They also run art workshops for all ages throughout the year.

SEE IT ! ***The museum is at Southey Works, off Carding Mill Lane just north of Keswick town.***

305

Become a world champion stone-skimmer on Easdale

HIGHLANDS & ISLANDS // Disused slate quarries, a decaying pier and a lonely pub. Hardly makes for an intriguing trip, does it? But there's a profound 'but' to visiting Easdale, the smallest permanently inhabited island in the Inner Hebrides. This car-free outcrop welcomes you with a dramatic ferry crossing and unrivalled views of the Firth of Lorn. And the flooded quarries are used both for the unlikely-sounding World Stone Skimming Championships and as a home for a thriving population of birdlife. No matter man's intentions, nature overcomes.

SEE IT ! ***The World Stone Skimming Championships takes place in September. Ferries run from Ellenabeich.***

306

Freewheel along Alderney's rugged, windswept coast

CHANNEL ISLANDS // The windswept shores of remote Alderney provide clues to the island's past role as an important strategic naval base. Perfect beaches are bookended with crumbling Victorian forts and the rusting metal of Nazi fortifications. Cycle along the 10-mile coastal loop, pausing to peek into gaping bunkers at Bibette Head, climb the Mannez lighthouse and admire the beaches of Corblets and Braye Bay. Near the airport, take the unpaved path to the top of the western cliffs to hear the clamour of the offshore Les Etacs gannet colony.

TRY IT ! ***Rent an electric bicycle or else cycle the loop clockwise to avoid the steep climb up Tourgis Hill near the airport.***

© PJ photography / Shutterstock

307

Discover the perfect Cotswolds town in Painswick

OXFORD & THE COTSWOLDS // The sinking sun casts an eerie glow across a web of gently sloping streets, flanked by medieval inns and stone houses and backed by a 14th-century Perpendicular Gothic wool church, encircled by tombs and 99 lollipop-like yew trees. Though there's strong competition, Painswick is up there with the Cotswolds' prettiest towns – but shh, its undiscovered-ness is a big part of the charm. Explore England's only rococo garden, an exquisite 1740s Benjamin Hyett creation strewn with Gothic follies, and seek out the delightfully old-world Woolpack pub in the teensy neighbouring village of Slad, a long-standing favourite of writer Laurie Lee, who channelled the area's bucolic beauty into *Cider with Rosie*. See it for yourself on the famous Cotswold Way, with wonderful walks fanning out from Painswick into the surrounding countryside.

SEE IT ! *If you aren't driving, hop on a train to nearby Stroud or Cheltenham. Painswick is connected to both by bus.*

© Paul Richardson / Alamy

308

Smell the smoke on the North Yorkshire Moors Railway

YORKSHIRE // All aboard! The cry of the guard, the hoot of a steam whistle and the clanking of carriage couplings mark the beginning of your journey back into England's past. The UK's most popular heritage railway runs for 18 miles from Pickering to Whitby, passing through a landscape little changed in the last hundred years. Lovingly restored steam locomotives pull period carriages with wood-panelled compartments, calling at stations which have been restored to different periods in time – Pickering (1937), Levisham (1912), Goathland (1922) and Grosmont (1950s). Goathland is the most popular stop, having starred as Hogsmeade station in the Harry Potter films.

Don't miss the chance to get off and walk around, or even between, stations (Goathland to Grosmont is only 4 miles) – half the buzz is seeing the old steam trains puffing through the landscape.

TRY IT ! *Book online the day before travel to get a 10% discount and sidestep ticket office queues.*

© Jon Sparks / Alamy

© Chris Willson / Alamy

309

Tower over a slice of Shropshire at Ludlow Castle

MIDLANDS & THE MARCHES // With a gorgeous black-and-white timber-framed town like Ludlow, picking highlights can be hard, but few would question Ludlow Castle's dominance over the woodsy, wending valley of the River Teme. Domination was the only way to survive in the once-dangerous Welsh Marches, and Ludlow Castle rose to the occasion. This ring of 11th-century ramparts peeps above the treeline with the topography that once so impeccably protected the castle – the surrounding hillsides and river – now enhancing its appeal, along with the festivals regularly happening within its grounds.

SEE IT ! ***Ludlow is connected by rail via the Welsh Marches Line to Shrewsbury, 27 miles north and Hereford, 23 miles south.***

310

Sample authentic gingerbread from Sarah Nelson's Shop

CUMBRIA // Besides wistful poets, Grasmere's other great tradition is gingerbread, pioneered in the middle of the 19th century by local baker Sarah Nelson, who began producing the half-biscuit, half-cake delight in tiny Church Cottage in 1854. Nearly 170 years later, Sarah's descendants have resisted the urge to streamline the production to a more modern, off-site facility and insist on making gingerbread much as Sarah did, in the cramped kitchen using her (secret) recipe and even some of the original utensils. Staff don frilly pinafores and starched bonnets for maximum authenticity. The gingerbread, needless to say, is delicious.

EAT IT ! ***Grasmere is in the heart of the Lake District, 17 miles northwest of Kendal. Find the tiny shop in the middle of Grasmere.***

Majestic Tintern Abbey glories in its heritage and setting; see it at its glorious best from across the river in England

311

Feel spirituality flow from the riverside ruin of Tintern Abbey

SOUTH WALES // William Wordsworth was among the first to romanticise these abbey ruins on a meander along the woodland-flanked River Wye, in his poem 'Lines Composed a Few Miles Above Tintern Abbey': '...Once again / Do I behold these steep and lofty cliffs,/ That on a wild secluded scene impress / Thoughts of more deep seclusion...'

But Tintern Abbey had been drawing visitors for centuries before Wordsworth wrote his evocative verses. Established in 1131 by the Cistercian monks, renowned for choosing bucolic spots to build their churches, Tintern was only their second monastery on British shores. Most of the remaining ruins, apexed by the enchanting abbey church, hail from the 1130s to the 1530s, when the Dissolution of the Monasteries halted development. After ambling through the ancient arches and checking out the remarkable amount of surviving ornamentation, take time to appreciate these ruins from afar. Cross the river (into England!) and climb up through the woods, a designated AONB, to the Devil's Pulpit viewpoint: from here, the abbey takes centre stage in a sweeping, spectacular panorama.

SEE IT ! ***Tintern Abbey is in Tintern village, 5 miles north of Chepstow. Bus 69 runs there from Chepstow bus station.***

312

Wreck-dive WWI destroyers at Scapa Flow

HIGHLANDS & ISLANDS // Down, down, down you descend, until the darkness envelops you. What lies beneath gives enough of a thrill when you hear about it on land, but immersed in the icy currents, the excitement causes you to dragon-puff the air through your regulator with double quick time. Then, out of the gloom, emerges a ghostly German warship, scuttled on the seabed following the end of WWI.

To unpack this astonishing story, rewind to 21 June 1919, when the British had interred a German U-boat fleet on the Orkney Islands while negotiations took place over the ships' fate. Fearing the fleet would be seized, Admiral Ludwig von Reuter decided to sink the lot – with 52 of the 74 vessels claimed by Scapa Flow.

While many were salvaged, three 580ft-long battleships, four cruisers and a destroyer still remain frozen in time up to 148ft below the surface, creating one of Europe's premier wreck diving sites. You'll have to pinch yourself to believe it's real – but you'll also have to have a valid PADI Advanced Open Water qualification and recent drysuit experience in order to dive.

☛ TRY IT ! ***Scapa Scuba is Orkney's only dedicated dive centre.***

Jonny Bealby's Top Five Places

Film-maker and Royal Geographical Society lecturer Jonny Bealby is the founder of adventure-travel firm Wild Frontiers. He has done the old Silk Road by horse, searched for the mythical Kafiristan on foot, and biked from London to Cape Town.

01

SOUTH DOWNS NATIONAL PARK – I just love the fact that a 45-minute drive from London brings you to a place that could be the wilds of Scotland. It's great for a Sunday walk, and there are numerous pubs to enjoy a good lunch in afterwards.

02

CAMBER SANDS, EAST SUSSEX – While Britain might not be known for its beaches, this is a classic – endless sand and a vast open sky. It's the perfect place to go for a ride, a windsurf or a walk with the dog.

03

YORKSHIRE DALES – My parents-in-law recently bought a place in Skipton. When life gets too stressful, I head there to walk across the Dales. I particularly like Malham Cove, a wonderfully weird geological feature.

04

CHELTENHAM – For a weekend away, this beautiful spa town is easy to get to from London, has great museums – did you know Gustav Holst was born here? – lovely parks, epic Regency buildings and a Michelin-starred restaurant.

05

BOROUGH MARKET – For a lover of fine cuisine this place is great, an exciting cacophony of fine-food traders in the heart of the city. What you'll find there will delight the taste buds of any self-confessed foodie.

© Bernard Philpot / Alamy

© Malcolm McDougall Photography / Alamy

313

Drop in on the Bloomsbury Group at Charleston

SOUTHEAST ENGLAND // England's southeast may be chock-a-block with the stylish homes of yesterday's famous figures, but Charleston in the South Downs National Park is a unique place, a time capsule where art and beauty always took centre stage.

Painters Vanessa Bell and Duncan Grant, Bell's two children and Grant's lover David Garnett moved into the house in 1916. Charleston soon became the rural meeting place for the Bloomsbury Group, including Roger Fry, Virginia Woolf and JM Keynes, who were keen to explore alternative artistic lifestyles and united by their anti-war stance. Bell and Grant adorned the rooms with artworks and antiques, many of which can still be found in situ today. Although the last resident, Grant's daughter Angelica, left in 1980, the interiors look as they did in the 1950s, packed with valuable objets d'art from the first half of the 20th century.

SEE IT ! ***Bus 125 runs between Eastbourne and Lewes, stopping near the house in Firle. By car, Charleston is signposted off the A27.***

314

Go highbrow and get chilled out at the Port Eliot Festival

SOUTHWEST ENGLAND // Literature and landscape were the two main selling points for this genteel southwest festival when it started back in 2003, although it's since branched out into live music, film, theatre, dance and workshops. But this is no grungy Glasto: it's more the kind of festival where smart folk in puffer jackets and expensive wellies sip flutes of prosecco while discussing the merits of the latest Booker nominations.

It's all set in the bucolic surroundings of the Port Eliot Estate, the family seat of the Earl of St Germans (if you can, try and wangle your way into the main house, where there's a truly stunning mural by the late Plymouth-based artist Robert Lenkiewicz). Spend your time lounging by the river, wandering the grounds, listening to book readings and watching the odd band. Nothing too strenuous, mind – Port Eliot is so laid-back, it's almost horizontal.

SEE IT ! ***The festival is held in late July. Trains run to St Germans station nearby.***

© Daniel Di Paolo

© Andrew Duke / Alamy

315

Sup with notable scribblers at Ye Olde Cheshire Cheese

LONDON // For a pint with a pedigree, look no further than Ye Olde Cheshire Cheese, a one-time haunt of Fleet St journalists, and, before them, a watering hole for Charles Dickens, Mark Twain, Arthur Conan Doyle, Alfred Lord Tennyson and Samuel Johnson, who lived around the corner on Gough Square.

While Fleet St journalism died a death, the pub's cosy interiors still hark back to a slower time, when the big news of the day was discussed not over takeaway lattes, but long (often very long) liquid lunches. Today, it's owned by the Samuel Smith Brewery, popular with students for pocket-friendly prices.

TRY IT ! *City Thameslink station is right on the doorstep of Ye Olde Cheshire Cheese, just a hundred yards west along Fleet St.*

316

Seek inspiration in a poet's footsteps on Keats' Walk

SOUTHERN ENGLAND // One crisp autumn day in Winchester in 1819, a young poet called John Keats took a walk. He trudged out across the misty meadows to the old Hospital of St Cross, taking in Wolvesey Castle, and when he returned to his lodgings, he sat down and composed perhaps his best-loved poem, 'To Autumn' (the one that begins 'Season of mists and mellow fruitfulness...').

You can still follow the poet's trail, a round trip of about two miles, perhaps finishing with a pint at the cosy Bell Inn on St Cross Road. Who knows, if the spirit of Keats is with you, you might even be inspired to pen your own ode...

SEE IT ! *Keats' Walk is clearly signed from Wolvesey Castle; pick up a trail leaflet at Winchester's tourist office.*

317

Have a crack at the World Conker Championships

MIDLANDS & THE MARCHES // Sports don't come more British or bonkers than this annual autumn meet-up of conker hotshots in rural Northamptonshire. The event was conceived in Ashton's village pub in 1965 by a group of friends disappointed because it was too wet for fishing. Their replacement recreation idea – to make a contest out of the bounty of the village green's horse chestnut trees – quickly caught on. A run of successful conker championships meant the venue had to move from Ashton to its current location, Southwick's Shuckburgh Arms.

TRY IT ! ***Southwick is 14 miles southwest of Peterborough by car; Peterborough has regular direct trains to London.***

© Oli Scarff / Getty Images

318

Enjoy art in the open air at the Yorkshire Sculpture Park

YORKSHIRE // Promoted with the tagline 'art without walls', this could be described as a safari park for sculpture. Set in a sprawling 18th-century country estate, its landscaped grounds are dotted with stunning sculptures and installations by a star-studded list of international artists, from Andy Goldsworthy to Ai Wei Wei. Curvaceously abstract reclining figures, immediately recognisable as the work of Yorkshire artist Henry Moore, stand boldly on sloping lawns, while Sophie Ryder's giant figures, half human, half hare, peer menacingly from among the trees.

SEE IT ! ***The park is 12 miles south of Leeds, just off Junction 38 on the M1 motorway.***

© Jonty Wilde

The Jacobite steam train crossing Glenfinnan Viaduct in the Scottish Highlands

319

All aboard the Hogwarts Express - aka the Jacobite Railway over Glenfinnan Viaduct

HIGHLANDS & ISLANDS // It appears indistinct at first, a series of blurred outlines between the trees. As the train judders around a bend, the tracks click-clack and the noise builds to a crescendo as windows are flung open. Within moments, the extraordinary arches of the Glenfinnan Viaduct railway bridge are revealed in slow motion. There is a momentary pause as the train brakes, a whiff of locomotive steam in the air and a flurry of photos, then – as if it was all a misunderstanding – the train accelerates north to Lochailort, Morar, Arisaig and Mallaig.

It's not so long ago that all rail travel was like this: the ever-changing countryside could be soaked up from the comfort of a cabin compartment. But seeing Scotland's West Highland Line at such a pace – the carriages shaking with a slo-mo rattle – is everyday business on the Jacobite steam train as it completes the 84 miles round trip from Fort William. This is train travel as it used to be. Yes it's a tourist operation geared towards trainspotters and Harry Potter fans keen to ride the same rails as the Hogwarts Express, but it's worth every penny.

TRY IT ! ***The Jacobite Railway is seasonal; out of season, take the cheaper ScotRail service.***

320

Head for heights at Salisbury Cathedral

SOUTHWEST ENGLAND // You can't possibly miss Salisbury Cathedral's spire, visible all over town, like a compass needle pointing out the route to heaven. At 404ft, the tower and spire combined are the highest of any British cathedral and a masterpiece of medieval masonry, dating from the early years of the 13th century. Come 1668, Sir Christopher Wren noticed that the spire was actually on a tilt, and advised that supporting scissor-shaped arches be added in the nave. Lean notwithstanding, a tower tour is obviously obligatory – but don't overlook the cathedral's other points of interest, including the west front, an original copy of the Magna Carta, and what may be the world's oldest working timepiece.

SEE IT ! ***Salisbury is less than two hours' drive from London. Entry to the cathedral is free, with a requested donation.***

321

Turn back time at the Black Country Living Museum

MIDLANDS & THE MARCHES // If you are going to celebrate an Industrial Revolution that was hell for the people working it, best do it right. Black Country Living Museum does. Fifty-odd original buildings from the Black Country boroughs of Dudley, Wolverhampton, Sandwell and Walsall – including a blacksmith's forge, coal mine, pub and school – have been reassembled here, with costumed characters telling the tales. The eateries are part of the fun too: anyone for 1930s-style fish and chips or a bag of sweets from an old-fashioned sweet shop?

SEE IT ! ***The Black Country Museum is in Dudley, 9 miles northwest of Birmingham.***

322

Wish in Mother Shipton's Cave

YORKSHIRE // Said to be England's oldest tourist attraction (first mentioned in 1630), this natural limestone cave and wishing well was once home to a soothsaying witch. Mother Shipton, born Ursula Southeil (1488–1561), is said to have dwelled in the cave, and made a living by foretelling the future. Among her many predictions were the defeat of the Spanish Armada, the Great Fire of London and the invention of iron ships.

Near to the cave is the Petrifying Well, a cascade of highly mineralised water from an underground lake that can turn objects to stone in less than six months.

TRY IT ! ***The cave is in the attractive town of Knaresborough, 4 miles east of Harrogate.***

323

Heal thyself with a stroll in the Chelsea Physic Garden

LONDON // You couldn't ask for a more characterful-sounding organisation than the Worshipful Society of Apothecaries, the official company for medieval chemists. In 1673, they set up this gorgeous secret garden in which to grow medicinal herbs that could be used to treat patients at London's fledgling hospitals, and its existence was only revealed to the public in 1983. The walled garden is a calm haven in the busy streets of Chelsea; look out for the gates topped by an emblem of a sun-headed Apollo fighting the dragon of disease.

SEE IT ! ***The Physic Garden is a hike from Sloane Square Tube; it's a more pleasant walk from Battersea Park over Albert Bridge.***

© Sam Thompson / 500px

324

Romp through 1000 years of shenanigans at Warwick Castle

MIDLANDS & THE MARCHES // Erected by William the Conqueror as one of his first English fortresses, this moated colossus is a glorious memento of the last millennium, flamboyantly using multiple exhibits and festivals to showcase a past that reads like a *Game of Thrones* script. The oldest part is the mound from the castle's motte and bailey days, dating from 1068; stone towers were raised from the 12th century onwards. The crowning glory in the deluxe suites of furnished rooms is the splendid Kenilworth Buffet, carved from a single oak and depicting scenes from Sir Walter Scott's novel *Kenilworth*. Outside, the pièce de résistance is one of the world's largest-ever siege machines, painstakingly reconstructed from 700 year-old drawings, while down below dressed-up characters loom out of the dungeons to shock.

☛ SEE IT ! ***Warwick Castle is 22 miles southeast of Birmingham, to which it is connected by half-hourly trains.***

© UrbanImages / Alamy

325

Take off for a flight into the colonial era at the once-grand Croydon Airport

LONDON // Believe it or not, until WWII Croydon Airport was the main airport for the whole of the UK, and the bustling international terminal for Imperial Airways, Britain's first national carrier. After the war, expanding passenger numbers and bigger planes spelled the death knell for this tiny aerodrome, but in its heyday, Croydon Airport welcomed holidaymakers and dignitaries from across the globe.

Why visit today? Well, nostalgia for one thing, plus the chance to dip into aviation history and feel a bit like Humphrey Bogart at the end of *Casablanca*. Fronted by a mounted de Havilland Heron, Airport House is a timeless piece of colonial-era neoclassical architecture. Inside, aviation-enthusiast volunteers staff an intriguing museum and guide visitors around the airside buildings.

☛ SEE IT ! ***Waddon railway station is 10 minutes' walk north of the old aerodrome along Purley Way, or jump on the 289 bus.***

© Chris Howes / Wild Places Photography / Alamy

326

Step back in time in Jersey's WWII bunker turned stellar museum

CHANNEL ISLANDS // Descend into the subterranean gloom of a former German military hospital to enter Jersey's best and most poignant museum. In tunnels cut from sheer rock by slave labour, frozen tableaux interactive exhibits and grainy video footage capture the islanders' gruelling wartime experience under Nazi occupation from 1940 to 1945. Peer into the hospital room and witness a Jersey family in their kitchen, and hear individual islanders' stories which are, by turn, uplifting and demoralising: the 'Jerry bags' (unattached young women) who fraternised with the Germans; the Nazi collaborators who gleefully informed on their neighbours; the courageous individuals who showed kindness to Eastern European slave labourers. The museum challenges you to answer: what would you have done in their place?

☛ SEE IT ! ***Wrap up warm, since it's chilly inside the tunnels even in summer, and get your tickets online to skip the queues.***

© Colin McPherson / Getty Images

327

Whizz through the Zip World Slate Caverns in Blaenau Ffestiniog

NORTH WALES // Zip World sports three zip-wire sites in Wales, but unlike a lot of aerial runways, the Blaenau Ffestiniog one does not need dimensional boasts (longest, fastest etc) to illustrate its uniqueness: this is an electrifying swoop, clamber and scramble through an old slate cavern, abandoned since the 19th century. In a one-of-a-kind underground adrenaline rush, you whoosh through the remains of the one-time nucleus of the world's slate-mining industry. Europe's first four-person zip wire, plus a heart-in-mouth mix of cables, ladders and rope bridges, transport you through 5 miles of quarries, mines and subterranean chambers, together comprising the continent's biggest zip zone. OK, that was two boasts, but what is surely one of the most original outdoor playgrounds deserves some championing.

☛ TRY IT ! ***Zip World Blaenau Ffestiniog is 32 miles southeast of Bangor. Two attractions are all-weather, one is weather-dependent.***

328

Sip, taste, try and buy at trendy Tooting Market

LONDON // Tucked behind an art deco frontage on Tooting High St, the hip, covered Tooting Market has major foodie appeal. While nearby Broadway Market covers the essentials, Tooting is given over to vintage glad rags, tribal masks, juice stands and offbeat eating options, a reflection of the trendy reinvention of this once workaday corner of London. When you tire of browsing for pre-loved designer labels, you can head to Unwined for inspired wine tastings, Graveney Gin for a sip of Tooting's finest spirit, or the Secret Bar for cocktails and chorizo.

☛ SEE IT ! *Tooting Broadway Tube is close by; weekends are the busy time, both for lunchtime eats and evening quaffing.*

329

Stay on trend with London Fashion Week's fashionistas

LONDON // A week is a long time in fashion, but chic Londoners block out the dates for London Fashion Week a year ahead of time. Like fellow It girls Paris and Milan, London is a stylish dame, and the collections launched on Fashion Week catwalks in February and September set the tone for red carpets and gala dinners across the planet. Secure a ticket and you'll step into a world of sculpted cheekbones, air-kissing fashion editors and superstar designers. And at the very least, you'll get the inside skinny on fashion dos and don'ts for the coming season.

☛ SEE IT ! *The main Fashion Week events use post-industrial spaces at the Vinyl Factory on Soho's Marshall St, near Oxford Circus Tube.*

330

Dine on gourmet pub food at coastal Kent's Sportsman

SOUTHEAST ENGLAND // Kent isn't described as the Garden of England for nothing; its orchards and fields yield some of the country's tastiest produce. These local ingredients take pride of place at the Michelin-starred Sportsman pub, near Whitstable. If you think gourmet food is all about £200 tasting menus, check this place out – a normal pub serving exceptional and (relatively) affordable local dishes, with the focus firmly on fish, lamb and Kentish fruit. However, unlike your local boozer, you'll have to book a table at least a month in advance.

☛ TRY IT ! *The pub is just west of the village of Seasalter. Local buses from Whitstable and Faversham stop outside.*

331

See the trees and the wood at Bedgebury Pinetum

SOUTHEAST ENGLAND // Around 10 miles southeast of Tunbridge Wells lies a little patch of conifer paradise, a family-friendly forest attraction with heaps of activities on offer. Some come for the tranquillity or to birdwatch, others to jump around the treetops courtesy of Go Ape. There's also horse riding, miles and miles of cycling trails suitable for all ages and abilities, and a large cafe. Although this is no untamed wilderness, it's the ideal place to digitally detox and fill your lungs with fresh Kentish air.

☛ SEE IT ! *Bus 254 from Tunbridge Wells passes quite close to the forest, but it's best reached by car. Parking costs a weighty £10 to £13.*

332

Flaunt your fascinator and have a flutter on the fillies at Royal Ascot

SOUTHERN ENGLAND // At first glance, Royal Ascot is just a horse race meeting. But look closer, and you'll see one of the UK's major festivals, where the rich and powerful rub shoulders with 15-minute celebs and common folk, and getting trolleyed on gin or Champagne is totally fine as long as you wear the right hat. The event was founded by Queen Anne in 1711, and since then has been attended by the monarch of the day, hence the 'royal' epithet. Tradition dictates that activities begin with a regal procession of horse-drawn carriages, accompanied by mounted outriders. Then the crowd gets down to the serious business of placing a bet, or just seeing and being seen – far more important than the racing, certainly for the paparazzi, who focus on the designer outfits and especially the outrageous headgear for which Ascot is most famous.

SEE IT ! *Ascot (pronounced 'Ascut' locally) is west of London. The Royal Ascot meeting is held in June.*

Tom Aikens' Top Five Places

Award-winning head chef and restaurateur Tom Aikens became the youngest chef to win two Michelin stars, aged only 26. He runs Tom's Kitchen Canary Wharf and Tom's Kitchen Chelsea and is the author of three cookbooks.

01

BLAKENEY, NORFOLK – I lived in Norfolk as a child and went to Blakeney most summer weekends. It's still one of my favourite places. You can go to the point to see the seals, go crab-fishing and get great fish and chips.

02

DINGWELL, SCOTLAND – This is where I get my hand-dived scallops. It's the most stunning area, just north of Inverness in the heart of the Scottish Highlands, not far from Skibo Castle and Castle Leod. Beautiful views, fresh sea air and, of course, brilliant seafood.

03

NOSS MAYO AND NEWTON FERRERS, DEVON – This is one of the most beautiful places in the summer, right by the River Yealm estuary, where we always used to come as kids, sail in my father's boat and catch mackerel.

04

ORFORD, SUFFOLK – This coastal village has a lot of charm and some great walks along the beach, plus a very old castle from the Anglo-Saxon times to run around in and lots of sailing along the coast.

05

SALCOMBE NORTH SANDS, DEVON – Also in Devon, this is a beautiful stretch of coast. As a family we would come here on summer holidays. It has a perfect beach – really sheltered and great for exploring, swimming and sailing.

© Sion Hannuna / Shutterstock

333

Admire Georgian terraces and fine views in Clifton

SOUTHWEST ENGLAND // Banksy's home town has long been known for its alternative edge, but you'll find a more genteel side to the city on the hillside along the Avon Gorge.

Since the late 18th century, the smart suburb of Clifton has been Bristol's most coveted postcode, and its streets are lined with handsome Georgian buildings that would look much more at home in belle-of-the-ball Bath than gritty old Brizzle. The similarities don't end there. Like Bath, Clifton once sat on its own natural hot springs, which attracted many wealthy tourists in the mid-1800s and transformed the area into a chic haunt for spa-lovers and socialites (indeed, you can still experience the hot waters for yourself at the Bristol Lido).

Don't miss a stroll along the Royal York Crescent – it's Clifton's most desirable terrace, offering splendid views over the city.

☛ SEE IT ! *Clifton is an easy uphill walk from Bristol city centre. Alternatively, cheat and catch bus 8.*

© Will Slater / Lonely Planet

334

Walk with the 'living dead' at Greyfriars Kirkyard

EDINBURGH // In Edinburgh, graveyards aren't houses for the dead. An entire industry has grown up around grave-spotting and here well-schooled crowds saunter among carved-stone tombstones. St Cuthbert's Graveyard is a delight to stroll in, and the Edinburgh Castle Dog Cemetery is as quirky as it gets, but one in particular stands out: Greyfriars Kirkyard.

A burial site since 1561, it's renowned as the place where Harry Potter author JK Rowling found inspiration for plenty of her characters' names. Among the strange bedfellows are 'Tom' Riddle, Moody, Scrymgeour, McGonagall and the Potter family clan. That's not to forget the final resting place of Greyfriars Bobby. The Skye terrier guarded his master's grave for 14 years and inspired Walt Disney to retell his tale for Hollywood. When it comes to ghoulish theatre, Greyfriars is the world's most overdramatised cemetery.

☛ SEE IT ! *Maps are available for a frighteningly cheap 50p in the Kirk shop. The Kirkyard is open 24 hours a day.*

Messing about on the river in the hope of landing a fine catch on the Tay at Ballathie in Tayside

335

Fly-fish a salmon on the River Tay

HIGHLANDS & ISLANDS // 'Now we wait,' the gillie says, pausing with intensity. 'The fish know we're here. You can sense it in the ripples. But we have the benefit of time – which gives us the upper hand.' It is hard to imagine a Scotland without salmon, especially while standing on the banks of the Tay, the king of salmon rivers.

And you don't have to be a fishing fanatic to find your footing by the waterside, either. There are dozens of guides and companies that can lend you a hand while fishing Britain's largest river, either from a boat, bank or while wading in knee-deep currents. You'll make the swiftest progress with a private lesson, but following a successful catch-and-release policy to shore up salmon stocks, even a novice can land a heavyweight 30lb fish – up to 10,000 rod-caught salmon are landed each season. Time moves slowly, but lose yourself in the art of reeling and casting for long enough and it becomes its own reward.

TRY IT ! ***World-renowned beats abound, particularly near Scone Palace, Pitlochry, Dunkeld and Lochs Tay and Tummel.***

336

Stargaze at the Standing Stones of Callanish

HIGHLANDS & ISLANDS // Talk about Celtic charm. This series of unexplained prehistoric ruins on the Isle of Lewis, made of nearly 50 slabs of gnarled gneiss, is enough to make anyone believe in a heavenly body. How on earth were the stones transported to this hilltop in 3000 BC? What were the 15ft monoliths used for? And why do the stones align with the sun and the stars? Add a perplexing burial chamber to the riddle and it's an almighty head-scratcher – best appreciated at sunset while overlooking the island-jewelled waters of Loch Roag.

☛ SEE IT ! ***Callanish is 18 miles west of Stornoway. The standing stones are free to visit and open 24 hours a day.***

337

Visit Agatha Christie's summer home at Greenway

SOUTHWEST ENGLAND // Where does a mystery maestro go on holiday? Well, in the case of Devon-born Agatha Christie, close to home. Her favourite summer sanctuary was the handsome Greenway, near Dartmouth, overlooking the River Dart, where she spent many holidays between 1938 and 1959. The house is still much as Christie left it – look out for her hats, antique china collection and Steinway piano, among other artefacts. There are two routes: on foot, via the 4-mile Dart Valley Trail from Kingswear, or even better, aboard the lovely Greenway Ferry.

☛ SEE IT ! ***Greenway is owned by the National Trust and closed in winter. A return ticket on the ferry from Dartmouth costs £8.50.***

338

Sink a hole-in-one at Scotland's ancient St Andrews

CENTRAL SCOTLAND // No other sporting destination in Britain has as much pulling power as St Andrews on the Fife coast. The expertly trimmed greens and fairways of its seven public links courses, where the game was first played 600 years ago, see 250,000 rounds each year, with the surrounding university city adding a well-groomed backdrop. Of the 18-holers, the Old Course is the one on everyone's bucket list, but equally soul-stirring are the rollercoaster greens of 'The Himalayas', the St Andrews Ladies' Putting Club.

☛ SEE IT ! ***You'll need to book a year in advance for the Old Course (from £88). The Himalayas costs £3, including equipment.***

339

Explore Margate's mysterious shell-lined grotto

SOUTHEAST ENGLAND // Margate has a secret. Behind a shopfront in an inconspicuous street just outside the town centre, steps and a short passage lead to a baffling attraction – a set of musty caves whose walls are covered in striking shell mosaics. They were discovered in 1835 and no one knows who built them or why. Shell grottos were popular garden features in 18th-century stately homes, but this example was found beneath farmland. Some think it may date to Roman days, others that it could be a hoax – decide for yourself in this mysterious space.

☛ SEE IT ! ***Via high-speed rail from London to Margate or the bus from Canterbury. In winter, the grotto is only open at weekends.***

340

Pay homage to King Richard III in Leicester city centre

MIDLANDS & THE MARCHES // King Richard III's death at the Battle of Bosworth Field in 1485 marked the end of both the Plantagenet dynasty and the Middle Ages in Britain. While the king's reputation was trashed by the Tudor regime and a Shakespeare play, the 2012 discovery of his skeleton in Leicester precipitated construction of this visitor centre to reinterpret the monarch's story and the pivotal times in which he ruled. The results – enthrallingly presented via multimedia exhibits – show that Richard III, day for day, did as much good as Henry VIII or Elizabeth I.

SEE IT ! ***The King Richard III Visitor Centre is on St Martins in Leicester city centre.***

341

Honour departed Londoners at Cross Bones Graveyard

LONDON // In medieval times, London's rich were interred under elaborate marble mausoleums, while the poor were shovelled under in modest paupers' graveyards. Southwark's Cross Bones Graveyard is a poignant memorial to the latter, founded as a burial ground for the Winchester Geese – prostitutes licensed, somewhat incongruously, by the Bishop of Winchester. Despite its maudlin backstory and eroded graves, the cemetery is given colour and life by a shrine of rainbow ribbons, tied to railings by visitors in tribute to London's forgotten dead.

SEE IT ! ***The graveyard is between London Bridge and Borough Tube stations; follow Borough High St and veer onto Union St.***

342

Discover the weird and wonderful land of the Viking Way

MIDLANDS & THE MARCHES // Anything north of East Anglia and south of Yorkshire in eastern England is an unknown, even for most Brits. The area has few blockbuster attractions, no national parks and is not really en route to anywhere. Enter this 147-mile path between Oakham, Rutland and the River Humber, in Yorkshire, which sets out to fill in the blanks. Named after this region's strong associations with Viking culture, highlights include the Lincolnshire Wolds AONB; the east of England's highest hills between Yorkshire and Kent, and the majestic Lincoln.

SEE IT ! ***Start in Oakham, 20 miles east of Leicester, and finish at the Humber. Allow 10 to 14 days for the whole walk.***

343

Go on a haute cuisine journey in Cumbria's Cartmel

CUMBRIA // Cutesy Cartmel was known for its 12th-century priory and historic racecourse, but more recently both have been overtaken by its gourmet rep. It's the purveyor of sticky toffee pudding, first made in the Lake District in the 1970s, but superstar chef Simon Rogan – Cumbria's answer to Heston Blumenthal – has also put his own stamp on the village, with two restaurants that garner consistently rave reviews: the double Michelin-starred L'Enclume, with a strong emphasis on foraging; and the adjacent Rogan & Co, a bistro that got its first Michelin star in 2018.

TRY IT ! ***Cartmel is just off the A590 in south Cumbria. You'll need to book in advance for a seat at Simon's tables.***

Viewed on a sunny day from the water, the village of Baile Mor on the Isle of Iona looks as pretty as a picture

344

Take the long road to Iona for divine inspiration, wildlife wonders and more

HIGHLANDS & ISLANDS // Time travelling on Iona is easy. Marooned in the middle of the Sound of Iona, 10 minutes from Mull, the island has become an irresistible draw for people looking for spiritual escape. The main attraction is Iona Abbey, the cradle of Christianity in Scotland in the 12th century, and where St Columba first landed from Ireland to found a monastery in 563.

That makes it glamour-central for churchgoers, but it's also a magnet for history and wildlife lovers – the sparsely inhabited island is alive with stories of Viking raids, adorned with stone crosses and sandy bays, which are circled by a healthy population of seals, dolphins and whales. The fact it is so hard to reach – a ferry first to Mull from Oban, a one-hour drive from Craignure, then a 10-minute ferry from Fionnphort – means it displays none of the mania associated with the more accessible Skye or Arran. The machair-backed, shell-sand beaches, Caribbeanesque tidal pools and aquamarine swimming spots are for local consumption only – and the spell they cast means savvy visitors who make the effort are amply rewarded.

SEE IT ! *Passenger ferries from Fionnphort to Iona run frequently, seven days a week.*

© John-Paul Bell / Alamy

© DrimaFilm / Shutterstock

345

Master a Munro with a scramble up Sgurr nan Gillean on Skye

HIGHLANDS & ISLANDS // It takes around seven hours to hike this 3162ft peak on the Isle of Skye, but a lifetime to shake its hanging crags from your mind. It's one of 11 Munros (mountains in Scotland exceeding 3000ft) on the Cuillin ridge, yet arguably the most famous because of its spine-shivering views and the feeling it elicits that an epiphany is never far off – when standing on the summit plateau, you realise you belong here.

The route starts by crossing a footbridge and continues past a waterfall and stone cairns until it reaches an ascent, for scramble-hardened hikers only, over heart-in-mouth boulders and rock slabs. Climbers test themselves on the peak's two rope-required routes, but a head for heights is essential, as is enough fuel in the tank to complete the leg-jangling 7.5-mile round trip.

SEE IT ! ***To begin, park off the Dunvegan road from Sligachan. Need a helping hand? Hire a fully qualified mountain guide.***

346

Get the big picture at Glasow's Kelvingrove

SOUTHERN SCOTLAND // Best approached on foot through oh-so-photogenic Kelvingrove Park, this is the ultimate Glasgow day out and Scotland's most popular museum with good reason. For starters, the baroque facade hides a mind-boggling maze of 22 themed galleries and some 8000 exhibits, including art, ancient Egyptian sculpture – and a Spitfire. From every angle, it bombards you with stories about Glasgow and how it conquered the world to become the second city of the Victorian empire. Like your art? There's a Dutch gallery, packed with 17th-century watercolours and old masters, a French gallery paying homage to Monet, Renoir and Pissarro, plus the world's definitive collection of works by the late-19th-century Glasgow Boys. Your final reward? A gallery dedicated to Charles Rennie Mackintosh, featuring furniture, decorative panels and rooms blueprinted from his designs.

SEE IT ! ***Like most museums in Glasgow, entry to Kelvingrove Art Gallery and Museum, plus guided tours inside, are free.***

347

Follow nature's best narrator at Darwin's Down House

SOUTHEAST ENGLAND // Just south of London, Down House was the Darwin family home between 1842 and 1896. It was here that Charles Darwin developed his most important theories and wrote *On the Origin of Species*. Like Kent's other historical homes, the building provides both an intriguing insight into the everyday life of the family, as well as examining Charles Darwin's work. Particularly interesting are the gardens and greenhouses where he carried out botanical experiments. The audio guide is voiced by none other than Sir David Attenborough.

☛ SEE IT ! ***Local buses link Downe village (half a mile away) with Orpington and Bromley. Parking is free.***

348

Savour car park cocktails with a view at Frank's Cafe

LONDON // Could Frank's Cafe be any more streetwise? It's run by the Bold Tendancies arts collective, serves negronis and hot wings overlooking the mean streets of Peckham, and is perched on top of a multistorey car park. Offbeat art installations only add to the buzz.

Frank's is only open in the summer, when the rooftop becomes a sun-kissed penthouse terrace, packed with arty south Londoners and the odd pilgrim from north of the river. Come early to secure a spot by the concrete perimeter wall for prime London skyline views.

☛ SEE IT ! ***Frank's is tripping distance from Peckham Rye Overground station.***

349

Tuck into traditional afternoon tea at Betty's of Harrogate

YORKSHIRE // Introduced by the seventh duchess of Bedford in 1840, afternoon tea is a typically English ritual, and Betty's is the perfect place to take it. Dainty sandwiches, delicate cakes, fruit tarts and oven-fresh scones with strawberry jam and clotted cream are all beautifully presented, and washed down with a nice cup of tea. Betty's was founded in 1919 by a Swiss immigrant who embraced the traditions of his adopted country with the zeal of the convert, and a hundred years later it feels as English as cricket, warm beer and losing at penalty shoot-outs.

☛ TRY IT ! ***Reservations are limited, so if you haven't made one you may have to queue for a table, especially at lunchtime.***

350

Make an ascent of lofty Leith Hill to see London and the sea

SOUTHERN ENGLAND // Southeast England isn't known for its snow-capped peaks, so even a modest hill can provide magnificent panoramas. That's certainly the case with Leith Hill, southwest of Dorking, which at 965ft above sea level is the highest point in the region. But what makes this spot extra special is the 18th-century viewing tower, which adds another 64ft to the elevation. Open every day except Christmas Day, it's claimed that on a clear day you can see 13 counties from it, with views to the English Channel and London.

☛ SEE IT ! ***Leith Hill is best reached by car. It's 3 miles from Holmwood train station on the London to Horsham line.***

© Jim Holden / Alamy

© travelibUK / Alamy

351

Wander through the Hundred Acre Wood in search of the real Poohsticks bridge

SOUTHEAST ENGLAND // Any fans of Winnie-the-Pooh and friends will be familiar with the Hundred Acre Wood. But few people know that the wood is a real place: Ashdown Forest, around 500 acres of woodland near Crowborough in East Sussex. The Milne family had a weekend house nearby and watching his son Christopher Robin at play sowed the seed for AA Milne's Pooh Bear books.

The wooded area is large so it's best to do a bit of research before you arrive – finding locations associated with the Pooh stories isn't difficult but can take a bit of legwork. In fact, hiking is the other reason to visit, with miles of trails criss-crossing this Area of Outstanding Natural Beauty, which also inspired EH Shepard's much-loved illustrations for the books.

SEE IT ! *The forest is a 3-mile walk from Crowborough station, served by trains from London Bridge and bus 29 from Tunbridge Wells.*

352

Refresh yourself with a wild swim near Grassington, Yorkshire

YORKSHIRE // The River Wharfe is one of Britain's best for wild swimming, and the handsome Georgian village of Grassington is its epicentre. The river is blessed with countless rock pools, waterfalls, chutes and natural water slides – just upstream from the village is Ghaistrill's Strid, a mini-gorge that offers great fun with an inflatable ring. But the most delightful swimming spot is downstream near Appletreewick, where a lovely pool with a rocky island waits invitingly beneath the trees. For those who haven't ventured beyond the confines of a swimming pool before, there's entry-level wild swimming to be enjoyed at Grassington Weir, immediately south of the village. On a hot summer's day the grassy riverbank meadow here will be crowded with picnicking families, kids and adults alike splashing, swimming and riding inflatables.

TRY IT ! *Grassington is 8 miles north of Skipton. The national park visitor centre in the village provides info on parking close to the river.*

© Paul Weston / Alamy

353

Don't be surprised to see a film crew in Wiltshire's olde-worlde Lacock

SOUTHWEST ENGLAND // Longing for a village that sums up a vision of olde-worlde England? Look no further than Lacock, where all the clocks seem to have stopped somewhere around the late 18th century. There are no telephone poles, no street lights and no cars, leaving its cobbled lanes and ivy-covered cottages blissfully free of 21st-century trappings.

Unsurprisingly, Lacock is a favourite film location (Harry Potter, *Downton Abbey* and numerous costume dramas have been shot here). The village also has a fine medieval abbey and a fascinating museum dedicated to one of the pioneers of photography, William Henry Fox Talbot. Bring your camera for the annual scarecrow festival and let his spirit guide you before enjoying a pint in one of the two pubs.

☛ SEE IT ! ***Lacock is 4 miles south of Chippenham, on the train line to London Paddington.***

© Chris Herring / Alamy

354

Nosy around the servants' quarters at Jacobean Blicking Hall in Norfolk

EAST ANGLIA // Elegant and ornate, the Jacobean mansion of Blickling Hall is framed by a lake and yew hedges. Curving gables and slender towers rise up from a perfectly proportioned facade. Inside, the aptly named Long Gallery seems to go on for ever, and elaborate staterooms are stuffed with fine Georgian furniture, pictures and tapestries.

The house was largely remodelled in the 17th century for James I's Chief Justice, while at one point the estate was owned by the family of Henry VIII's ill-fated queen, Anne Boleyn. It's far from a museum piece, though. Life in the contemporary house comes vividly to life during expertly led tours. These guide you through the servants' attic quarters, the gardens and the housekeepers' cleaning routines – no easy task, considering all those chandeliers, paintings and porcelain.

☛ SEE IT ! ***National Trust-owned Blickling Hall is 8 miles from North Walsham train station.***

The precipitous Yorkshire town of Staithes tumbles down to the tidal river of Staithes Beck

355

Escape the modern world in the old fishing village of Staithes

YORKSHIRE // With its steep cobbled lanes and higgledy-piggledy houses, Staithes seems to hide away from the modern world, focusing instead on its centuries-old connection with the sea. Looking a little like a cross between Whitby and Robin Hood's Bay, this old fishing village is set on a precipitous hill overlooking a tiny harbour, and split by the tidal river of Staithes Beck. But it's a lot smaller than Whitby and less touristy than Robin Hood's Bay – the houses are less prettified, and there are lobster pots stacked at the edge of the working harbour.

The village's main claim to fame is that 18th-century explorer Captain James Cook worked here as a boy. Legend says that fishermen's tales of the high seas, and bad treatment by his employer, led him to steal a shilling and run away to Whitby. By the end of the 19th century the village was home to an artists' colony, the Staithes School, inspired by the French Impressionists. The tradition continues today, and you can admire the work of local artists in Staithes Gallery before enjoying an excellent pub lunch and pint at the Cod & Lobster.

SEE IT ! ***Staithes is 11 miles northwest of Whitby. Cross the footbridge and climb Cowbar Bank for the best view of the village.***

© Andrea / Obzerova

© Sam Stephenson

356

Dance until dawn in Edinburgh at the world's biggest Hogmanay party

EDINBURGH // Stand amid the throng on Princes St at the turn of midnight on New Year's Eve and you're a guest at the world's most in-your-face street party. It starts with the arrival of an international tartan army, dressed in kilts-to-the-max and crammed beneath Edinburgh Castle to ceilidh and quaff whisky. It ends with everyone pogoing from Waverley Bridge to The Mound, feeling cuddly, cockeyed and very Caledonian.

If you don't manage to get tickets to party, there are lots of events in the evenings leading up to it, including concerts and a torchlit procession.

SEE IT ! *The official street party is a ticketed event, running from 7pm to 1am.*

357

Dress up and stimulate the senses at Glyndebourne Festival

SOUTHEAST ENGLAND // Fed up of having to travel to see performances and scrabble for tickets, in 1934 John Christie and his opera singer wife Audrey Mildmay decided on a radical solution – why not build a 1200-seat opera house in a garden in the middle of nowhere (actually a lovely spot just outside Lewes in East Sussex)?

Many would assume such a bold project was doomed to failure, but Glyndebourne has since become one of the UK's leading opera venues, its festival a highlight of the English summer season. Tickets are like gold dust, smart attire is expected, and tradition demands a picnic feast during the conveniently long interval.

SEE IT ! *Glyndebourne is just outside Lewes, which is linked to the nearby village of Glynde by train.*

The Steam Yacht Gondola, chugging along serenely on the Lake District's Coniston Water

358

Travel back in time aboard the Steam Yacht Gondola on Coniston Water

CUMBRIA // The Lake District trades heavily on its visible connections to the Victorian age, and one of the most satisfying experiences of yonder times is a ride aboard the Steam Yacht Gondola on Coniston Water.

A cross between a Venetian vaporetto and a traditional English houseboat, the screw-propellered steam yacht was built in 1859 to ferry passengers from the Furness and Coniston railways. She was retired from commercial service in 1936, eventually being converted into a houseboat after WWII. In 1979, the by-then derelict boat was given a complete refit by the National Trust, including the restoration of its fancy cushioned saloon.

The Gondola is the loveliest way to enjoy the lake, especially if you're visiting Brantwood, John Ruskin's home overlooking Coniston. Ironically, the author of *The Stones of Venice* was a fierce critic of steam power and would have undoubtedly baulked at the sight of the original Gondola, which plied its daily circular route in full view of his house. A more enthusiastic author was Arthur Ransome, who used the craft as inspiration for Captain Flint's houseboat in *Swallows and Amazons*.

TRY IT ! ***You can board the boat at Coniston Jetty; there's a 10% discount for National Trust members.***

359

Explore Scotland in miniature on the island of Mull

HIGHLANDS & ISLANDS // When Scots rave about the benefits of visiting the Isle of Skye or the Orkney Islands, they're trying to talk you out of visiting Mull. But it's a ridiculously tempting alternative, with castles (Duart, Glengorm and Moy), a distillery (Tobermory), wildlife extravaganzas (eagles, puffins, otters, seals and sharks), lighthouses, caves and stone circles, and one of Scotland's most gratifying hill walks (Ben More). Base yourself in pastel-painted harbour town Tobermory, and you'll understand the urge to keep it to yourself, too.

SEE IT ! ***Ferries to Craignure leave from Oban regularly (46 minutes). Alternatively, take a boat from Lochaline or Kilchoan.***

360

Barn dance it up at Cecil Sharp House

LONDON // Folk venues once filled London like mushrooms after rain, but today just a handful of stalwarts still fly the flag for fiddles and close harmonies. Cecil Sharp House is a standout, a vibrant centre for traditional English folk music and dance, preserving traditions that predate the folk revival of the 1960s by centuries.

In life, Cecil Sharp toured the UK and backcountry America to record the traditional music and dance of the English-speaking world. Attend today, and you might hear tin-shack reels from the Appalachian mountains and the clip-clop of Morris dancers – a surprising find in 21st-century Camden.

SEE IT ! ***Cecil Sharp House is walking distance from Camden Town Tube. The scenic route is through Regent's Park from Great Portland St.***

361

See chocolate-box cute cottages at Arlington Row

OXFORD & THE COTSWOLDS // Famously labelled 'the most beautiful village in England' by celebrated 19th-century textile and decorative arts designer William Morris, Bibury epitomises all that makes the Cotswolds sparkle. Arlington Row's perfect cluster of honey-coloured cottages sits in riverside bliss, gazing out on the Rack Isle wildlife refuge and River Coln. Originally a monastic wool store dating from 1380, this historic row was transformed in the 17th-century into weavers' cottages – you can even rent no 9, for the quintessential Cotswolds stay.

SEE IT ! ***Bibury is 8 miles northeast of Cirencester, which has good bus and train links. Swing by early on to beat the crowds.***

362

Road-trip through Cheddar Gorge

SOUTHWEST ENGLAND // All right, it's not exactly the Grand Canyon, but Cheddar Gorge is still an impressive sight – England's deepest ravine, 453ft high, carved from the soft limestone hills by the course of the Cheddar Yeo. Further erosion has gouged out numerous subterranean caves, some of which were inhabited since long ago: the skeleton of a 9000-year-old man was discovered here, as well as polished skulls that some archaeologists believe may have been used as prehistoric cups (cheers!). If you want to delve deeper you can do a caving expedition, or just admire the view while ambling along the 3-mile clifftop trail.

SEE IT ! ***The gorge is 11 miles northwest of Wells in Somerset. Traffic is heavy in summer, so come in spring or autumn to avoid the jams.***

© Matt Munro / Lonely Planet

The fairy-tale-like St Michael's Mount; get there via the causeway, but watch out for those tides!

363

Cross the causeway to St Michael's Mount

SOUTHWEST ENGLAND // Rising in the middle of Mount's Bay, the island abbey of St Michael's Mount looks like it's been picked up out of a fairy tale and plonked on the horizon opposite Penzance. This peculiar lump of land has been inhabited since at least the Bronze Age (an axe-head, dagger and intact metal clasp have been found here), and some archaeologists believe it may be the island of Ictis, where ancient Greeks and Romans came to trade for copper and tin.

There's been a chapel on the Mount since at least the 5th century, but it's the island's medieval castle and priory, built between the 12th and 14th centuries, that draws all eyes: the ancestral seat of the St Aubyn family, it's stuffed with grand rooms and priceless antiques, and encircled by gorgeous subtropical gardens.

But the best bit of all about the Mount is getting there: at low tide, you can cross over to the island via the cobbled causeway, just as pilgrims have done for the last thousand-odd years. If you're in luck, low tide might coincide with sunset, to magical effect.

SEE IT ! ***The causeway to St Michael's Mount runs from the nearby village of Marazion. You can also take a ferry.***

© s0ulsurfing - Jason Swain / Getty Images

365

Turn plundering pirate at the Ulster Museum in Belfast

NORTHERN IRELAND // Housed in a bright, modern building, the Ulster Museum is no musty provincial institution – it's packed with fascinating treasures, artworks and interactive displays. The Armada room contains the spoils of the *Girona*, a Spanish galleon wrecked off the north Antrim coast in 1588, while the Egyptian room is home to Takabuti, a 2500-year-old Egyptian mummy unwrapped in Belfast in 1835. Yet more artefacts can be found in the Early Peoples Gallery, including the bronze Bann Disc, a superb example of Iron Age Celtic design.

SEE IT ! ***The museum is in the Queen's Quarter's Botanic Gardens. Don't miss the Palm House and Tropical Ravine greenhouses nearby.***

364

Find a beach that's perfect for you on the Isle of Wight

SOUTHERN ENGLAND // Everyone knows about the southwest's beaches – but you'll likely find quieter strands on the Isle of Wight. The island is ringed by a cluster of sandy coves, perfect for sunbathing, sandcastle-building and (as long as you can stand the chilly Channel temperatures) even a spot of swimming. Our tips? Try Shanklin if you're en famille, Chilton Chine if you're bringing your pooch, Binnel Bay for escaping the crowds, Blackgang Beach for skinny-dipping or Compton Point if you're after a romantic sunset walk.

SEE IT ! ***You'll need a car to reach many of the Isle of Wight's beaches. A good road map comes in very handy.***

366

Get under the capital's skin at Chislehurst Caves

SOUTHEAST ENGLAND // These 22-mile-long man-made caves in the outer reaches of southeast London were first excavated back in the 13th century, mined for flint and chalk. Since operations ceased in the 19th century, the caves have served as an ammunition store, a mushroom farm and a WWII air-raid shelter.

Nowadays the chalky underworld is revealed on guided tours, atmospherically lit by oil lamps. Take a jacket or sweater as it's cold down there!

SEE IT ! ***Chislehurst train station is nearby, on the line from Charing Cross and London Bridge. Bus 269 runs from Bromley.***

367

See hip London on a human scale at Broadway Market

LONDON // Community markets turned hip hang-outs abound in London, but Broadway Market has come through the change with more soul than most. Cutting north from the Regent's Canal to London Fields, the strip is lined with funky places to eat and drink, but the lack of a Tube station keeps the crowd local and the vibe family-friendly and fun. The definitive Broadway Market day starts with a stroll along the canal, followed by a flat white and some artisan picnic shopping, before carting the spoils off to a shady spot in London Fields.

☛ SEE IT ! ***The Overground stations at London Fields and Cambridge Heath provide easy access.***

Apple Juice with
MIXED Fruit
Chegworth
STRAW
£2.50 ea
CHEGWORTH
VALLEY
gluten
free!
P

368

Take in the thrills and spills of the TT on the Isle of Man

NORTHWEST ENGLAND // The annual Tourist Trophy (TT) is one of the most famous motorcycle competitions in the world, drawing in 50,000 petrolheads for the two-week event in late May/early June. The 37.75-mile circuit covers most of the island in a loop that begins and ends in Douglas: all the roads are closed and almost every available bed is taken up by participants and fans. You can watch from pretty much anywhere along the route, but if you can't get a seat in the main grandstand, two other decent viewing spots in Douglas are Braddon Bridge and Bray Hill.

SEE IT ! ***There are regular flights from Liverpool, London and Manchester, and ferry services from Liverpool and Heysham.***

369

Ramble woodlands at Westonbirt National Arboretum

OXFORD & THE COTSWOLDS // Whether dressed in dainty spring florals or parading rich autumnal reds, Britain's 600-acre national arboretum (near Tetbury) charms, whatever the season. Westonbirt is both a key conservation project and a delight to explore: its 15,000-tree collection of 2500 species is one of the world's finest, with sections dating back to its foundation in the 1850s by the super-wealthy Holfords. Trails meander past endangered sapphire dragons, the country's most beautiful incense cedars and nearly all of its native trees.

SEE IT ! ***Travel by public transport and receive a discount on your admission fee. Westonbirt is renowned for its autumn maples.***

370

Gawk at the mighty defences of 13th-century Conwy

NORTH WALES // Embellished by some of the best-preserved town walls in Britain, the mighty medieval fortifications of Conwy flex their bulk at the golden sandy estuary alongside, while the Snowdonia mountains rear behind in a scene that couldn't make for a prettier postcard picture. Conwy Castle, raised between 1283 and 1289 and honoured with Unesco status, along with English King Edward I's other colossal North Wales fortresses, steals the show among the town's many historic attractions.

SEE IT ! ***Four miles south of Llandudno and 44 miles west of Chester, Conwy has a railway station on the North Wales Coast Line.***

371

Go potty over ceramics at the World of Wedgwood

MIDLANDS & THE MARCHES // With a name synonymous with top-quality ceramics that can trace its pedigree back 260 years to entrepreneur founder Josiah Wedgwood, this is easily Britain's foremost interactive pottery experience. A museum swelling with wares from Wedgwood's centuries of worldwide domination of the fine china and porcelain market, this is also Wedgwood's working factory, a series of studios where wannabe potters can try their hand at clay crafting before breaking for afternoon tea (no prizes for guessing what it's served on).

SEE IT ! ***World of Wedgwood is 4 miles south of Stoke-on-Trent. A combo includes afternoon tea, plate designing and museum visits.***

372

Smell the fumes at the National Motor Museum in Beaulieu

Ian Dagnall / Alamy Stock Photo

SOUTHERN ENGLAND // This is one that's got motorheads written all over it. If riding a replica of a 1912 London bus, stepping into a country garage *c*.1930 or seeing the original Chitty Chitty Bang Bang sounds like a fun day out, you'll be in seventh heaven here.

Founded in 1952 by the third Baron Montagu of Beaulieu, in honour of his motor-mad father (the first man to drive a car to the Houses of Parliament), the museum houses more than 250 classic cars, including Del Boy's Robin Reliant van from *Only Fools and Horses*, Mr Bean's Mini and the flying Ford Anglia from *Harry Potter and the Chamber of Secrets*. It's also surely the only museum in England that has its very own monorail. Vroom-vroom.

SEE IT ! ***Beaulieu is on the southern side of the New Forest, about 14 miles south of Southampton. It is open year-round.***

Laura Penhaul's Top Five Places

Two-time world record holder Laura Penhaul was team leader of the first all-female crew to row across the pacific. She works alongside Paralympic athletes as a physio and performance coach.

01

CHAPEL PORTH BEACH, CORNWALL – There's a really cute cafe here where they serve *croque de la mer* sandwiches (toasted garlic bread with melted cheese and crab salad). It's beautiful, and a great place to run.

02

MOUNT EDGCUMBE COUNTRY PARK, CORNWALL – This place has incredible scenery but hardly anyone knows about it. Adventure Segway there is a brilliant way to explore the area, whatever your fitness levels. My parents even did it for their 40th anniversary.

03

SKYE, SCOTLAND – There's a really sweet bothy up in the Isle of Skye called Ollisdal and it's a great way to get away, with no phone signal. It's close to the route of the brilliantly wild clifftop walk from Ramasaig to Orbost.

04

DANS LE NOIR?, LONDON – This restaurant is hosted by people who are visually impaired. You go into a room where you can't see your hand in front of your face and they serve up the most incredible food. It's great fun.

05

GWITHIAN TOWANS BEACH, ST IVES – I love sleeping out among the stars with friends – riding our bikes and just bedding down wherever. There are loads of places here where you can stay sheltered among the sand dunes and stargaze well into the night.

© Edwin Remsberg / Alamy

373

Tread in the steps of Richard III at Middleham Castle

YORKSHIRE // The imposing walls, towers and buttresses of grey stone that dominate the village of Middleham look for all the world like a youngster's doodle of a medieval castle. Heavy, squat and four-square, bristling with portent, they emanate power. Set at the eastern end of Wensleydale, where it guarded the royal road between Skipton and Richmond, Middleham Castle's biggest claim to fame is that it was the childhood home of King Richard III.

The massive Norman keep in the centre is one of the biggest in the country, built towards the end of the 12th century, with a magnificent great hall at its centre. It replaced an earlier motte-and-bailey fortress, whose remains are at William's Hill, a pleasant 10-minute walk south of Middleham. Climb to the top for stunning views over the castle's 14th-century curtain walls and corner towers, and west to the rolling skyline of the Yorkshire Dales.

SEE IT ! ***Middleham is 12 miles south of Richmond. Staff celebrate the birthday of Richard III each 2 October, complete with cake!***

© CL - Medien / Shutterstock

374

Feel the spirit of Scotland's founding fathers at Scone

CENTRAL SCOTLAND // Standing amid the hush of Douglas firs, surveying what was the capital of the Picts 1500 years ago, it's hard to imagine this palace as a frenzy of political activity. But it was once the seat of parliaments and the crowning place of Scots kings, including Macbeth and Robert the Bruce. Here, any visitor automatically becomes a history expert.

Beyond the ludicrous splendour of the grounds and treasures of the state apartments, there are plenty of compelling stories to be told. None more so than of Moot Hill, where a small Presbyterian chapel stands to mark the spot where Scots kings were coronated on the Stone of Scone, a powerful symbol of Scottish independence. Today, a replica sits in front of the chapel – the original is at Edinburgh Castle – but excavations around Scone's lost abbey continue to unearth riches to stir any imagination.

SEE IT ! ***Scone Palace is open from March to October and located 3 miles north of Perth. Trains from Edinburgh take one hour.***

© Gillian Pullinger / Alamy

375

Find a natural talent at Gilbert White's House in Selborne

SOUTHERN ENGLAND // While you may well not have heard of Gilbert White, this pioneering parson was, in his own modest way, the 18th century's answer to David Attenborough. A passionate gardener and horticulturalist, he devoted much of his life to the study of the natural world – or at least, the natural world of his local parish of Selborne in Hampshire. Unusually for the time, White believed in hands-on practice and the value of studying animals in their natural environment. From bats to bees, harvest mice to earthworms, and willow warblers to woodpeckers, Gilbert White studied them all. His magnum opus, *The Natural History and Antiquities of Selborne*, published in 1789, has become a nature-writing classic and, famously, it's never been out of print. You can still visit his house and wander the gardens, which are planted and maintained according to White's own methods. All hail a horticultural hero.

SEE IT ! ***The closest railway station is in Alton, about 5 miles to the north. There's a bus service connecting the town with Selborne.***

© John McGovern / Alamy

376

Learn how Glasgow conquered the world at the People's Palace

SOUTHERN SCOTLAND // There is something cinematic about this museum, with eclectic films and photo exhibits competing for your attention at every turn. First conceived as a palace of 'pleasure and imagination', to provide distraction for Glasgow's working classes in the late 19th century, it's a trick that still delivers plenty of razzamatazz today.

There are paintings and personal stories riffing on the city's social history, from the time of the tobacco lords in the 1750s to post-WWII trade unions, but also displays dedicated to two of the city's obsessions: dancing and having a right good laugh (cue: Sir Billy Connolly's legendary banana boots).

Adjoining the palace is the Winter Gardens, a botanical house that transports visitors from Glasgow Green, the city's beloved park, into a world of tropical palms.

SEE IT ! ***The People's Palace is best reached by walking along the Clyde Walkway. It's a 25-minute (1-mile) walk from Central Station.***

© PDerrett / Getty Images

378

Take the fast train to arty Margate

SOUTHEAST ENGLAND // A decade ago Margate was down in the dumps, a semi-derelict, long-forgotten seaside resort town. But then along came the spectacular Turner Contemporary gallery, a world-class art space that has helped spin the fortunes of this Thanet community 180°. JMW Turner admired the refracted light in Margate – now the town draws his fans and hip day trippers from London who perusing the gallery's temporary shows then head into the rejuvenated old town for a bite to eat and a mooch around the artisan stores and retro clothes emporia.

SEE IT ! *Margate is linked to London by direct high-speed train and to Canterbury by local bus.*

377

Seek out angels and demons at Rosslyn

EDINBURGH // It's not all Dan Brown's fault. This rural sanctuary was one of the most mysterious chapels on Earth, long before the American author penned *The Da Vinci Code*. The success of the book – and movie spin-off – has brought in the busloads, who try to find connections to the Knights Templar, but it's still a riot to join them in feeling stupefied. Why? Because you're looking at some of the most spectacular church interiors in Europe and at 200-plus pillar, archway and keystone carvings that cover the nave, apse and altar. Wow, and double wow.

SEE IT ! *Rosslyn Chapel is in the village of Roslin, which is a 30-minute drive south from Edinburgh.*

379

Get into Godard at HOME, Manchester

NORTHWEST ENGLAND // This arts venue has two theatre spaces, five cinema screens, a ground-floor bar and a decent café-restaurant. All of which makes it one of the city's most popular gathering spots: even if you're not attending one of its well-regarded plays or performances (think provocative work), or to see the latest indie movie release, HOME is a wonderful space to just hang around in, drink coffee and discuss film and avant-garde theatre. This being Manchester, however, there's a low pretension threshold and a fairly high bar for creative endeavours. Just what you'd want from one of Britain's best arts centres.

SEE IT ! *HOME is on First St, a short walk southwest from Oxford Road station.*

© age fotostock / Alamy

© Keith Douglas / Alamy

380

Find your inner horticulturalist at West Sussex's West Dean Gardens

SOUTHEAST ENGLAND // Billed as one of the UK's greatest restored gardens, West Dean Gardens near Chichester is an unmissable spot for anyone with even slightly green fingers.

There has been a garden of some kind here since the early 17th century and the site has been enhanced over the centuries. Additions include still-working Victorian glasshouses, a 295ft-long Edwardian pergola, sunken gardens and a walled kitchen garden from the 1990s.

The sheer number of plants on display here is overwhelming, from blooming borders to a rainbow of lettuce varieties in the kitchen garden; and from figs in the glasshouses to 100 varieties of apple. And when it's watering and feeding time for humans, make for the award-winning café and restaurant.

☛ SEE IT ! ***There are local buses every 20 minutes from Chichester to the village of West Dean. The gardens are closed in January.***

381

Clamber up the 288 steps to lord it over the Fens at Ely Cathedral

EAST ANGLIA // They call it the 'Ship of the Fens', and it's easy to see why – in East Anglia's flat, fenland landscape, Ely's 215ft tower punctures the sky, visible for miles around. Inside, the early 12th-century nave soars up in clean, uncluttered lines. You'll also spot the entrancing ceiling, the masterly 14th-century Octagon, and towers that surge up in shimmering colours. A cathedral since 1109, Ely's past is, inevitably, chequered – look out for the empty niches in the 14th-century Lady Chapel. These once held statues of saints and martyrs, but were hacked out unceremoniously by iconoclasts during the English Civil War.

For more evocative details, be sure to take the free ground-floor guided tours. And book ahead for the superb tower tours, which deliver behind-the-scenes glimpses, up to 288 steps and remarkable views.

☛ SEE IT ! ***Visit during evensong (5.30pm Monday to Saturday, 4pm Sunday) or a choral service (10.30am Sunday) for the best atmosphere.***

382

Home in on cute Crickhowell for some top walks

MID-WALES // Roving along the hedge-lined lanes of the Brecon Beacons National Park brings you to Crickhowell, a fudge-tin pretty town sitting astride the River Usk. Winner of the Great British High Street Awards in 2018, its old-fashioned appeal is obvious: neat rows of Georgian houses, a butcher, baker, bookshop and raft of independent shops, and a glorious 600-year-old pub, The Bear, with sagging beams. The town is the starting point for some cracking walks, including the short but steep ascent to Crug Hywel Iron Age hill fort.

SEE IT ! ***Abergavenny, 7 miles away, has the closest railway station. Crickhowell is on the main A40 through the Brecon Beacons.***

383

Give the mountains a break at Surf Snowdonia

NORTH WALES // Snowdonia's natural attractions (vast mountains, lovely lakes) did not deter developers from adding a non-natural one which, since completion in 2015, commands real reverence from a very different demographic to the region's traditional thrill seekers: surfers.

Surf Snowdonia, which can generate a 6ft-high wave claimed by many to be the planet's biggest manufactured break, is the UK's only artificial surfing lake. An off-road pump track and a new on-site hotel are next on the cards.

TRY IT ! ***Surf Snowdonia is in Dolgarrog, a village 9 miles south of Conwy. It has a railway station on the Conwy Valley Line.***

384

Unravel scientific wonders at Woolsthorpe Manor

MIDLANDS & THE MARCHES // As the one-time home of Sir Isaac Newton, this 17th-century yeoman's house inspired some of the world's most groundbreaking discoveries. The big one was gravity: watching apples fall from a still-standing tree here is supposedly how Newton happened upon his theory. A window into the scientist's times as much as his life, this attraction's master stroke is a wonderful science centre, where you can experiment with gravity and organise stargazing sessions: apt, in the house of the man who explained the tides and solar system.

SEE IT ! ***The manor is in Woolsthorpe-by-Colsterworth, 8 miles south of Grantham.***

© Peter Conner / Alamy

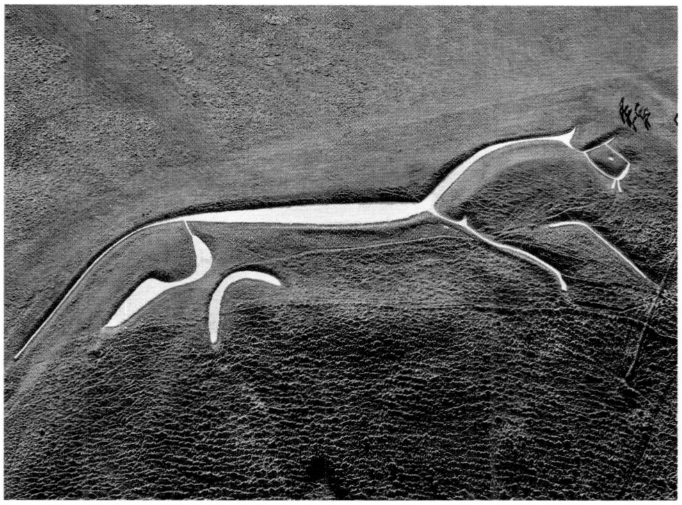

© Iconpix / Alamy

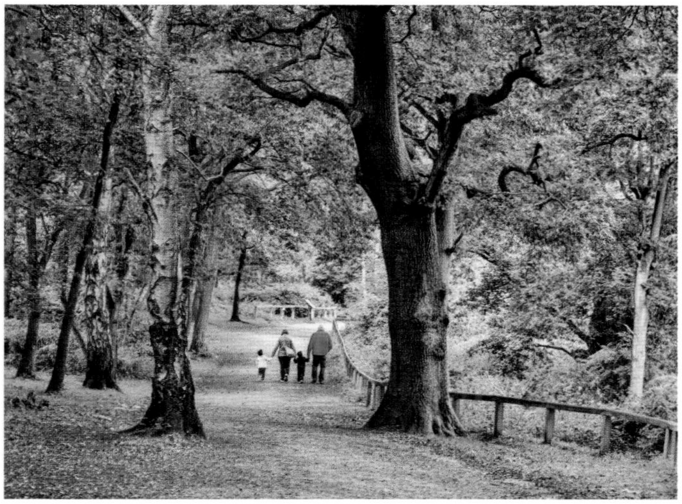

© Travellinglight / Alamy

385

Uffington White Horse – the UK's Nazca Lines?

OXFORD & THE COTSWOLDS // Southeast from Oxford lie the whaleback hills of the Berkshire Downs, and the great prehistoric work of art that is the Uffington White Horse. Revealing the chalk below the turf, Bronze Age people created a hilltop figure over 100ft tall that has dominated the region for millennia. While today's visitors can reach the horse, it's hard to make out at close quarters so better seen from a distance. In fact, its striking appearance from the air has led some observers to link its origins to UFOs or the mysterious crop circles often seen in this area.

Back down to earth, other Bronze Age features in the surrounding area include the giant ditch defences of Uffington Castle, while a 3-mile round-trip walk goes to Wayland's Smithy, a Neolithic burial chamber, where – according to local legend, and to maintain the equine theme – horses left overnight are magically re-shod by an invisible blacksmith.

☛ SEE IT ! *The nearest town is Faringdon, northeast of Swindon. The villages of Longcot and Fernham offer great views of the White Horse.*

386

Join Sherwood Forest's Merry Men (and women)

MIDLANDS & THE MARCHES // Sherwood Forest, as even nascent Nottinghamshire aficionados know, was Robin Hood's stomping ground, and if ever you were to emulate the outlaw and his band of brigands, this high ropes course would be the initiation test, suspended from the same trees Locksley & Co no doubt swung from. The Tree Top Adventure here features outdoor activities company Go Ape's longest tree-to-tree zip wire, alongside a melee of Tarzan swings, rope ladders and precarious paths at around 9m high.

The site, 19 miles north of Nottingham and 6 miles northeast of Mansfield, offers an equivalent children's course, and the little 'uns can also go wild at Nets Kingdom, where they can bounce high above the forest floor on nets. The setting for this almighty adrenaline rush is the largest remaining tract of publicly accessible forest in the East Midlands, Sherwood Pines.

☛ TRY IT ! *Stagecoach bus services 14 and 15 stop in Kings Clipstone, a mile away from Go Ape Sherwood Pines.*

387

Brave the stories of Real Mary in the grisly King's Close

EDINBURGH // Trust the residents of Scotland's bewitching capital to do a fine job of scaring the pants off you. That's the appeal of this entombed labyrinth of frozen-in-time streets and claustrophobic rooms hidden underneath the Royal Mile – a walk here feels like falling through a trapdoor into a 17th-century time warp. There are costumed actors to talk you through the close's grisly history, which saw the passageways buried following the Black Plague of 1645, but it's all family-friendly fun. In short, something wicked this way comes.

SEE IT ! ***Due to the historic layout, the hour-long tour can't accommodate wheelchairs and it isn't unsuitable for under-5s.***

388

Discover a visionary space at Stoneywell

MIDLANDS & THE MARCHES // A unique example of an intact 1890s Arts and Crafts movement house, Stoneywell is surrounded by beautiful old woodland, but it is this cottage's construction – built directly into a slope with rooms on seven levels – and its furnishings that most impress. The story of Stoneywell's founding says it all. Ernest Gimson, an architect subscribing to the Arts and Crafts ethos that one should be able to build what one designs, retreated to this rural pocket of Leicestershire and did just that. The cottage remains a pooling of innovative 19th-century design ideals from Gimson and the craftsmen he enlisted to build it.

SEE IT ! ***Stoneywell is in Ulverston, a hamlet 8 miles northwest of Leicester.***

389

Sample local goodies at St George's Market in Belfast

NORTHERN IRELAND // Built in 1896, St George's is Ireland's oldest continually operating market; these days the atmosphere is festive, with live music most Sundays. Over recent years, Northern Ireland has experienced a boom in locally grown and artisan produce, and St George's Market is the ideal place to while away a morning, sampling everything from Belfast tea to traditional baked goods, flavoured cooking oils, and meats and cheeses from nearby farms. Stalls packed with local arts and crafts are perfect for souvenir hunters.

SEE IT ! ***St George's Market opens is open Friday to Sunday. It's a short walk from Belfast city centre.***

© Design Pics Inc / Alamy

© Daniel Di Paolo

© Meibion / Alamy

390

Enjoy the perfect pie and pint combo in a London boozer

LONDON // Steak and kidney is one of those inspired combinations, like bacon and eggs or mac and cheese. Add a pint of locally brewed bitter, served in the convivial surroundings of an old London boozer, and you've come close to perfection. A few ground rules first, however. The pastry should be rich and shortcrust, not fluffy or flaky. Onion, steak, kidney and ale are the only approved fillings – start adding things like red wine and Mediterranean herbs and you're going well off-piste.

Rules apply to the beverage, too – American IPAs and German wheat beers are verboten, as is anything artisan or fruit-flavoured. The pint should be real ale, brewed inside the M25 and hand-pulled, ideally by a Cockney bartender whose gran sang for the troops in the war. Recommended pubs for this London treat include Mayfair's Guinea Grill and The Windmill, and Columbia Rd's Birdcage.

☛ TRY IT ! *Bond Street and Green Park Tubes are handy for Mayfair; for Columbia Rd, take a stroll from Hoxton Overground.*

391

Feel the sand between your toes at Camber Sands

SOUTHEAST ENGLAND // If all those shingle beaches along the south coast have left you longing to feel some grains between your toes, there's no better place to head than the dunes and golden flats of Camber Sands near Rye. Extending for almost 2 miles along the coast from the mouth of the River Rother, there's plenty of towel space for everyone here, even on hot sunny days.

The seafront is almost wholly undeveloped, lending the beach a wild feel – so desolate are parts of Camber Sands that they have stood in for various deserts on screen.

On a windy day, this long stretch of flat sand is ideal for kitesurfing, kite landboarding and kite buggying – or simply flying a kite! There are a couple of hire centres on the seafront road and instructors on hand to show you the ropes.

☛ SEE IT ! *Local buses running between Rye and Dover stop in the village of Camber. There are three car parks.*

© Courtesy of River Cottage

Fresh fruit and veg are the order of the day at River Cottage, where most of the produce is grown in the garden

392

Learn to cook at River Cottage

SOUTHWEST ENGLAND // Since the late 1990s, chef and environmental campaigner Hugh Fearnley-Whittingstall has been serving up his version of the good life from his family's own rural idyll in the depths of Dorset, River Cottage. Through cookbooks and TV shows, Fearnley-Whittingstall has fronted campaigns covering tricky topics such as marine sustainability and waste, and educated the nation with his rustic, seasonally inspired cuisine. If you've been motivated by his ethos, why not consider booking a bespoke cooking course at the place where it all began?

Covering everything from meat and fish preparation to foraging, food-preserving, baking, jam-making, cheese craft, beekeeping and even hedge-laying, there's a course to suit all interests (although you're unlikely to meet the main man himself, what with all his commitments). And after you've learned the basics, it would seem silly not to dine at the restaurant to see the theory being put into practice: the Sunday lunch is legendary, and of course, much of the produce comes direct from the farm and kitchen garden.

TRY IT ! ***River Cottage is about 4 miles south of Axminster. A one-day cooking course costs around £240.***

393

Make time for a cuppa at Falling Foss Tea Garden

YORKSHIRE // Tucked away in a hidden fold of the North York Moors, this must be a contender for the most enchanting tea room in northern England. Set in the garden of a cute Georgian cottage known as Midge Hall, it's surrounded by native woodland and sits within earshot of Falling Foss, a 33ft-high waterfall that cascades in a silvery veil down a moss-cushioned pancake stack of Jurassic shale. Although there's parking a few minutes from the cottage, the best approach is to hike the half-mile nature trail downstream from May Beck car park.

SEE IT ! *The waterfall walk is open year-round, but the tea garden operates April to September only.*

394

Saddle up for the Whole Earth Man V Horse Marathon

MID-WALES // Whatever is in the water supplying Llanwrtyd Wells, it must make people nuts. This former spa town has swapped taking the waters with hosting two far madder and less leisurely pursuits. The Whole Earth Man v Horse marathon, in which two-legged athletes take on four-legged ones over 22 miles, complements the equally silly world bog snorkelling championships on the town's wacky events calendar. Race records show a man has actually beaten a horse: twice. Since 2007, though, horses have reined supreme.

SEE IT ! *Llanwrtyd Wells, 12 miles southwest of Builth Wells, can be reached (with difficulty) by train from Swansea or Shrewsbury.*

© Robert Harding / Alamy

395

Watch the best of Britain's regattas at Cowes Week

SOUTHERN ENGLAND // As you'd expect from a nation of seafarers, nowhere knows how to do a regatta better than Great Britain, and the reigning monarch of regattas is Cowes Week – the largest in the world, with more than 1000 boats and 8000 competitors. It's been held on the Isle of Wight since 1826; throughout the eight-day festival, vessels of all shapes and sizes race across the choppy waters of the Solent, and at the end of the week, a grand fireworks display lights up the skies over the Channel.

SEE IT ! *Cowes Week is usually held in the first week of August. Accommodation is usually booked up, so reserve well ahead.*

396

Take in the swirl of murmurations above the Somerset Levels

SOUTHWEST ENGLAND // Forget Glastonbury, Somerset's most spectacular gathering happens in the winter months. From late September, hundreds of thousands of starlings migrate to the UK from colder climates, and one of their favourite roosting spots is the Somerset Levels. Here, when the conditions are right, they gather in huge swooping formations known as murmurations. Head to the RSPB Ham Wall wetland area to see the massive avian acrobatic show, in which thousands of birds dive, twist and whirl in breathtaking unison.

SEE IT ! ***RSPB Ham Wall is 4 miles west of Glastonbury and has parking and boardwalk trails through the wetlands.***

Is this the best pub location in the world? Probably. Head to the village of Porthdinllaen to find it

397

Sink a pint at Ty Coch Inn in Morfa Nefyn

NORTH WALES // Raise a pint to the third-highest-positioned pub on this list (find the others at #315 and #330), which could claim to be Britain's number-one watering hole without too much whinging from any of the competition.

The Ty Coch sits on the beach in the National Trust–owned fishing hamlet of Porthdinllaen, a settlement of about two dozen houses around the beach from Morfa Nefyn – about a mile's walk away along the coast. And it is some beach: a silvery sandy crescent below a steep arcing promontory, which forms your route to the pub, on foot, as vehicle access is restricted.

The pub building, dating to 1823, actually started life as a vicarage. Then the reverend relocated and left his housekeeper to open Ty Coch tavern in 1842, serving the needs of the beach's drink-deprived sailors. Mariners once had four pubs in minuscule Porthdinllaen to choose from: Ty Coch is the sole survivor. Going to the bar? Make yours a glass of the Ty Coch's delicious cider and slurp it in the atmospheric beamed interior or at one of the tables overlooking the sands outside.

TRY IT ! ***Morfa Nefyn lies on the Llŷn Peninsula in Gwynedd, 19 miles west of Porthmadog.***

© John Potter / Alamy

© Bildarchiv Monheim GmbH / Alamy

398

Get off the beaten track in the Yorkshire Wolds

YORKSHIRE // David Hockney fans will recognise the landscapes of the Yorkshire Wolds – rolling chalk downs, rich farmland, mighty beech trees and overgrown country lanes. Lacking any major tourist attractions, it's a part of the country where you can escape the crowds and enjoy a ramble without meeting another soul.

The Wolds curve in a lazy crescent from the Humber estuary west of Hull to meet the North Sea at Flamborough Head. Their lonely allure is epitomised by the walk between the hamlet of Thixendale (the location for Hockney's most famous series of Wolds paintings) and the abandoned medieval village of Wharram Percy, whose ruined church rises above the grassy outlines of long-gone streets and cottages. Picturesque beyond words, the secluded path follows a dry valley in the chalk, through woods and fields that seem little changed since the 1960s.

SEE IT ! ***Thixendale and Wharram Percy lie on minor roads between Malton and the A166 York–Driffield road.***

399

Visit Red House, the family home of William Morris

SOUTHEAST ENGLAND // Celebrated for his textile designs and his association with the British Arts and Crafts movement of the late 19th and early 20th centuries, William Morris built this family home in the then Kentish village of Upton in 1860. With the help of architect Philip Webb, the father of Arts and Crafts architecture, as well as some of the leading artists of the day, Morris created a work of art inside and out. As lovely as it was, 'the beautifullest place on earth' according to Edward Burne-Jones, Morris sold the house after five years and moved to a flat in fashionable Bloomsbury.

In the hands of the National Trust since 2003, Red House is an idyllic property that showcases the best of Arts and Crafts design, from exquisite stained glass and furniture designed by Webb and Morris to Pre-Raphaelite paintings.

SEE IT ! ***Bexleyheath is the nearest train station, with services from London Victoria, Charing Cross and Cannon Street.***

400—500

400

Traverse a cliffside coastal walk at the Gobbins, Co Antrim

NORTHERN IRELAND // Billed as the most dramatic walk in Europe, the Gobbins is an exhilarating coastal path that follows the curves of the cliffs through a series of tubular and suspension bridges, tunnels, caves and narrow crevices. Walks along this dramatic part of the east Antrim coast are accompanied by guides, who explain the history and geology of the site and point out seabirds. A feat of engineering, the Gobbins opened in 1902 and in its heyday was more popular than the Giant's Causeway. After 60 years in a state of disrepair, it reopened in 2015.

SEE IT ! ***Guided tours set off from the visitor centre at Islandmagee. The nearest train station is Ballycarry, 1.8 miles away.***

401

Explore the Abbey Garden on Tresco

SOUTHWEST ENGLAND // Few islands can boast a horticultural treasure as precious as the Abbey Garden. Nurtured by the balmy Gulf Stream, it was established in 1834 by botanical collector Augustus Smith and is home to all kinds of subtropical blooms and exotic plants that struggle to survive elsewhere in the UK: spiky succulents, crimson flame trees, majestic palms, king protea and blue-purple tree echium. Admission also covers the fascinating Valhalla Museum, with many figureheads salvaged from ships wrecked on the Isles' rocky shores.

SEE IT ! ***There are no cars on Tresco, so everyone gets around on foot or by bicycle – bikes can be hired right beside the main quay.***

402

See a circle of life at Philiphaugh Salmon Viewing Centre

SOUTHERN SCOTLAND // In Scotland, a salmon is more than the king of fish. It is an entry point into golden days spent by the river casting lines. It is breakfast, an appetiser and a main course (but it is most certainly not deep fried). And when scrutinised in its native habitat on the Ettrick River, at this viewing gallery in Selkirk, it is a fish that makes you marvel at the world's precious natural order. As the rainbow-skinned salmon leap their way upriver to spawn, the epic journey seems like something of an aquamarine dream.

SEE IT ! ***The Philiphaugh Salmon Viewing Centre is 1 mile east of Selkirk and is open seven days a week.***

403

See grass roots cricket in Sewerby

YORKSHIRE // Few pastimes are as quintessentially English as watching a cricket match. But for the true village-green experience, eschew the glamour of county cricket for the quieter pleasures of amateur leagues. Sewerby, northeast of Bridlington in East Yorkshire, is unusual in having a cricket pitch with a wonderful clifftop location overlooking the North Sea, and stunning views across Bridlington Bay. Instead of a grandstand, the pitch is lined with park benches, affording everyone a view of the action. And afterwards, you can take a stroll along the coastal path.

SEE IT ! ***Matches are played on most Saturdays from May to September, starting at 1pm. Bring a picnic.***

404

Swing by Sherwood Forest National Nature Reserve

MIDLANDS & THE MARCHES // No wonder Robin Hood adored Sherwood Forest: the majesty of the 900-odd ancient oaks in this one-time royal hunting ground and 1000-acre reserve is mesmeric: and there are trees aplenty in which it is easy to imagine his outlaws hiding out. Most renowned amongst the arboreal residents is the Major Oak, nigh-on a millennium old, where Robin and all the Merry Men supposedly slept! An innovative visitor centre, added in 2018, helps you plot your explorations and a much-loved Robin Hood Festival entertains each August.

SEE IT ! ***The forest visitor centre is just north of Edwinstowe, 7 miles northeast of Mansfield.***

405

Take a stroll around Derry's city walls

NORTHERN IRELAND // From the Bogside murals to the Fountain estate and the River Foyle, most of Derry can be seen from the vantage point of the old city walls. Completed in 1619, these are the only city walls in Ireland to survive almost intact, though the four original gates (Shipquay, Ferryquay, Bishop's and Butcher's) were rebuilt in the 18th and 19th centuries, when three new gates (New, Magazine and Castle) were added. Walking the circumference of the walls encircling the city centre is a great way to get a feel for Derry's layout and the city's past.

SEE IT ! ***It's easy to walk the walls unguided, but you'll learn more if you join a tour such as City Walking Tours.***

406

Quench your thirst in England's highest pub, the Tan Hill Inn

YORKSHIRE // There aren't many pubs where you have to step over a couple of lambs lounging at the front porch and shoo a cat off the bench before you can take a seat and enjoy your pint of bitter. The 17th-century Tan Hill Inn is just such a pub, sitting in glorious isolation in the midst of sheep-spotted Stonesdale Moor on the northern edge of the Yorkshire Dales National Park. At 1732ft above sea level it's England's highest pub and a favourite stop for hikers walking the Pennine Way, which runs right past the front door.

SEE IT ! ***The pub is 27 miles west of Richmond, on a minor road leading to Brough in Cumbria.***

407

Visit Jane Austen's house in Chawton

SOUTHERN ENGLAND // There's something odd about standing on the spot where great works of literature were created – it can almost feel like the writer in question has simply stepped away, due to return at any moment. So it is at Chawton, near Winchester, in the cosy red-brick house where Jane Austen lived with her mother and sister from 1809 to 1817, and where she penned some of her best-known books (including *Mansfield Park*, *Emma* and *Persuasion*). Look out for Austen's own writing desk and first editions of several of her novels.

SEE IT ! ***The museum is 18 miles east of Winchester; local buses run fairly close to Chawton village.***

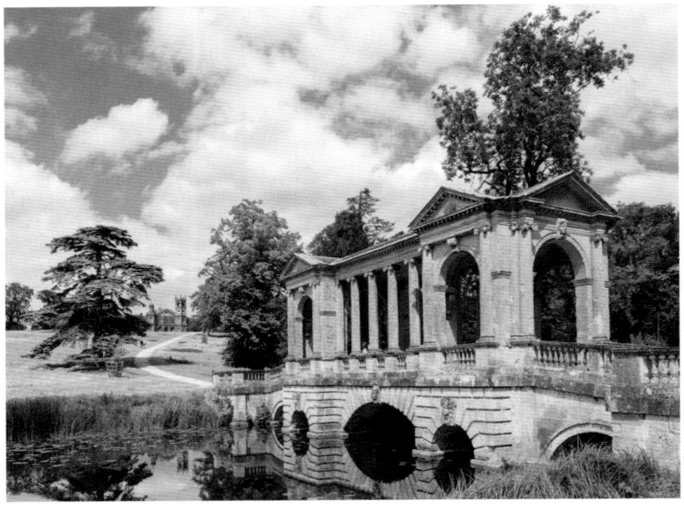

© Ian Dagnall / Alamy

© Alamy Stock Photo

408

Uncover the secret temples and follies of Stowe Gardens

SOUTHERN ENGLAND // Britain's greatest landscape architect, Lancelot 'Capability' Brown, may have risen to sculpt the nation's most renowned parklands, but he honed his talents in the 1740s as head gardener to the prosperous Temple-Grenville family, whose deftly designed country gardens grace the grounds of Buckinghamshire's neoclassical Stowe House. Zipping along majestic, 1.5-mile-long Stowe Ave, the house and gardens lie hidden from view – the beauty is in discovering them on foot, slowly unravelling Capability Brown's signature subtle dips, playful tricks on the eye and his man-made 'natural' aesthetic. Wander between lakes, fountains, cascades and bridges to reach the sweeping Grecian Valley, sprinkled with yews, pines and, famously, temples and follies. Elegant Stowe House itself is now an exclusive private school: study its staterooms on guided tours.

SEE IT ! *Stowe is 3 miles northwest of Buckingham; the nearest train stations are at Milton Keynes and Bicester North.*

409

Bask in the glow of the Chagall windows at Tudeley

SOUTHEAST ENGLAND // The tiny All Saints' church in Tudelely, less than three miles from Tonbridge in Kent, has the distinction of being the only church in the world whose stained glass windows are all designed by Russian-born artist Marc Chagall, and the contrast between the humble church and the rich European modernism of the artist's swirling blues and golds is unmissable. Chagall's hauntingly lovely twelve windows were bought about by the tragic death in 1963 of a young modern art lover, Sarah d'Avigdor-Goldsmid, whose parents commissioned the artist to design the large east window as a tribute to their daughter. Arriving at the medieval church in 1967 to install the window, Chagall apparently exclaimed, 'It's magnificent. I will do them all.' The vibrantly coloured scenes encompass traditional Chagall tropes of hope and joy, such as angels, asses, birds and horses.

SEE IT ! *The church is 2.5 miles southeast from Tonbridge Station. The church is open daily during daylight hours.*

© Dave Porter / Alamy

© The National Trust Photolibrary / Alamy

410

Marvel at Southwell Minster's interior decoration

MIDLANDS & THE MARCHES // The faithful have worshipped on the site of Southwell Minster for 1300 years, and parts of the existing building are thought to date from as early as the 9th century, putting this cathedral right up there with England's most venerable religious places. Despite being the spot where King Charles I was captured during the English Civil War, history is not the cathedral's strongest suit; ornamentation, however, most certainly is, and its Romanesque interiors are some of the Church of England's most interesting. The striking cynosure is the fine polygonal 14th-century chapter house, festooned in the most exquisite naturalistic carvings of the day, and without equal elsewhere in the country. Motifs include leaves based on nearby woods and hedgerows, animals and, intriguingly, green men.

SEE IT ! ***Southwell is 2 miles northwest of Fiskerton railway station, on the Lincoln–Nottingham line, and 12 miles southeast of Mansfield.***

411

Play lord of the manor at Dorset's Kingston Lacy

SOUTHWEST ENGLAND // Not many stately homes can claim to have their very own Iron Age hill fort, but this Dorset dazzler does. The ancient fortification known as the Badbury Rings sits within Kingston Lacy's grounds, along with a Japanese-style teahouse, Victorian fernery, rose garden, water meadows, acres of woodland and even the remnants of a Roman road. And then there's the house: built in the mid-1600s to resemble an Italian palazzo, it's crammed with antiques, Egyptian artefacts and even a few Old Master paintings (including works by Rubens and Titian). The house was originally owned by the Bankes family, who unfortunately backed the wrong side during the Civil War; their former home, Corfe Castle, was blasted to bits by Roundhead forces, so they had to make do with this little country pad instead.

SEE IT ! ***Kingston Lacy is 2.5 miles west of Wimborne in Dorset, and has been owned by the National Trust since 1982.***

412

Get happily lost in the topiary gardens of Levens Hall

CUMBRIA // Attached to an impressive Elizabethan manor home, built around a fortified pele tower, are the even more impressive 12-acre topiary gardens laid out between 1689 and 1712 by French gardener Guillaume Beaumont. They've remained largely unchanged since then, so the extraordinary Alice in Wonderland-like vision of pyramids, swirls, curls, pom-poms and peacocks you'll see is close to what Restoration-era guests would have beheld. As you make your way through the gardens, you're met with a series of ever-more dramatic set pieces.

SEE IT ! ***Levens Hall is 2 miles south of Sizergh Castle on the A6, south of Kendal.***

413

Ponder the art at Jupiter Artland

SOUTHERN SCOTLAND // In West Lothian, they say the Guggenheim's got competition – and the reason is this sprawling sculpture park and art gallery in the grounds of Bonnington House. An iron cage installation by Anish Kapoor? Find it hidden by a copse of oak. A skeletal tangle of wire by Anthony Gormley? Overlooking a swathe of farmland. Charles Jencks' concentric land sculptures? Swirling around four lakes and a causeway. Call it what you will: Narnia for artists, or a garden of discovery. One thing's for sure: you'll never view a gallery the same way again.

TRY IT ! ***Jupiter Artland is open from May to September. It's a 30-minute drive from Edinburgh.***

414

Marvel at the fabulous follies of Stourhead

SOUTHWEST ENGLAND // If an Englishman's home is his castle, then his gardens are his kingdom – which must make the 2650-acre gardens of Stourhead an empire. They're a triumph of 18th-century English landscaping, designed by Henry Hoare II, and laid out between 1741 and 1780. Inspired by the dreamy Italianate landscapes of painters such as Claude Lorrain and Poussin, the gardens are a horticultural fantasy-land of temples, lakes, woods, bridges and follies, chief of which is the 164ft-high King Alfred's Tower, offering sweeping views across the estate.

SEE IT ! ***National Trust-owned Stourhead is off the B3092, 8 miles south of Frome.***

415

Feel awestruck at Gloucester Cathedral

OXFORD & THE COTSWOLDS // Architecture-lovers won't want to miss Gloucester's glorious cathedral: having started life as a Saxon abbey, later re-imagined as a 12th-century Norman church, it's now one of the finest and earliest examples of the distinctive English Perpendicular Gothic style. Ingeniously uniting Gothic and Norman Romanesque design, the cathedral houses the intricate alabaster tomb of King Edward II, who died (suspiciously) at Gloucestershire's Berkeley Castle in 1327. The 1367 Great Cloister – almost unparalleled in its beauty – flaunts England's original fan vaulting and is cameoed in several Harry Potter films.

SEE IT ! ***Gloucester is well connected with London and beyond. Extend your trip to by exploring the Cotswolds or Forest of Dean.***

© Mark Andrews / 500px

© SWNS / Alamy

416

Have old-fashioned seaside fun at the 'Queen of Welsh Resorts', Llandudno

NORTH WALES // Wales' main beach resort, Llandudno, retains vestiges of its Victorian heyday and a striking natural setting that make it among the most attractive of Britain's bigger seaside towns. The sheltered sandy sweep of its North Shore Beach, the longest pier in Wales (longer also than Blackpool's and Brighton's) and the 1902 Great Orme Tramway hauling passengers up to a headland high above town, all helped establish it as a leading tourist destination by the turn of the century, and have kept it up there ever since.

Just outside town is the impressive country mansion of Bodysgallen, but it's the refreshing presence of one of Wales' best contemporary art galleries, Mostyn, that shows Llandudno is anything but resting on those 19th-century laurels.

SEE IT ! ***Llandudno, 46 miles west of Chester, is well connected to the national railway network.***

417

Dodge the pagans and Flaming Tar Barrels of Devon's Ottery St Mary

SOUTHWEST ENGLAND // Here's a novel way to spend an evening. Get yourself a wooden barrel. Coat it with tar. Set it on fire, then strap it to your back and run around the streets of a little English village, trying not to ignite either yourself or the hordes of onlookers who have gathered to watch your antics.

Normally, any person attempting this kind of lunacy would be packed off to the nearest psychiatric unit, but for one night of the year, running about with a flaming barrel strapped to your back is considered the height of jolly japery by the locals of East Devon's Ottery St Mary. Apparently it's all something to do with the Gunpowder Plot and pagan fire rituals; regardless, it's probably not a good idea to try it at home.

SEE IT ! ***The Flaming Tar Barrels festival is held on 5 November, starting at around 5pm. It's hugely popular so get there early.***

City workers and sightseers alike make use of Leadenhall Market, a Victorian oasis in London's financial district

418

Uncover Victorian London between the skyscrapers at Leadenhall Market

LONDON // With skyscrapers seemingly endlessly on the up, the old City of London is vanishing under a wave of polished chrome and sheet glass. Thank heavens then for Leadenhall Market, a gorgeous piece of Victoriana within sight of the Gherkin, Cheesegrater and Lloyds of London.

In a grand covered market that's all curving cast iron, lanterns and cobbles, it only takes a tiny leap of imagination to transport yourself back to Dickensian times, when the clerks and actuaries of the City retreated here for boozy lunches in pubs like the Lamb Tavern and New Moon.

The covered arcades linking Gracechurch St, Lime St and Whittington Ave (named for that famous cat-owning Whittington) were created by Victorian market maestro Sir Horace Jones, who was also behind Smithfield and Billingsgate. And although stuffed today with modern chain stores, cocktail bars and bistros, the uniform shop frontages still feel more Victorian than millennial – no surprise then that it's stood in for Victorian London in dozens of film and TV dramas, including *Harry Potter & the Philosopher's Stone*.

SEE IT ! ***Monument and Aldgate provide the nearest Tube access; Fenchurch mainline station is just metres away.***

© Alamy Stock Photo

© Tony Smith / Alamy

419

Be awed by Hexham's grand Augustinian abbey

NORTHEAST ENGLAND // Along Hadrian's Wall, the largest town, Hexham, is dominated in every sense by its immense abbey. This is Early English architecture at its finest: built for Bishop Wilfrid as a Benedictine monastery, Hexham still has its 7th-century Saxon crypt constructed from inscribed stones from Corstopitum in 674. Despite repeated raids by the Vikings and the Scots (and subsequent modifications), the fact that it's still here is testament to some creative thinking during the Dissolution of 1537, which saw the monastery rebranded as Hexham's parish church, a role it maintains today.

SEE IT ! *Hexham is midway between Newcastle and Carlisle. The most scenic way to travel from either city is by train.*

420

Wet your beak at the Philharmonic pub, Liverpool

NORTHWEST ENGLAND // True, there aren't that many heritage-listed lavatories in Britain, but maybe that's because they haven't been designed by the same team that built the Lusitania. And while the marble men's toilets in the Philharmonic Dining Rooms (to give it its full and proper name) are indeed gorgeous, the rest of the bar – resplendent with etched and stained glass, wrought iron, mosaics and ceramic tiling styled in the manner of a traditional gentleman's club – is one of the most beautiful watering holes in all of England. It was commissioned between 1898 and 1900 and named after the concert hall opposite.

TRY IT ! *The Philharmonic is at 36 Hope St, directly across from the Philharmonic Concert Hall.*

© Joanna Kossak / RHS

© Archive PL / Alamy

421

Find inspiration at the mothership of British gardens, RHS Wisley

SOUTHERN ENGLAND // The Royal Horticultural Society's gardens at Wisley, often described as the world's greatest, are the last word in horticultural excellence, and a couple of hours exploring the mixed borders, conifer plantations, rose beds and Mediterranean terraces more than confirm the fact. As does the million visitors a year.

Wisley was established in 1878 by RHS member George Wilson as an experimental garden – within 20 years the subsequent owner gave the site to the society. Today, Wisley covers an incredible 240 acres and is as much about professional garden design as inspiring ordinary members of the public to go forth and create their own patches of greenery. The most popular attraction is the Bicentenary Glasshouse with desert, tropical and temperate sections.

☛ SEE IT ! *Reaching Wisley without a car takes patience. Trains run from London Waterloo to Kingston, from where there's an hourly bus.*

422

Lose count of the thousands of objects at Snowshill Manor and Gardens

OXFORD & THE COTSWOLDS // At the start of the 20th century, an eccentric aristocrat (is there any other kind?) named Charles Wade bought Snowshill Manor to use as a giant display cabinet for his vast collection of artefacts. There are thousands of sundry objects here, from model boats to full-sized suits of samurai armour, via stuffed fish, wooden bicycles, paintings, violins, clocks and toys.

Wade's admiration for William Morris and the Arts and Crafts movement is clear from the ceramic bowls, shoe-making lasts and spinning wheels in the collection. After wandering the house, take a break in the garden – even this was laid out by Wade as a series of 'rooms', an opportunity to display yet more sculptures and objets d'art among the carefully tended lawns and flower beds.

☛ SEE IT ! *Snowshill is near the town of Broadway, connected by bus to Moreton-in-Marsh or Evesham. Both are on the train line to London.*

423

Backpack to the edge of Britain at Kearvaig Bothy, but beware gunfire

HIGHLANDS & ISLANDS // The handwritten sign posted at Durness Post Office only hints at the heightened thrills awaiting you on Cape Wrath. 'Live ammunition will be fired and pyrotechnics discharged on dates and times shown below...' reads the message. At first, you're confused, but checking the date and time, there is thankfully no clash with your plan to overnight at this off-grid beach refuge, located on land regularly used for target practice by the Ministry of Defence.

But that's not all. You'll have to carry all your supplies across 5 miles of tough terrain. Firewood is scarce, so you'll have to haul some of that with you, too. Is it worth it? You betcha. A night at Britain's loveliest bothy is what backpacking dreams are made of.

☛ SEE IT ! ***Take the passenger ferry and minibus from the Kyle of Durness (summer only) before beginning the hike.***

424

Try not to blush at the impressive size of the Cerne Giant's weapons

SOUTHWEST ENGLAND // Oo-er, missus. This giant 180ft-high chalk warrior stands proud on the hillside above the sleepy village of Cerne Abbas in Dorset, and wields a hefty club above his head – but that's not the only weapon he has on show. Prodigiously, unashamedly priapic, the Cerne Giant's unmissable feature is his gigantic upstanding phallus, almost a fifth as long as his body.

The first recorded mention of the giant was during the 18th century, although it's possible he was based on an earlier figure dating from the Iron Age. Some scholars believe he represents the Greco-Roman hero Hercules; others think he is a pagan fertility god, and maybe once carried a cloak and a severed head on his left arm. Good luck explaining him to the kids, that's all we can say.

SEE IT ! ***The Cerne Giant is about 9 miles north of Dorchester. The site is owned by the National Trust, and is free to visit year-round.***

425

Escape to the Roseland Peninsula

© Alamy Stock Photo

SOUTHWEST ENGLAND // In contrast to the stark cliffs, big waves and rugged character of the north Cornish coast, the rural Roseland presents a markedly gentler side to the Duchy. Bordered to the west by the Fal Estuary and to the east by St Austell Bay, this quiet corner of Cornwall is characterised by pretty villages, gently sloping fields, out-of-the-way farms and little-visited coves. It's also worth stopping at the clover-shaped Tudor castle at St Mawes – a favourite of Henry VIII himself.

SEE IT ! *The Roseland is busy in summer, but outside July and August it's much quieter. Cross the River Fal on the King Harry Ferry.*

The Collyer Twins' Top Five Places

Jordan and Loanne Collyer are fashion bloggers, DJs and presenters. They have collaborated with Puma, Tommy Hilfiger, Converse and ASOS, and have featured in Vogue's influencer series.

01

SALCOMBE – A little hidden treasure, Salcombe is a quaint seaside town full of candy-coloured houses and coves. Head to the Winking Prawn for the infamous bucket of 'beer prawns'.

02

THE PIG, BATH – The perfect place for foodies who want to escape city life and relax in a gorgeously cosy country home. Here you can indulge in delicious locally sourced food, unwind with a spa treatment and clear the cobwebs with beautiful country walks.

03

GREENWICH PARK – Our favourite park in London and a world heritage site with arguably the best view of the city. Bring a picnic on a summer's day to enjoy the views, and make sure to visit the Royal Observatory.

04

PORT LYMPNE SAFARI PARK – This animal park set over 600 acres of beautiful Kent countryside is perfect for a weekend escape. Hire buggies and tour the park, stay in a glass tree house and sip wine among giraffes and rhinos.

05

FED BY WATER, LONDON – A little gem in Hackney, Fed By Water single-handedly dispels the myth that vegetarian and vegan food is boring. This plant-based, authentic Italian restaurant boasts the most delicious, wholesome pasta and pizza dishes.

426

Discover museums and magnificence at Woolaton Hall

MIDLANDS & THE MARCHES // Woolaton Hall is that rare result of a working man taking on the aristocracy and outdoing them at their own game: it was with coal-mining wealth that Sir Francis Willoughby raised this audaciously spectacular mansion in the 1580s, eclipsing most mighty 'prodigy houses' being constructed at the time by Elizabeth I's richest courtiers. Nottingham's Natural History and Industrial Museums are here too, and away from the ornamented five-towered house are a deer park, botanic garden and extensive grounds with a lake to cross.

SEE IT ! ***Woolaton Hall is 3 miles west of Nottingham. Jump on bus 30 from Nottingham Victoria bus station.***

© ACORN 2 / Alamy

427

Seek the truth at the Greater Manchester Police Museum

NORTHWEST ENGLAND // One of Manchester's lesser-known highlights is this museum dedicated to the fuzz, or at least their 19th-century predecessors. Inside the old Victorian police station – which has been restored to its creepy, authentic self – you can visit cells and sit in the old magistrate's court (dating from 1895), where justice was dispensed for crimes both big and small. You can even examine the case histories – complete with mugshots and other bits of evidence – of some of the more notorious names to have appeared here over the years.

SEE IT ! ***The museum is only open on Tuesdays, and then for only a few hours, so check opening and closing times before setting out.***

© brinkstock / Alamy

The St Ives Bay branch line, running from St Erth, transports passengers along a lovely stretch of Cornish coastline

428

Take the train from St Erth to St Ives

SOUTHWEST ENGLAND // If there's one town every visitor to Cornwall wants to tick off their bucket list, it's St Ives: an artistic icon, fishing village and seaside stunner, all rolled into one improbably photogenic, quintessentially Cornish jumble of magic. The only trouble is that during the summer months you're as likely to find a free parking space as you are to sight a dodo instead of a seagull down by the harbour.

Happily, there is an especially fine solution to the St Ives conundrum – and that's to let the train take the strain. In this case it's the dinky branch railway that rattles like a toy train along the coast from the nearby village of St Erth, offering vistas of beaches, cliffs, dunes and sea.

The journey might only last 11 minutes, but in terms of scenic trips, this is a train ride that's up there with the best of them – and you won't have to waste a moment negotiating perilously narrow streets and troublesome traffic jams.

It's one of those trips that proves the old adage: sometimes, to travel really is better than to arrive.

TRY IT ! ***Trains run every half hour or so from tiny St Erth, which is on the main line between London Paddington and Penzance.***

429

Browse Saffron Walden's postcard-pretty market

EAST ANGLIA // On sunny days it's the perfect scene: an ancient town square framed by photogenic buildings, crowded with shoppers and lined with brightly coloured stalls. Here retail goes old school. Very old – a market has been held in Saffron Walden since 1141. These days, stalls groan with eclectic wares, from retro threads to slices of gourmet heaven. If you ascribe to the travel axiom that nothing conveys the essence of a place quite like a market (and you should), head to this produce-packed showcase of Britain at its best.

SEE IT ! ***Market days are Tuesday and Saturday. Trains run to Audley End (2 miles away), buses and taxis connect with the town.***

430

Unleash your inner warlord exploring Carreg Cennen castle

SOUTH WALES // Protruding from a westerly flank of the Brecon Beacons, the photogenic ruins of Carreg Cennen top a precipitous crag and bear a past entangled with Welsh military greats. Rhys ap Gruffydd, head of the medieval Deheubarth dynasty, was the likely founder of the fortress, while Owain Glyndŵr, last Welshman to hold the title 'Prince of Wales', laid siege here for months in vain. A path from the main site snakes underground, beckoning plucky adventurers down to a dark limestone cave.

SEE IT ! ***The castle rises 4 miles south of Llandeilo in Carmarthenshire, above the village of Trap.***

431

Imagine centuries of monarchical stories at Kenilworth Castle

MIDLANDS & THE MARCHES // Marrying medieval castle with Elizabethan mansion, Kenilworth must have witnessed the most colourful royal goings-on of any English residence: Edward II was imprisoned here, it was the Lancastrian kings' preferred haunt-cum-hunting ground, and Elizabeth I's favourite Robert Dudley had the gardens laid out for his Queen's private use. Whether you are wandering the tower where Queen Bess had her quarters or the Great Hall that entertained a string of kings beforehand, ghosts of erstwhile heads of state always feel close.

SEE IT ! ***Kenilworth railway station is a 1-mile walk away, with hourly Monday–Saturday connections to Coventry (10 minutes).***

© Joe Dunckley / Alamy

432

Find Hardy country in London at St Pancras Old Church

LONDON // If London's graveyards could speak, they'd spin tales of triumph and tragedy. You'll get a little of both at the curious Hardy Tree, a sturdy old ash tree in the churchyard of St Pancras Old Church. Around its base, hundreds of uprooted gravestones are stacked in concentric circles, like a Buddhist mandala executed in Christian stonework. Credit for this artistic arrangement goes, surprisingly, to the writer Thomas Hardy, who worked for the architecture firm charged with moving the dead of the St Pancras graveyard to make space for the expanding railways. As the youngest employee, he was given the dirty job of overseeing the exhumation of bodies and reburials. Quite what inspired him to create his ornamental swirl of salvaged tombstones is unknown, but it has endured beyond Hardy's lifetime as a memorial to London's self-reinvention, and the forgotten generations ploughed under with each new wave of development.

SEE IT ! ***Oft-overlooked St Pancras Old Church is north of King's Cross Tube and St Pancras International station, along Midland Rd.***

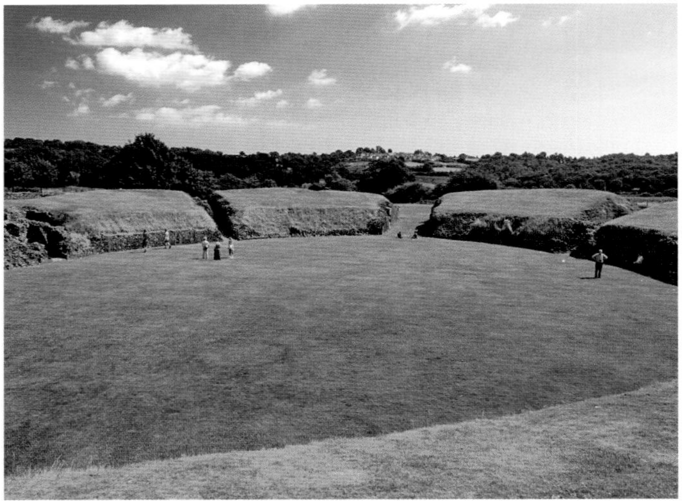

© Hemis / Alamy

433

Rome through ruins and Arthurian myths at Caerleon

SOUTH WALES // The sort of history you wish you could have studied at school bubbles to the surface in Caerleon, where legends of legionnaires and tales of King Arthur loom large.

One-time Iron Age hill fort and capital of the medieval Kingdom of Gwent, Caerleon is nevertheless most fabled for its Roman heritage. The extent of Roman remains is due to the fact that Caerleon was one of only three permanent British Roman settlements; consequently, many facets of life in the Second Legion Augusta, stationed here from AD 74 until well into the 3rd century, are visible.

The standout sights are undoubtedly the most complete examples of a Roman bathhouse, amphitheatre and barracks anywhere in the country. But Caerleon is among the most plausible locations of Camelot, too, with the amphitheatre believed to have been one potential site of the Round Table.

SEE IT ! ***Caerleon is 4 miles northeast of Newport, Gwent, which has a railway station on the main London–Swansea line.***

434

Fall hook, line and sinker for Aberaeron and its dolphins

MID-WALES // While many British resorts are crumbling, Aberaeron is booming with independent shops, restaurants and cafes. In the crook of Cardigan Bay, this cute-as-a-button harbour town has rows of brightly painted Georgian houses and sea walls bearing the brunt of ferocious Atlantic storms. Good food? You bet. Go for fish 'n' chips at the New Celtic, honey ice cream at The Hive or creative riffs on local seafood at the boutique-chic Harbourmaster. Look out for bottlenose dolphins on the 6-mile coastal ramble over gorse-clad cliffs to New Quay.

☛ SEE IT ! ***Aberaeron is on the A487 which runs along Cardigan Bay. The nearest train station is in Aberystwyth, 16 miles north.***

435

Go up country and agricultural at the Royal Welsh Show

MID-WALES // Fleeces fly amid rapid-fire commentary as the sheep-shearing contest hots up. In the grandstand, the dairy cattle parade by in the hope of being named 'Champion of Champions'. Welcome to Europe's biggest agricultural show, spread across an enormous 250-acre showground and packing in 200,000 visitors. This is the UK's go-to event for all things farming, whether you want to watch competitive tree felling, stock up on local cheese, cider and honey, eye up a new combine harvester, or simply admire the woolly superstars.

☛ SEE IT ! ***The four-day event is held in late July. The showground is located where the A470 and A483 cross at Llanelwedd, Builth Wells.***

436

See the spectacular panoramas of Plas Newydd, Anglesey

NORTH WALES // One of the most wonderful places to soak up views of the Menai Strait, separating dreamy Anglesey from the mainland, complete with Thomas Telford's talismanic Menai Suspension Bridge and Snowdonia swooping up behind that, is this 15th-century house and grounds. Traditional seat of the Marquesses of Anglesey, highlights of Plas Newydd house include the estate landscape painted by Rex Whistler, while the woodland-dotted grounds feature Italianate gardens and a delightful arboretum.

☛ SEE IT ! ***The estate is near the village of Llanfairpwllgwyngyll, which has a train station on the North Wales Coast Line.***

Fishing boats and dinghies lie beached on the sand during low tide at Mousehole Harbour

437

Snap a sunset shot of Cornish Mousehole

SOUTHWEST ENGLAND // First, let's get the pronunciation right: it's Mowzel, not Mouse-hole. Next, the facts: it's a small Cornish fishing village, three miles west of Penzance, and it overlooks the expanse of Mount's Bay. Now, a couple of things you probably won't know: it puts on a dazzling display of Christmas lights, and is the only place on the planet where you can tuck into stargazy pie (a pilchard pie in which fish heads are left poking up through the crust). In summary: Mousehole is probably the prettiest, pleasantest, most picture-perfect Cornish coastal village you will ever have the privilege to visit.

Granted, the village is irritatingly busy in summer, it has way too many second homes and there's practically nowhere to park. And yes, it's more or less a ghost town outside summer. But if you want that classic sunset view of a Cornish fishing village, Mousehole's the place. After bagging your shot, we recommend you retire for a congratulatory pint at the Ship Inn – as salty a Cornish pub as you could ever wish to find.

SEE IT ! ***Local buses shuttle from Penzance via Newlyn, or you can follow an easy 3-mile walk along the coast path. Avoid summer if you're averse to crowds.***

438

Find a life of crime at the National Justice Museum, Nottingham

MIDLANDS & THE MARCHES // The very entrance steps of this museum were once used for executions, and the walk through British crime and punishment history gets more grisly inside. Here, amid the UK's largest collection of law, order and criminal artefacts, you can delve into horrors from medieval trials to chillingly recent 20th-century techniques, like the force-feeding apparatus used on suffragettes. Costumed characters add to the ghoulishness, emphasised by the fact that this was a real jail and courthouse for over six centuries.

SEE IT ! *Combine a visit to the National Justice Museum with an equally spine-shuddering tour of the caves beneath Nottingham.*

439

Go deep down at the National Coal Mining Museum for England

YORKSHIRE // The term 'museum' may be a bit misleading here – this is no dry and dusty collection of artefacts, but what was once a real, working coal mine that can be explored in a thrillingly atmospheric way. You get to don hard hat and head torch and, with an ex-miner as your guide, enter the 'cage' (mine elevator) and descend 459ft into the darkness. The guide's banter and knowledge take the edge off any anxiety, and bring the mine's history vividly to life – it was first opened up in the 1770s and remained an active pit until 1985.

SEE IT ! *The museum is 10 miles south of Leeds on the A642, and can be reached from Junction 40 on the M1.*

440

Walk the length of the Long Gallery at Montacute House

SOUTHWEST ENGLAND // The Long Gallery is long. Really long. At 172ft, to be precise, it's the longest room of its kind in England. Once a space for socialising, dancing and sword fighting, these days the Long Gallery is notable for the pictures that line its walls: you might come face-to-face with Walter Raleigh, Francis Bacon or even Queen Bess herself. Throw in lavish 16th- and 17th-century interiors and a landscaped park, and it's no wonder that Montacute is a film-maker's favourite: *The Libertine*, *Sense & Sensibility* and *Wolf Hall* were all shot here.

SEE IT ! *The National Trust-owned Montacute House is 5 miles west of Yeovil off the A3088.*

441

Visit the Victorian wonderland of colourful Cragside

NORTHEAST ENGLAND // Surrounded by grottos, whimsical follies, wild moors, five lakes and over seven million trees, this vision of Victorian architecture is the work of the first Lord Armstrong, an industrialist who made his fortune manufacturing ships and hydraulic cranes. His 1880s mock-Tudor country retreat was not only filled with an extraordinary cache of art, but also featured hot and cold running water, a telephone and alarm, and – in a world first – hydroelectric power. Lady Margaret Armstrong oversaw the landscaping and its 40 miles of walking trails.

SEE IT ! *Cragside is 1 mile northeast of Rothbury. Visit from late May to mid-June, when the gardens are ablaze with rhododendrons.*

442

Join the servants at early Jacobean Audley End

EAST ANGLIA // In a country not short of stately mansions, positively palatial Audley End holds its fine head high. Inside, lavishly decorated rooms glitter with silverware, outside, one of Lancelot 'Capability' Brown's finest landscapes sweeps off all around, dotted with structures by neoclassical designer Robert Adam. But it's the creative, witty events that help you really feel part of life at Audley End. Where else can you Be a Groom for a Day, meet the staff in a Victorian service wing, and learn to be the very best servant at Butler School?

SEE IT ! *Audley End house is 1.5 miles away from Audley End train station, on the London Liverpool Street–Cambridge main line.*

443

Hang out with the cool kids in the Baltic Triangle, Liverpool

NORTHWEST ENGLAND // When it comes to nights out and general entertainment, Liverpool's cutting-edge credentials are best expressed in the Baltic Triangle, an old neighbourhood of warehouses and factories just southeast of Albert Dock. After decades of dereliction, the whole area has come alive as the city's digital and creative hub, with a bunch of cool bars, cafes and event spaces springing up alongside a growing number of design studios. Urban gardens, street food and vintage caravans... it's *the* place to find the latest indie trends.

SEE IT ! *The Baltic Triangle is between the city centre and the docks, just north of Toxteth.*

444

Fly (if you're lucky) the skies of Bristol in a beautiful balloon

SOUTHWEST ENGLAND // What's not to love about hot-air balloons? Elegant and ethereal (albeit not terribly ecofriendly), there are few sights more heart-warming than a hot-air balloon sailing silently through the skies. Which explains why we think the Bristol International Balloon Fiesta is one of the UK's most entertaining summer shindigs. Held just outside Bristol, it's Europe's largest balloon-themed gathering, and welcomes well over a hundred hot-air balloons from around the world. If you're lucky, you might even get to hitch a ride on one.

SEE IT ! *The event is held over four days in August at the Ashton Court Estate, 3 miles west of Bristol city centre.*

445

Hike to Hayburn Wyke's hidden picnic spot in Yorkshire

YORKSHIRE // The Yorkshire coast is filled with hidden nooks and crannies, but few are as memorable as Hayburn Wyke. A steep path leads down from a country pub through a wooded valley to emerge at a cliff-bound cove. A double waterfall, fringed with greenery, splashes straight onto the foreshore. There's no beach as such, just an expanse of rocks and boulders ideal for rock-pooling and fossil hunting. After a picnic lunch, you can hike south along the top of the cliffs to the neighbouring bay of Cloughton Wyke.

SEE IT ! *The cove is 5 miles north of Scarborough. Drive to the pub car park, or cycle from Scarborough along the Cinder Track.*

446

Uncover island life at the Cregneash Village Folk Museum on the Isle of Man

© Neil McAllister / Alamy Stock Photo

NORTHWEST ENGLAND // This fascinating folk village museum, located on an upland plateau overlooking the Calf of Man on the island's southern tip, explores the history and tradition of crofting, a form of small-scale communal farming practised on the island until the early part of the 20th century. In short, arable land would be divided into 'crofts' and farmed, while the poorer quality hill ground would be used for communal grazing.

One of the things you'll find is a typical cottage where you can see how the crofters lived, while the surrounding fields are home to four-horned sheep and tailless Manx cats – petting is encouraged.

SEE IT ! *Fly from Liverpool, London or Manchester or take the Isle of Man Steam Packet ferry from Liverpool and Heysham.*

Anna Hansen's Top Five Places

Anna Hansen is one of the UK's top female chefs. In 2006, she opened The Modern Pantry in Clerkenwell and has published a cookbook of the same name. In 2012, she was awarded an MBE for her services to the restaurant industry.

01

THE PIG, BROCKENHURST – This is the perfect place to retreat to when things get busy. It's has a wonderful kitchen garden. There's a wealth of wildlife too and it's great for long bike rides in the New Forest.

02

ISLE OF PURBECK – There is so much to explore in this 60-sq-mile stretch in southeast Dorset. I love to take long walks around the villages, hills and stunning Jurassic coast beaches, coves and coastline.

03

SNOWDONIA – I love camping and hiking in the wild landscapes of Snowdonia National Park. It's such an escape from reality.

04

HOTEL ENDSLEIGH, NEAR TAVISTOCK – This superb Devon hotel is set in lush Grade I-listed gardens (one of Humphry Repton's last commissions). It's owned and designed by hotelier Olga Polizzi and is just fantastic.

05

JIKONI, LONDON – This is currently one of my favourite London restaurants. Run by Ravinder Bhogal, it focuses on flavours and culinary traditions from Africa, Asia, Britain and the Middle East.

© Courtesy of Andrew Hayes-Watkins

© jenifoto / Getty Images

© Justin Kase / Alamy

447

Match film locations to real-world spots in Castle Combe

OXFORD & THE COTSWOLDS // If it hadn't been declared the 'prettiest village in England' and caught Hollywood's eye in the mid-1960s, Castle Combe might have remained an obscure settlement, hidden in a steep-sided valley in the southern Cotswolds. Instead, the narrow main street, with its delightful hotchpotch of honey-stone cottages, has featured in numerous TV shows and films, from *Dr Doolittle* to *War Horse*. All the moviemakers need to do is cover the 'no parking' signs and other modern accoutrements, and hey presto, it's instant Olde England.

Visitors will find it's the same deal: a village virtually unchanged for centuries. After drinking in the history, quench your thirst for real ale at one of the local pubs. Or head for the tea room, passing the public telephone box – another relic of bygone days.

SEE IT ! *The nearest city is Bath, making Castle Combe popular with summer visitors. Come in winter to escape the crowds.*

448

Go on the hunt for a treasure hoard at Beeston Castle

NORTHWEST ENGLAND // Some of northern England's most picturesque ruins are the crenellated remains of Beeston Castle, built atop a steep hill with splendid views of the surrounding Pennines and – on a clear day – as far as the Welsh mountains.

'The Castle of the Rock' was built by Ranulf, 6th Earl of Chester, in the 1220s on the remnants of an Iron Age hill fort. It was seized by Henry III in 1237 and remained in royal hands until 1645 and the defeat of Charles I in the Civil War, after which it was partially destroyed. The ruined castle has been a tourist attraction since the middle of the 19th century, with visitors coming to enjoy the views and look for Richard II's 'lost' treasure, which legend has it was hidden in the castle's deep well in 1299. It's never been found, but you can console yourself with an amble around the absorbing museum and the 40-acre wooded estate.

SEE IT ! *The English Heritage-managed castle is 11 miles south of Chester, just off the A49.*

449

Come face to face with creatures of The Deep in Hull

YORKSHIRE // Is this Britain's most spectacular aquarium? From the outside, The Deep is one of the most striking structures in Hull, rearing above the muddy waters of the Humber estuary like a menacing shark's head. But the inside is every bit as exciting. The main display tank, known as Endless Ocean, is home to huge shoals of horse-eye jack and trevally, several species of shark and stingray, and a pair of loggerhead turtles. You can view it from a transparent tunnel, and take an underwater elevator back to the surface.

SEE IT ! ***Be there at 2pm on weekdays to see scuba divers feeding the inhabitants of the Endless Ocean tank.***

450

Visit the Arts and Crafts bounty that is Blackwell House

CUMBRIA // A glorious example of the 19th-century Arts and Crafts movement, Blackwell House was designed between 1898 and 1900 by Mackay Hugh Baillie Scott for brewer Sir Edward Holt. The house is a Grade I example of outstanding British domestic architecture, and inside it is a trove of original furnishings and objects, all created according to the Arts and Craft ethos of precise workmanship. Highlights include the mock-medieval Great Hall and the light, airy White Drawing Room, while there are sensational views of Windermere from the cafe.

SEE IT ! ***Blackwell House is 2 miles south of Bowness on the B5360.***

451

Ceilidh like a pro at the Feis Ile festival of music and malt

HIGHLANDS & ISLANDS // There's a correct way to party on Islay and yelping, singing, clinking and drinking are just the start. Practise hard enough, and you'd be a fool to miss the week-long Feis Ile, the Islay Festival of Music and Malt, which sees the Inner Hebridean island invaded by ceilidh bands, whisky drinkers and Highland dancers. It's a boot-stomping, fiddle-bowing spectacle, first introduced 33 years ago to safeguard the islanders' fragile Gaelic culture. And it's worked. Regardless of where you're from, partying here feels like a homecoming.

SEE IT ! ***Feis Ile is held in the last week of May every year. Ferry tickets and itineraries are available from Caledonian MacBrayne.***

© Lakeland Arts

The ferry arrrives at tiny Lundy Island, 12 miles – and a two-hour crossing – from the north Devon coast

452

Bird-watch and star-spot on Lundy Island

SOUTHWEST ENGLAND // Three miles long and half a mile wide, little Lundy feels like a glimpse of England *c.*1950. There are no cars, a population of 28, a handful of shops and just one pub (the Marisco Tavern).

Nature still holds sway in this tiny, idyllic spot: basking sharks cruise the shoreline; wild ponies, sika deer and Soay sheep roam free; and vast colonies of seabirds roost along the rugged coast (the island's Viking name, Lund-ey, translates as the 'Island of Puffins').

Twelve miles off the north Devon coast, the island was privately owned until 1968, but is now leased by the Landmark Trust, which manages and maintains it. The fun begins with the journey to the island, via the two-hour ferry crossing from Bideford or Ilfracombe on the MS *Oldenburg*. Once docked, rangers lead hiking and snorkelling safaris, but you're free to hike, bike and wander the place at will – Lundy has an endearingly old-fashioned vibe that's hard not to fall for. But there's another compelling reason to visit – the island's fabulous night skies. Few places in the British Isles offer such a clear window to the wonders of the Milky Way.

SEE IT ! ***The ferry runs between April and October. The winter-only chopper flies from Hartland Point from November to March.***

453

Take the pilgrim's route to the wonders of the Borders Abbeys

SOUTHERN SCOTLAND // Of all the wonders of the Scottish borders, none capture the imagination more than Jedburgh, Melrose, Kelso and Dryburgh Abbeys. They have crumbling chapter houses and cloisters and are relics of a monastic life that thrived prior to the Protestant Reformation of 1560. But amid the highlights, Melrose Abbey wins hearts and minds for its collection of medieval sculpture and Robert the Bruce connection (spoiler alert: at the warrior king's request, his heart was buried here).

☛ SEE IT ! *Historic Environment Scotland oversees all four properties. To do your own pilgrimage, consider the 68-mile Borders Abbeys Way.*

454

See the lights of Diwali on Leicester's Golden Mile

MIDLANDS & THE MARCHES // Leicester's Belgrave Rd (aka the Golden Mile) with its jewellery shops, sari sellers, curry houses and spice bazaars, is about as close as Britain gets to a typical Indian street scene, and the Hindu festival of lights, Diwali, is the time to see it at its brilliant best. Over 35,000 people descend on this vibrant hub of the city's Asian community for the biggest Diwali celebrations outside the subcontinent. A fortnight of cultural events across Leicester starts with a spectacular switch-on of 6,000 lights and ends with a banging fireworks display.

☛ SEE IT ! *Diwali runs from late October to early November. The Diwali Leicester guide, stocked citywide, lists all events.*

455

Find a bard's genius at the Robert Burns Birthplace Museum

SOUTHERN SCOTLAND // Alloway was a fitting birthplace for Scotland's national bard. The ploughmans' cottages, the golden fields of barley, the hedgerows populated by mice and beasties – all were an inspiration for his sonnets and poems. There are six sites to visit, from the three-room cottage where he was born to the cobblestone Brig o' Doon and the Alloway Auld Kirk, as featured in the poem 'Tam o' Shanter'. As for the museum, it isn't just filled with artworks, books and manuscripts – it's a shrine to the 'Auld Lang Syne' author and a life well lived.

☛ SEE IT ! *Trains run from Glasgow to Ayr (50 minutes), from where there's a local bus service to Alloway.*

456

Dodge the ghosts of the Crumlin Road Gaol in Belfast

NORTHERN IRELAND // If you feel the echoing corridors and cramped cells of this former jail are haunted, you might be right. 'The Crum' was the scene of 17 executions between 1854 and 1961, and remained a working prison until 1996, housing a host of historic figures. Their stories are recounted on guided tours which take in the tunnel beneath Crumlin Rd, built to transfer prisoners from the courthouse across the street, the notorious C-Wing and the chilling execution chamber. If you're brave enough, take one of the night-time 'paranormal tours'.

☛ SEE IT ! *The jail's pedestrian entrance is on Crumlin Rd; the car park entrance is reached via Cliftonpark Ave to the north.*

© Shutterstock / Chris JG White

© RHS / Jason Ingram

457

Look out for Cornish piskies in the waters of St Nectan's Glen

SOUTHWEST ENGLAND // If you've always dreamed of stumbling upon a fairy glade, hightail it to the north Cornish coast, detour to Tintagel, head along the B3263 to Trethevy, and keep your eyes peeled for signs to St Nectan's Glen. Park your car, follow the track, and before long you'll find yourself in the enchanted glade of your imagination: a 60ft cascade framed by trees and climbing ivy, gushing into a deep kieve (plunge pool).

It's a mystical spot, supposedly frequented by Cornish piskies (pixies), and legendarily associated with King Arthur – you'll see ribbons and offerings dangling from the surrounding trees. The water's icy-cold year-round, but only the sissiest of bathers would dare don a wetsuit here. There's a little cafe for post-dip sustenance, and a walkway leads to two other small waterfalls nearby.

☛ SEE IT ! *Take the B3263 coast road from Tintagel towards Boscastle, and head for the car park at Trethevy. From here, signs lead to the glen.*

458

Flex green fingers at Harlow Carr Botanical Gardens

YORKSHIRE // There's something about Harrogate that attracts the green-fingered. Not only does this genteel Yorkshire spa town host two of Britain's biggest gardening events (the spring and autumn flower shows), it's also home to Harlow Carr, the northern showcase of the Royal Horticultural Society. Famed for its wildflower meadows and bluebell woods, other highlights include a stream-side garden fringed with ferns, primulas and irises, and a scented garden fragrant with the perfumes of jasmine, lilies, roses and wisteria.

Keen cooks can take inspiration from the kitchen garden, where carrots and beetroot thrive in serried ranks of raised beds and peas and runner beans cling to climbing frames of living willow. Even in winter the gardens look amazing, especially during the run-up to Christmas when the evening illuminations add a festive sparkle to the scene.

☛ SEE IT ! *Harlow Carr is 1.5 miles southwest of Harrogate town centre. You can walk there on a waymarked trail from Valley Gardens.*

459

Follow in the footsteps of royalty at Traquair House

SOUTHERN SCOTLAND // When Scotland's oldest inhabited house comes into view, at the end of a densely forested driveway, there's a moment when you hold your breath to take it all in. Its white stone turrets and baronial architecture smack of *Downton Abbey* grandeur, albeit with a tartan trim, while the ancient woodlands (home to pygmy goats!) were once a royal hunting ground. The highlight? The 19 public rooms, which welcomed 27 kings and queens – including Mary, Queen of Scots – and the secret stair used as an escape route for those fleeing persecution.

SEE IT ! ***Traquair House is open from April to October and weekends in November.***

© Ian Linton / Alamy

460

Find a little bit of ancient Greece at Little Sparta

SOUTHERN SCOTLAND // Over the rough-and-tumble Pentland Hills from Edinburgh, artist and poet Ian Hamilton Finlay made his home, and this 7-acre Arcadian garden is a lasting tribute to his brilliance. It is scattered with artworks, including poetry in sculptural form, stone-carved philosophical aphorisms and Greek temples caught between the trees and bushes. In line with his wishes, the garden is only open in summer – ensuring that when in bloom, it is a living, breathing, ephemeral work of art in its own right.

SEE IT ! ***Little Sparta is open from June to September and is a one-hour drive from Edinburgh or Glasgow. There is no public transport.***

461

See revolutionary architecture at Cromford Mills

MIDLANDS & THE MARCHES // The Derbyshire peaks that thrill today were once more important as feeds for the rivers that powered Britain's cotton industry. Along the Derwent Valley north of Derby, a mini-empire of mills and millworkers' housing sprang up during the 1770s, spearheaded by cotton baron Richard Arkwright. His Cromford Mills complex, the world's first example of water-driven cotton-spinning mills, heads up a brilliantly intact legacy of early Industrial Revolution buildings built to cover all his workers' supposed needs.

SEE IT ! ***Cromford Mills is 2 miles south of Matlock; nearby Cromford railway station has hourly trains to Derby.***

462

Walk down 'the most beautiful pier in England' at Clevedon

SOUTHWEST ENGLAND // Britain has plenty of piers, but the one at Clevedon is prince among them: poet Sir John Betjeman described it as 'the most beautiful pier in England' and it's been Grade I–listed since 2001 (the only pier to have that status since the collapse of Brighton's West Pier). Over 1000ft long, it was built in the 1860s to receive paddle steamers running pleasure cruises into the Severn Estuary, but it suffered badly over the following decades. By 1970 the pier was all but derelict, but it's now been handsomely restored.

☛ SEE IT ! *Clevedon is 13 miles from Bristol. The pier is open from 10am to 5pm.*

© Danield Di Paolo

463

Relive Charles I's final days at Carisbrooke Castle

SOUTHERN ENGLAND // For nigh on a millennium, the motte-and-bailey castle of Carisbrooke has stood watch over the Isle of Wight and the English Channel. It's withstood sieges and threats of invasion but is probably best known as the place where the doomed monarch, Charles I, spent his final days before his trial and execution. The structure is still in fairly good repair, and it's possible to see the Great Hall, Great Chamber gatehouse and chapel, as well as a working well which is still operated by donkeys, as it has been for centuries.

SEE IT ! *The English Heritage-owned castle is about seven miles south of Cowes.*

464

Hunt ghosts among the secret follies of Culzean Castle

SOUTHERN SCOTLAND // In a country that overdoses on castle folklore, it's hard to fathom how one exists with quite so many enviable traits. But Culzean has it all, and it encourages notions of fantasy. Below the 16th-century country house's cliff-hugging perch, secluded coves recast the Ayrshire coast as the Adriatic. There are woods, secret follies, a walled garden, clock tower, deer park and swan pond to discover, too. Stewards say it's haunted by seven ghosts, including a piper, but with this much make-believe to enjoy, who's counting?

SEE IT ! *Culzean Castle is 12 miles south of Ayr. The castle is open from March to October.*

465

Salute the missing sailor at the Hot Cross Bun Ceremony

LONDON // Every year on Good Friday, the Widow's Son Inn honours a touching local legend. The widow who formerly lived at this site waved her sailor son off to war, promising a fresh hot cross bun would be waiting for him on his return at Easter. Sadly, he never made it back, but she continued to make a bun in his memory each Good Friday, and after her death a net full of buns was discovered in the attic. Sailors still gather at the pub to continue the tradition, in a poignant memorial to the old missing sailor and to their own lost colleagues.

SEE IT ! *The nearest Tube station to the Widow's Son Inn is Bromley-by-Bow.*

466

Climb the Great Laxey Wheel on the Isle of Man

NORTHWEST ENGLAND // The Isle of Man's most impressive structure is the Lady Isabella Laxey Wheel, built in 1854 to pump water from a nearby mine and today the largest surviving waterwheel of its kind in the world. You can still see the 72ft wheel turn, drawing an impressive 250 gallons of water per minute from a depth of 1800ft – how's that for Victorian engineering and ingenuity? The story of the Laxey miners is told in the mine trail, and you can climb to the top of the wheel for fab panoramic views across the Glen Mooar Valley.

SEE IT ! *The wheel is halfway between Ramsey and Douglas; it is closed in winter.*

467

Set the seafood standard with an Arbroath smokie in a harbour shed

© Alamy Stock Photo

NORTHEAST SCOTLAND // A family-run harbour shed is probably not where you'd expect to find Scotland's most glorious seafood delicacy. But order an Arbroath Smokie – salted, smoke-cured haddock, hung and dried on charred wooden rods – and you'll be hooked for life. The appeal of the copper-gold fish soon makes sense: smokies have been around since the late 1800s, apparently after a local storehouse accidentally caught fire, smouldering barrels of fish preserved in salt. Two places to try are M&M Spink and Iain R Spink.

SEE IT ! ***Arbroath is 20 minutes north of Dundee.***

Jon Rotheram & Tom Harris's Top Five Places

Jon Rotheram and Tom Harris are the chefs behind Hackney's Michelin award-winning pub The Marksman – one of East London's best-loved drinking dens and dining rooms – and bunshop in Victoria.

01

WHITSTABLE, KENT – TH: It's the place to go for great crab and oyster dinners with friends and family, crabbing for the kids and walks along shingle beaches. It's a relatively short walk to The Sportsman for a fancy lunch too.

02

GWYTHIAN BEACH, CORNWALL – TH: We often rent a beach house here. The beach is extraordinary on a warm summer's day, and pretty special even on a rainy one. The kids love a sunset picnic on the cliffs above the beach, it's a lovely way to end the day.

03

HOLKHAM, NORFOLK – JR: Best known for its beautiful sandy beach, it's perfect for the kids to run around and play and also great for foraging sea purslane and sea beets. There's plenty of lovely seafood in the area too.

04

ORFORD, SUFFOLK – JR: This is a lovely little town where you can get great smoked fish from Pinneys of Orford, and great pastries from Pump Bakery.

05

MERSEY ISLAND – JR: Mersey is great for a family break. We'll go for a delicious meal at The Company, which has the freshest oysters and loads of other good shellfish. There are some nice coastal walks there too, and it's not too far from London.

468

Hobnob with royalty in Glamis Castle's rose-tinted turrets

NORTHEAST SCOTLAND // You can't argue with one thousand years of history. Glamis is a fortress graced by Mary, Queen of Scots, James V, and the Old Pretender to the throne, James VIII. It has William Shakespeare's *Macbeth* in its DNA. And it is rose-pink, turreted, and so magically over the top that it speaks more of L Frank Baum's *Land of Oz* than *Outlander*. Inside and out, from clock tower and crypt to Italian garden and sculpture trail, it's astonishing enough to brighten the murkiest Scottish day.

SEE IT ! ***Glamis Castle is 12 miles from Dundee, and can only be visited on a guided tour. It's open from March to December.***

© Gimas / Shutterstock

469

Stroll around Erddig, one of Wales' most stately stately homes

NORTH WALES // This 17th-century mansion and gardens deserves its moniker of the 'Welsh *Downton Abbey*'. The rambling, ruddy-hued house was furnished according to the most extravagant fashions of the day: think Chinese embroidered silks, blue damask and silver leaf. The activities of its erstwhile owners, the Yorkes, colour the house still: over two centuries and seven generations, the family accumulated a diligently cared-for collection of 30,000 artefacts, meaning Erddig has now become one of the National Trust's greatest museums, too.

SEE IT ! ***Erddig is 2 miles south of Wrexham. Come between March and October to see all the sights, as some close in winter.***

© Jane Redfern Jones / Alamy

Faskally Wood in Scotland is illuminated every autumn by the Enchanted Forest light show

470

Watch a woodland come alive at Perthshire's Enchanted Forest

HIGHLANDS & ISLANDS // The light falls pure and still. The noise of nearby Pitlochry has faded away, and the silence and shiver from the trees transforms the world anew. Like some long-forgotten ceremony, Faskally Wood awakes with a luminescent glow and sound carries through the branches, as if the 1000-year-old trees are communicating an ancient message. Then, softly, softly, you proceed through the forest, your footsteps tracked by series of choreographed movements, the thrills heightening the deeper you delve into the woodland.

This is no regular autumnal evening in Perthshire. It's what awaits at the Enchanted Forest, a family-friendly *son et lumière* performance – or night-time sound and light show – that's regularly lauded as the UK's most spellbinding outdoor attraction. Begun in 2001 as a three-night event to inspire locals to get outdoors, it has grown to see more than 80,000 tickets sell out during its annual five-week run. Complemented by technical wizardry, innovative design and an original music score, it's a rare example of man and nature working together in perfect harmony.

SEE IT ! ***The event runs for a one-month season each October. Buses to Faskally Wood from Pitlochry are included in the price.***

© Bruce Benson/ Alamy

© Guy Brown / Alamy

471

Take the ferry to Plymouth's Royal William Yard

SOUTHWEST ENGLAND // The city of Plymouth has played a central role in Britain's maritime history for centuries: Francis Drake supposedly spied the Spanish Armada here while playing bowls on Plymouth Hoe, and the city remains an important naval base and dockyard. Austere and imposing, the limestone buildings of the Royal William Yard were constructed between 1825 and 1831 to provide victualling for the Royal Navy fleet. Covering some 16 acres, it's hard to believe such a grand structure was commissioned solely to dish out rations of salt pork, hard tack and ship's biscuit. The complex is now home to cafes, restaurants and bakeries, including the excellent Column Bakehouse. The best way to get here is aboard the Royal William Ferry, which runs across from the Barbican – another area steeped in maritime history.

SEE IT ! ***The ferry trip takes 20 minutes and runs hourly in summer, as well as some weekends in spring and autumn.***

472

Discover your inner artist at Guernsey's Moulin Huet Bay

CHANNEL ISLANDS // Gazing on Moulin Huet Bay, you might see placid turquoise waters lapping lazily at the beach. Or perhaps you'll be there on an overcast day, watching white-crested waves break angrily against the large rocks at either end of the bay. You haven't been here before and yet these rocky contours and waters invoke an eerie sense of déjà vu. Perhaps you've seen this landscape rendered in hazy impressionist strokes by Renoir, who fell in love with Moulin Huet while visiting in 1883, and used it as inspiration for 15 of his paintings. Or maybe you've admired a contemporary take by artist Sara Serafin of this moody, ever-changing sea. Whether you're an artist yourself, a rock-pooling enthusiast, or simply looking for an isolated spot for peaceful contemplation, Moulin Huet will charm you too.

SEE IT ! ***Watch the sunset from the cliffs, or come here during inclement weather to admire the bay at its most stormily picturesque.***

473

Explore the best of Scottish nature at Inverewe Garden

HIGHLANDS & ISLANDS // How many sweet flowers grow in a Scottish country garden? Visit this 19th-century masterpiece, set over 800 hectares on the shores of time-nibbled Loch Ewe, and you'll struggle to count. The floral perfumes come from dog's-tooth violets, adder's tongues and blooming Himalayan poppies – all the result of the Gulf Stream meeting the Highlands head-on. It's backed by the Sawyer Gallery, plus there are wildlife hides where you can spot Scotland's big five – red squirrels, red deer, otters, seals and golden eagles.

SEE IT ! ***The gardens are 50 miles south of Ullapool. Free guided walks are available from May to September.***

474

Descend 270 steps to pretty Petit Port beach on Guernsey

CHANNEL ISLANDS // If you want to combine an idyllic beach visit with a serious thigh workout, then Petit Port, off Guernsey's south coast, is just the ticket. Reachable via 270 steep steps – count em' – this sandy, sheltered cove, nestles just off the west side of craggy Jerbourg Point. If luck's on your side, you'll have the place to yourself, and if those steps are an insufficient challenge, then how about a scramble along the rocks of Jerbourg Point to the squat little lighthouse? Hungry? Then head to nearby Hotel Jerbourg or The Auberge for a meal.

SEE IT ! ***Visit in the afternoon, when the beach gets the best of the sun's rays. Catch a bus from St Peter Port.***

475

Board Britain's oldest afloat fighting ship in Hartlepool

NORTHEAST ENGLAND // Hartlepool's national naval museum is a total winner. Its centrepiece is the permanently moored HMS *Trincomalee*, Britain's oldest still-buoyant warship, which was built in Bombay in 1817. Climb aboard to see its captain's quarters, hold and 46 guns. The Fighting Ships experience incorporates a vivid narration of life aboard the HMS *Prosperity* as its crew prepare for battle. On the quayside, costumed guides enthral with tales from the recreated 19th-century seaport, dotted with businesses such as a gunsmith and swordsmith.

SEE IT ! ***Trains link Hartlepool with Newcastle in just under an hour, while buses run to/from Durham in just over an hour.***

476

Leaf through first editions at Armagh Robinson Library

NORTHERN IRELAND // Somehow it seems the stories have seeped into the walls, imbuing the place with a sense of wonder and learning – such is the magic of this charming little library, founded in 1771 by Archbishop Robinson. Bookworms will be in heaven as they peruse the shelves: treasures include a first edition of *Gulliver's Travels*, published in 1726 and annotated by Swift himself, Sir Walter Raleigh's 1614 *History of the World*, the *Claims of the Innocents* (pleas to Oliver Cromwell), engravings by Hogarth and theological works dating from the 1480s.

SEE IT ! ***The Robinson Library is near the Church of Ireland Cathedral in Armagh city centre. Ring the bell for entry.***

477

Survey Wrest Park's très jolie landscape

SOUTHERN ENGLAND // If you want a typically English stately home, don't come here. Wrest Park was designed in an unashamedly French style by owner Thomas de Grey in the early 19th century, after a visit to Paris. But what you should come for is the gardens surrounding the mansion, a joyous celebration of styles and eras, with sweeping walkways, symmetrical borders and manicured lawns, dotted with statues, ponds and fountains. Beyond the gardens lies the great park, its grassy expanses fringed with woodland groves, owing much to England's best-known landscape architect, Lancelot 'Capability' Brown.

SEE IT ! *Wrest Park is north of London, about 30 miles northeast of Oxford, and easiest to reach by car.*

478

Take in Yorkshire from a grand height

YORKSHIRE // As you walk into its cobbled marketplace you can immediately see what makes Richmond special. One of the biggest market squares in England spreads before you, overlooked by one of the country's most imposing Norman castles. The setting is magnificent, perched on a rocky crag high above a waterfall in a bend of the River Swale, atop the 'Riche Mont' ('strong hill') that gave the town its name. The view from the top of the castle tower is one of the finest in Yorkshire, west towards the high moors around Swaledale, and east across the Vale of York.

SEE IT ! *Visit in late September to take in the excellent Richmond Walking and Book Festival.*

479

Lose your heart to the beautiful Arran

HIGHLANDS & ISLANDS // The senses that draw you in to the many magical pleasures of Arran are simple, timeless ones, dominated by sight, sound and smell. It might be the salty breeze on Blackwaterfoot Beach at low tide. Or a fruity single malt from the Isle of Arran Distillery. The chirp of a sparrowhawk above the stone circles on Machrie Moor. The crack of lobster shell at Lamlash while contemplating the Firth of Clyde. The view to the Mull of Kintyre from Goat Fell. Days on Arran pass by in slow motion, but all live long in the memory.

SEE IT ! *Ferries run regularly from Ardrossan to Brodick (55 minutes), and from Claonaig in Kintyre to Lochranza (30 minutes).*

480

Follow the path of Ireland's patron saint

NORTHERN IRELAND // Follow in the footsteps of St Patrick, the missionary who brought Christianity to Ireland, by hiking 82 miles along a signposted trail similar to the Camino de Santiago pilgrimage in Spain. During his time in Ireland, Patrick travelled widely, performing miracles, converting pagans and baptising chieftains as he went. The trail links the site of Patrick's first church in Armagh with Downpatrick Cathedral, where he is buried, passing Armagh's orchards and the Newry canal towpath and crossing the magnificent Mourne Mountains along the way.

SEE IT ! *Walking the entire trail from Armagh to Downpatrick takes six to 10 days. The trail is marked, but bring a map.*

© Hilda Weges Photography / Shutterstock

481

Learn lots about mining at brilliantly authentic Blaenavon

SOUTH WALES // The mining industry of the 18th, 19th and 20th centuries transformed Wales more than any other phenomenon in its history. And there is no better place than Blaenavon to begin understanding what things were like for those who worked down the pit. Blaenavon town developed in the 1780s, initially around an ironworks, continued growing through coal mining from the 1860s onwards, and is still a functioning town today.

Near the town, vestiges of its redundant industries, from furnaces to winding engines and workmen's cottages, slew across a 12.7-sq-mile area of stark uplands now protected as a Unesco Industrial Landscape. The highlight? The Big Pit, a museum in the former colliery, where you can descend 300ft underground with a real (well, ex) miner to experience life down a mineshaft.

SEE IT ! ***Blaenavon is 7 miles southwest of Abergavenny. The Industrial Landscape's attractions are a short walk or drive apart.***

© Stephen Dorey / Alamy

482

Commune with a higher power at Les Vauxbelets

CHANNEL ISLANDS // Imagine the pointed Gothic turrets of the Basilica in Massabielle, Lourdes, reaching for the sky. Imagine crowds of faithful coming in search of miracles, kneeling in the grotto; the murmur of solemn voices. Now remove the crowds. Shrink the Basilica. In front of you is the Little Chapel at Les Vauxbelets, measuring just 9ft by 6ft, the sunlight glinting off thousands of ceramic shards and seashells.

Some come here for silent communion with a higher power, others to marvel at this pint-sized sanctuary, whose construction took over half a century. This is the third incarnation of a labour of love begun in 1914 by Brother Déodat Antoine, an exiled French monk. The first was criticised, the second demolished because the Bishop of Portsmouth wouldn't fit through the doorway, while the final version was completed with the islanders' help in 1965.

SEE IT ! ***Visit in the morning, when the sun illuminates the delicate stained-glass windows. Frequent buses run from St Peter Port.***

© Alamy Stock Photo

Bushy Park, surrounding Hampton Court Palace in west London, is home to herds of red and fallow deer

Ben Ainslie's Top Five Places

Ben Ainslie CBE is one of the most successful competitive sailors in Olympic history, having competed and medalled at five Olympic games. He is now the Team Principal and Skipper of British America's Cup INEOS Team UK.

01

THE HAVEN BAR AND RESTAURANT, LYMINGTON – This fantastic restaurant overlooks the river and harbour. I love to see so many people having fun in their boats and enjoying the Solent.

02

THE PANDORA INN, FALMOUTH – Parts of this date back to the 13th century and it's actually where I had my first ever sail as a youngster in a small dinghy – I got sent up the creek on my own to meet my family for lunch there.

03

THE HUT AT COWELL BAY, ISLE OF WIGHT – This is one of the best spots on the south coast for the sunset. And the Espresso Martini is hard to beat.

04

VICTORIA PALACE THEATRE, LONDON – When we have some free time we always try and head to the theatre. The last play my wife Georgie and I saw was Hamilton here.

05

BUSHY PARK, LONDON – Hampton Court Palace was Henry VIII's favourite home, and I can see why. It's where Georgie and I got married, so it holds some really special memories for us, as do the surrounding parks.

483

Spend a penny at Victoria Pier's public toilets, Hull

YORKSHIRE // Public toilets? On a list of Britain's top 500 attractions? You can't be serious! But these are no ordinary public toilets, oh no. These are gorgeous temples of lavatorial luxury, built in Edwardian style with art nouveau flourishes, resplendent with gleaming white tiles, polished copper piping, varnished mahogany and a minor jungle of potted plants. Opened in 1926 to serve passengers waiting for the old Humber Ferry, they were restored in the 1990s and regularly win awards for best-kept public loos.

SEE IT ! ***The gents is the more impressive – ladies can ask the attendant for a guided tour when it's vacant.***

484

Squeeze into the UK's dinkiest residence at Quay House, Conwy

NORTH WALES // Good things *do* come in small packages. Guinness World Records–certified as the smallest house in Great Britain, Quay House extends a whitewashed terrace on the Conwy quayside by precisely 72 inches of width and 122 inches of height. Incredibly, the last inhabitant was a 6ft3in fisherman, Robert Jones, who was unable to fully stand inside: authorities declared the abode unfit for living in 1900 and forced him to move out. Today thousands descend on this dinky abode to glean an insight into the 16th-century Welsh lifestyle.

SEE IT ! ***Conwy is one of the main towns on the North Wales coast, 4 miles south of Llandudno and 44 miles west of Chester.***

© tipwam / Shutterstock

485

Listen to poetry at Seamus Heaney HomePlace

NORTHERN IRELAND // It's rare that a museum manages to lift poetry off the page and bring the words to life, but the exhibitions at Seamus Heaney HomePlace achieve just that. Much of Heaney's poetry is rooted in the rural village of Bellaghy where the late Nobel prizewinner grew up, and displays place the poems in the context of his home and surroundings. References to the local landscape, village life and the people who influenced him are highlighted, while audio guides allow you to listen to poems read by Heaney as you walk around.

☛ SEE IT ! ***Seamus Heaney HomePlace is in the village of Bellaghy, near Magherafelt. Belfast or Derry City are a 45-minute drive away.***

486

Explore the treasure trove of Elizabethan Burghley House

MIDLANDS & THE MARCHES // Elizabethan enthusiasts will get a gleam in their eye at the prospect of checking out this lavish country residence, one of the leading, showy 'prodigy houses' of super-rich 16th-century courtiers. The courtier in Burghley's case was William Cecil, Queen Elizabeth I's High Treasurer, whose descendants live here still. The multi-domed mansion, ensconced in grounds designed by Capability Brown, possesses a prodigious art collection, too: no wonder period films from *Elizabeth: the Golden Age* to *Pride and Prejudice* have been shot here.

☛ SEE IT ! ***Stamford, 12 miles west of Peterborough, is the nearest town: the house is 1.5 miles southeast of Stamford railway station.***

487

Marvel at the model English village of teeny tiny Bekonscot

SOUTHERN ENGLAND // The world's first and oldest model village, Bekonscot was originally built indoors in the 1920s by a wealthy gent, Roland Callingham, as a setting for his large model railway (originally inside his house – Mrs Callingham reputedly said either it went, or she did). Over subsequent decades the site was extended, as miniature houses, roads, cars and people were added. More recently, Bekonscot was renovated and all features returned to a 1930s' style. Kids love it, and nostalgic adults love it even more.

☛ SEE IT ! ***Bekonscot is in the centre of Beaconsfield, a town to the northwest of London, easily reached by (real) train.***

488

Face a private army at redoubtable Blair Castle, Perthshire

HIGHLANDS & ISLANDS // In *Game of Thrones* the Starks have Winterfell. In Perthshire, the Atholl family have Blair Castle, and they've kept it safe for seven centuries – in part thanks to the Atholl Highlanders, Europe's last private army. Putting such melodrama aside, this baronial manor is where the Cairngorms meet a cathedral-like glade, making the estate ripe for a Highland safari by 4WD or on horseback. The portraits and plush interiors, meanwhile, trace Scotland's history through the ups and downs of the Jacobites and Royalists who have called the castle home.

☛ SEE IT ! ***Located outside Pitlochry, Blair Castle is open from March to October.***

The subterranean world of Marble Arch Caves was first discovered by French cave explorer Edouard Alfred Martel in 1895

489

Ride a boat through the Marble Arch Caves, Co Fermanagh

NORTHERN IRELAND // Hidden beneath rolling hills near the southern inlets of Lower Lough Erne is a network of caves carved out of a limestone plateau by Fermanagh's abundant rainwater. This fascinating underworld of rivers, waterfalls, winding walkways and lofty, stalactite- and stalagmite-filled chambers can be discovered on an entertaining tour. Visits to the spectacular caverns – the main draw at Marble Arch Caves Global Geopark – begin with a short boat trip through the underground River Cladagh to Junction Jetty. Continuing on foot, the tour passes through more chambers, along the Moses Walk walled pathway sunk waist-deep into the river, and on to the Calcite Cradle, the complex's show cave. Though there are stairs and narrow passageways, rest assured this is spelunking-lite and very family-family.

SEE IT ! *The caves are 10 miles southwest of Enniskillen. To climb nearby Cuilcagh Mountain get a map from the caves' information desk.*

490

Rest and Be Thankful between sea and sky at Ardgartan

HIGHLANDS & ISLANDS // Even in a part of Scotland as scenic as Argyll, it's hard to comprehend the sublime vistas of Loch Long and its northern horseshoe of pine-skirted mountains when seen from the backwoodsy cabins at Ardgartan. You might gear up for the region's most spectacular scramble to the top of The Cobbler (2900ft), a distinctively anvil-shaped outcrop, or explore the surrounding Argyll Forest Park and the loch's western shoreline by pedal or paddle. Then there is the unmissable valley view from the nearby Rest and Be Thankful, one of the UK's most stunning mountain passes. Come evening, soak in a hot tub while gazing on a veil of stars, or fill up on tried-and-tested fish and chips from the local pub. Skinny dipping? You could give that a go, too.

☛ SEE IT ! *Ardgartan Argyll is part-owned by the Forestry Commission. Its 40 cabins are found 46 miles northwest of Glasgow.*

491

See Clachan's 'Bridge over the Atlantic'

HIGHLANDS & ISLANDS // Flying over Scotland on a clear day reveals much about its wave-nipped islands. There are plenty of bridges and crossings to them, but one that stands out by virtue of its design is the Clachan Bridge, which connects the mainland to the island of Seil.

What makes it so special? Granted, it's hardly an engineering marvel – just a simple humpback of masonry built in 1793 by engineer Robert Mylne – but its idiosyncratic location in the Clachan Sound, which connects at both ends to the Atlantic, makes it one of only a handful of bridges that crosses the ocean. In this case, all 77ft of it.

SEE IT ! *The Clachan Bridge is 8 miles southwest of Oban on the single-track B844.*

492

Get medieval in Carlisle Castle

CUMBRIA // Built with stones 'borrowed' from Hadrian's Wall, Carlisle's brooding castle was established in 1092 and refortified by successive English monarchs, including Henry II, Edward I and Henry VIII – all keen to maintain a sturdy bulwark against successive invasions from nearby Scotland. Its location in the 'Debatable Lands' means that it has seen quite a bit of action over the centuries, including the imprisonment of Mary, Queen of Scots and a pretty gruesome eight-month-long siege during the English Civil War. Today, the peaceful castle is home to the Cumbria Museum of Military Life.

SEE IT ! *Carlisle Castle dominates the north side of the city.*

493

Guard the keep at Enniskillen Castle

NORTHERN IRELAND // The word castle is sometimes bandied about rather loosely to describe grand manor houses and country estates, but this turreted stone fortress is the real deal, conjuring images of knights on horseback and battling armies.

It stands at the western end of Enniskillen's central island, looming over the cabin cruisers and speedboats on Lower Lough Erne. The former stronghold of the 16th-century Maguire chieftains, it now houses the Fermanagh County Museum, with a gallery dedicated to the county's monastic islands and waterways.

SEE IT ! *The castle is in Enniskillen town centre. The 3-mile-long Castle to Castle path connects Enniskillen Castle and Castle Coole.*

494

Find top culture at Manchester's Lowry

NORTHWEST ENGLAND // One of a trio of hallmark early millennium developments on Salford Quays (along with MediaCityUK and the Libeskind-designed Imperial War Museum), the Lowry Centre is home to two impressive theatres and a set of galleries showcasing the work of local and international artists – including 300 works by the Stretford-born artist who gave the centre its name, LS Lowry (1887–1976). The Lyric is the largest stage in England outside of London's West End, while the smaller Quays theatre hosts more experimental shows and performers on the rise.

SEE IT ! *The Lowry is easily reached by Metrolink; get off at Harbour City or MediaCityUK.*

495

Ponder ancient pilgrimage paths at Braich-y-Pwll

NORTH WALES // The sand-hemmed Llŷn Peninsula, dangling tantalisingly off western Snowdonia, gives up the ghost at this heather-dotted headland staring out at Bardsey Island, the last landfall in this direction until South America. This was the drama-heightened end point of one of medieval Britain's most important pilgrimages, with the mere matter of a treacherous 2-mile sea crossing left for the faithful. The holy island of Bardsey, the pilgrims' final stop, was purportedly the burial place of 20,000 early Christian saints.

SEE IT ! ***Hike to Braich-y-Pwll from the village of Aberdaron, or brave the Bardsey Island crossing from Porth Meudwy or Pwlheli.***

496

Learn to churn at Wensleydale Creamery

YORKSHIRE // 'Now then Gromit, how about a cup of tea and nice bit of cheese, hmm?' Fans of Wallace and Gromit will know that the favourite snack of Britain's most famous animated character is created in this modest factory on the edge of Hawes in the Yorkshire Dales. Visit it and you can watch as a master cheesemaker converts eight pints of fresh cows' milk into a pound of the crumbly white Wensleydale that has been made in this region for more than 900 years, and even try your hand at churning butter.

SEE IT ! ***Cheesemaking demonstrations are usually held on weekdays from April to October.***

497

Revel in the forlorn coastal beauty of Downhill Demesne

NORTHERN IRELAND // There might be more to life than capturing the perfect picture, but Downhill Demesne sure is photogenic. On lush green lawns, perched high above the sea (and a beach familiar to *Game of Thrones* fans), sits the colonnaded, dome-capped Mussenden Temple, built by the bishop of Derry for his library (or mistress, if rumours are to be believed). It's the star attraction of the 160-hectare demesne established by the bishop in 1774. The ruins of the abandoned house now stand forlornly on a clifftop, above beautiful landscaped gardens.

SEE IT ! ***Downhill Demesne is 28 miles east of Derry city. Tickets include entry to nearby National Trust property Hezlett House.***

© Thomas Bresenhuber / Shutterstock

498

Learn about 1066 and all that at Battle Abbey

SOUTHEAST ENGLAND // 'If there'd been no battle, there'd be no Battle' goes the local saying about the 1066 encounter between the forces of William Duke of Normandy and Anglo-Saxon King Harold – dubbed, as every British schoolchild knows, the Battle of Hastings. King Harold famously took an arrow in the eye, the English lost and William launched the Norman Conquest. The abbey built by William in Battle (what a coincidence!) as repentance for all the bloodletting now hosts an interactive exhibition examining the events of that fateful day.

SEE IT ! ***Battle is a short bus or train journey from Hastings and can be reached by train from London Charing Cross.***

499

Behold the fancy walls of fairy-tale Bolsover Castle

MIDLANDS & THE MARCHES // Originally intended to guard Henry II against a takeover by his own sons, elaborate Bolsover Castle reached its zenith as an opulent early 17th-century entertainment residence for Charles and William Cavendish. Within the crenellated confines, King Charles I attended one of the century's most decadent debauches, and courtier-poet William Cavendish taught the future Charles II to ride. The extent of the extravagance is evidenced in the Little Castle: grander than most fortresses, yet only William Cavendish's second home.

SEE IT ! ***Bolsover Castle stands 6 miles east of Chesterfield, Derbyshire. Buses 82 and 83 run to Bolsover village from Chesterfield.***

500

Flip out on Shrove Tuesday at the Olney Pancake Race

SOUTHERN ENGLAND // While most of the world is getting ready for the sexy spectacle that is carnival, the British are busy making pancakes. In the Buckinghamshire village of Olney, the locals have added a bit of excitement to proceedings by organising an annual Shrove Tuesday race, where contestants have to toss pancakes in a frying pan as they run. This pre-Lenten tradition can be witnessed in other places, but Olney claims to host the original (going back to 1445), though who first came up with the 'idea' is a factoid lost in the mists of time.

SEE IT ! ***Bus 42 from Bedford to Northampton stops en route in Olney twice an hour in both directions.***

Index

First Edition
Published in August 2019
by Lonely Planet Global Limited
CRN 554153
www.lonelyplanet.com
ISBN 978 1 78868 640 2

Printed in China
10 9 8 7 6 5 4 3 2 1

Managing Director, Publishing Piers Pickard
Associate Publisher Robin Barton
Commissioning Editors Dora Ball, Jessica Cole
Art Director & Layout Daniel Di Paolo
Editor Monica Woods
Image Research Ceri James
Proofreader Kate Turvey
Print Production Nigel Longuet
Thanks Flora Macqueen, Nick Mee, Yolanda Zappaterra

Written by: Isabel Albiston, Dora Ball, Oliver Berry, Joe Bindloss, Kerry Christiani, Fionn Davenport, Marc di Duca, David Else, Belinda Dixon, Anna Kaminski, Lauren Keith, Mike MacEacheran, Catherine le Nevez, Isabella Noble, Luke Waterson, Neil Wilson, Yolanda Zappaterra.

Lonely Planet offices

AUSTRALIA
The Malt Store, Level 3, 551 Swanston Street, Carlton Victoria 3053 Phone 03 8379 8000

IRELAND
Digital Depot, Roe Lane (off Thomas St), Digital Hub, Dublin 8, D08 TCV4

USA
124 Linden St, Oakland, CA 94607 Phone 510 250 6400

UNITED KINGDOM
240 Blackfriars Road, London SE1 8NW Phone 020 3771 5100

STAY IN TOUCH
lonelyplanet.com/contact